Your Psychic Potential

Your Psychic Potential

M.J. Abadie

Illustrations by

Mark Hasselriis

Adams Publishing
Holbrook, Massachusetts

Published by Adams Media Corporation
260 Center Street, Holbrook, MA 02343

ISBN: 1-55850-475-3
Printed in the United States of America

First Edition
J I H G F E D C B

Library of Congress Cataloging-in-Publication Data
Abadie, M. J.
Your psychic potential / M.J. Abadie—1st ed.
p. cm.
Includes bibliographical references.
ISBN 1-55850-475-3 (trade pbk.)
1. Psychic ability. 2. New Age movement. I. Title.
BF1031.A18 1995
133.8—dc20   95-13445
                                                                       CIP

This publication is designed to provide accurate and authoritative informa-tion with regard to the subject matter covered. It is sold with the under-standing that the publisher is not engaged in rendering legal, accounting, or other professional advice. If legal advice or other expert assistance is required, the services of a competent professional person should be sought.
—From a *Declaration of Principles*, jointly adopted by a Committee of the American Bar Association and a Committee of Publishers and Associations

This book is available at quantity discounts for bulk purchases. For information, call 1-800-872-5627.

Passages from *Hermes: Guide of Souls* by Karl Kerenyi (Spring Publishing) , used with permission. The author also gratefully acknowledges the permission to reprint an excerpt from a January, 1983 *Esquire* magazine article by Thomas Morgan.

To

MARK HASSELRIIS

Metaphysician *extraordinaire*
Companion on the Path
Fellow in the Work

In appreciation for the years of deep and abiding friendship

Contents

Preface

The Possible Human

The way to become human is to learn to recognize the lineaments of God in all of the wonderful modulations of the face of man.
—JOSEPH CAMPBELL
The Hero with a Thousand Faces

Imagine this scenario: You need information about the future ramifications of an impending decision regarding a major life change—it could involve your career, your marriage, a relocation, health, or a person close to you.

Instead of worrying and wondering and endlessly nagging yourself to come up with a right decision, you simply go to a special private place where you can be quiet and alone.

When you get there, you take a few moments to relax completely according to your preferred method. You slowly allow your conscious mind to sink to the deep level of your inner non-conscious mind. At a certain point, you ask a succinct predetermined question about the situation for which you desire counsel. Calmly, you feel this question becoming a part of your entire being. After a short time, you put the entire issue aside and out of your conscious mind, effectively forgetting about it, and go on about your daily life.

Later, you return to your special private place and once again relax yourself. You announce to your non-conscious mind that you are now ready to receive the answer to the question you have posed. Quietly, confidently, you wait. In a few minutes, like viewing a TV screen, you "see" and "hear" the correct answer. You now know exactly how to proceed, precisely what to do. You do it and the result is as desired. You have done this many times before. It always works.

Sound impossible? It isn't. Right now, today, you actually have this power. The problem is that you don't know you have it *and* you don't know how to use it. But in fact the computer (your non-conscious mind) is already programmed to give you the answers you want and need—you just don't know the correct keys to press to access the vast resources of information already in your mental software.

We humans are only at the beginning stages of discovering our almost unlimited capacities. Scientists say that we use, at best, only ten percent of our brain's capacities, and that's when we are being especially productive. Most of us jog along in our daily lives using only about five percent, or even less. Can you imagine what would happen if we all used substantially more of our innate capacity? All problems could be solved, personal, social, and political. Humans could be happy, productive, and economically secure all the time. The blights of war, greed, disease, overpopulation, ecological problems, and famine could all be abolished. Ridiculous, you may say. But many people are already aware that humans possess the potential to transform themselves and their environments.

One of France's most eminent brain specialists, Dr. Frederic Tilney, puts it bluntly: "We will, by conscious command, evolve cerebral centers which will permit us to use powers that we now are not even capable of imagining."

Many today, including scientists, educators, theologians, psychologists, and New Age practitioners, are fully aware that the potential for the human race is "almost infinite," in the words of Dr. Richard Leakey.

Is the idea of a fully developed human being new? Is it the product of highly technical, advanced scientific research? No, indeed. It is as old as the teachings of the Buddha, "the Enlightened One." Although most world religions are based on a divine being, the Buddha is a *human* being who has received enlightenment. Along with enlightenment have come extraordinarily stupendous powers.

At the end of recounting a long, richly baroque telling of the story of Buddha and his many accomplishments, Joseph Campbell, in *The Mythic Image*, states:

> To be remarked, however, is the idea of all these (to us) supernatural marvels proceeding, not from divinities, but from a fully realized human being....The godlike powers of the Buddhas and Bodhisattvas are to be thought of as potential within us all; not gained, but recovered, or in the Platonic sense "recollected,"

when the impediments of ignorance will have been either slowly purged away or suddenly transcended....

This idea is repeated by William Blake, in *The Marriage of Heaven and Hell*, where he writes:

If the doors of perception were cleansed, everything would appear to man as it is, infinite. For man has closed himself up, till he sees all things thro' narrow chinks in his cavern.

I think no one who has ever looked into the face of a newborn has failed to be awed at the sheer potential that lies dormant in this new human. What talents, what abilities, what accomplishments await? While marveling, we also wonder how much of this potential will reach fruition.

Like that infant, we possess marvelous potential right now, lying hidden within ourselves like the latent beautiful butterfly is concealed within the chrysalis. We are at the point of being able to realize talents we as yet don't even have terms to describe properly. According to neuroscientist Dr. Manfred Clynes, humans have reached the stage where it is possible to evolve states of mind and emotions entirely new to our experience!

And these potentials are not restricted to any one field of endeavor. There is a New Age tenet, "There are no limitations," which supports the point, but this idea is not only metaphysical in nature. It has been proved that expanding consciousness in one direction has the unexpected result of producing positive results in other, seemingly unrelated, areas. For example, a woman meditating on her next career move suddenly discovers that her chronic migraine headaches are gone. A writer, using visualization techniques to resolve health difficulties, discovers that his imagination has been ignited.

The point here is that we are whole persons. If we are to grow into our innate potential and become able to use more of "the little gray cells," we must learn to employ holistic methods to assist us in shucking the outmoded concept that the mind and body are two separate entities. Whatever your reason for reading this book, for wanting to develop your psychic potential, you must begin by recognizing the principle that you are a whole person, not a collection of mind and body parts.

Ever since René Descartes equated thinking with being in 1637 ("I think, therefore I am."), the Western world has been afflicted with a mind-body split, with the result that the links of communication between the conscious and the unconscious spheres of the human psyche have been sundered. The non-rational right brain has had to play second fiddle to the rational, linear-thinking left brain, while the body—long considered by the Church to be the evil repository of sin—comes in a miserable last. For centuries, therefore, analytical, logical, rational thinking has dominated our culture, and only now, standing on the threshold of the twenty-first century, are we finally ready to discard this outworn mental garment and declare ourselves to be, not only whole persons, but ones whose as yet undiscovered abilities are worthy not only of our consideration but of awe and wonder.

Most of us have heard of "right-brain" and "left-brain," and we know that the so-called left brain rules our analytical, rational thinking while the right brain presides over nonverbal, imaginative thinking. There is more to the story than this, but the essential theme is not only that both sides of the brain need to be engaged at the same time, but that the body must be recognized as being a significant partner and not merely the vessel containing the brain.

This holistic approach is not new; ancient traditions, especially in the Orient, have always acknowledged the whole person and recognized that the interactions among mind, body, emotions, and spirit need to be integrated in order to achieve mental acuity, emotional stability, and physical health. But in the West the holistic view has been confined to a relatively small group of thinkers and New Age practitioners, especially those in the healing arts, who have been considered "alternative" to the accepted ways of conducting life, approaching problems and maintaining health.

Becoming a whole person is not difficult, because you already are a whole person! When you go to the doctor because of a bodily complaint, you don't leave the rest of you at home. When you are working hard at the office, you may be aware only of your logical brain, but if your romantic interest calls unexpectedly, your mental gears shift abruptly to the right, imaginative side and your body may give you some very definite messages about its existence. And when you sleep and experience the theatre of your dreams, your body is still going about its accustomed duties of circulating and cleansing your blood and digesting your food, activities that are being directed by your brain.

However, *being* a whole person and *experiencing* one's self as whole are two different matters. Most of us, due to our upbringing, our society, our busy lives, our many roles, and our own inner conflicts, experience ourselves as divided, even fragmented. In the service of the separate parts of our lives, we have sliced ourselves into pieces—like a pie. One piece for the job, one piece for the family, one piece for school, one piece for the community, one piece for our parents, and so on until at the end of the day there isn't a piece left over for ourselves. Not only do we end up in sections, but these often don't seem to have much relation to one another. Bill's wife is Johnny's mother and Susie's sister and Janey's friend and Roger's boss and den mother to the Brownies. But who is this person who is all these different roles?

Getting yourself together, as the saying goes, is the difference between coping and being in control of your life. Many people who have learned to utilize the techniques described in this book have discovered that there is a quantum leap in their ability to accomplish *all* the disparate parts of their lives.

Releasing your psychic potential is a little like being the conductor of a great orchestra, except that you are also all the instruments. The conscious mind is the conductor, whose job it is to get all the parts going in concert, in harmony. At times, some parts may be silent, but their participation must be cued in at the proper time. When we are working at a job requiring logical thinking, our flights of imagination are not appropriate, just as stringed instruments don't play over percussion. But we must know the right time to bring them in.

The lesson is that even when some of the instruments in our internal orchestra are silent for good reason, we must nonetheless remain aware of their existence and know what they can add to the melody of our lives. The challenge is to learn to blend all of our parts into one harmonious whole, to allow each one to interact with and enhance the others. For example, in Bulgaria in the 1960s, a group of professional people were gathered to learn a foreign language through a new method employing specific right-brain techniques of relaxation and rhythmic repetition of words, with the left-brain nuts and bolts of vocabulary and syntax. To their utter amazement, they learned one thousand words in one day!

Once we understand that two sides of the brain are better than one and that the body is a significant partner in the total enterprise, we are in a position to tap the reserves of the mind for any purpose we wish. The power is yours to command, whether you want information about future events, greater prosperity, better relationships, renewed health, career advice, the right partner, increased self-esteem, enhanced performance, or other benefits.

And, although we are free to call upon ancient and non-Western traditions and techniques, we do not have to go to India and take up residence in an ashram or live in a monastery in Tibet to commune with our inner selves. We need only to accept the proposition that it is possible for us today to come to full human maturity within the existing parameters of our contemporary lives.

"Live," Nietzsche says, "as though the day were here."

M.J. Abadie
November 1994
New York City

Acknowledgments

My thanks go first and foremost to Pam Liflander, editor of this book, who not only opened the way to publication but contributed mightily to the finished product through her insightful commentary, lavish care, and exquisite consideration—a true collaborator.

And I salute Mark Hasselriis, whose fine drawings grace these pages, for his continuing involvement in my psychic process—as collaborator, interpreter, friend, and fellow along the Way.

Javier Amador-Peña is deserving of praise for the elegant and sensitive design.

My appreciation is extended also to my dear friend and fellow astrologer, Mary Orser, whose researches have consistently enriched my own and who continues to contribute to the field as a resource person.

Of all the influences, none has been more illuminating than that of Joseph Campbell, whom I revere as a spiritual father. Over the course of my long association with him, I was not only privileged to participate in his work, but I was inspired by his vision of an enlightened human being as the highest possible standard of attainment, a view reflected in these pages.

Over the years of intense psychic work, Blanche Meyerson was an unfailing support, offering encouragement, hospitality, an opportunity to be among like-minded people, and, finally, being the nucleus of a client referral group when I first started reading the Tarot professionally. In addition, her healing hands lifted me over many an obstacle.

German friends Catharine Born and Désirée Kahn were part of the synchronicity that put me in "the right place at the right time" to experience some of the psychic events described herein.

Christopher Santini of Tucson, AZ is thanked for introducing me to the works of Catharine Ponder, who has been an inspiration.

And I owe a debt of gratitude to Brendan Byrne for putting into my hand a copy of Ernest Holmes' *How To Use The Science of Mind* at a crucial point in my life.

One is not alone in investigating this field, and among many upon whose works I have drawn I would like especially to mention

Colin Wilson, whose books are both a repository of knowledge and a source of inspiration, and Sheila Ostrander and Lynne Schroeder, who pioneered bringing the Soviet research to Western attention.

Rupert Sheldrake's seminal work, which so amazingly fits into the psychic framework, has been important to me. I wish there were more scientists like him!

Closer to home, friends who contributed in diverse ways include Allen Erdheim, Ian Anderson, Gregory Mowrey, John Knox, Claudia Bader, and Charlotte Hunter. Nephews Vic Abadie and Paul Abadie and my brother George Abadie are thanked for their support.

In a book of this sort, it is proper to thank the Invisible Powers, and I acknowledge as patron the goddess Bast whose personal representative, the cat Mushkin, graces my life and helpfully "edits" my work by occasionally ripping manuscript pages to shreds.

Finally, I thank you, the reader, for being interested in this fascinating and rewarding subject, and it is my sincere hope that this book will serve as a guide to you along your own psychic Way.

Introduction

You Are Already Psychic

You have within yourself a source of great knowledge.
—PATRICIA GARFIELD,
Creative Dreaming

It has fallen to me to counsel others through various stages of psychic development. Many were scared and confused by visits from uninvited powers and some were spiritual seekers who already knew intuitively that there was a Way, an invisible path, to follow to empower and better their lives. As we stand on the verge of the long-awaited Aquarian Age, as well as that of the new millennium, it seems that many, many people are being brought along this course, some without their conscious choice, others because they seek a valid spiritual path to sustain them in these rapidly changing, often frightening, times. Because many of the people who have come to me for help have asked me to share my experiences and knowledge with a wider public, I have decided to break my own silence and write this book.

In my search for understanding a multitude of psychic experiences, my studies have encompassed psychology, especially that of C. G. Jung, mythology (through my long association with Joseph Campbell), metaphysics, dream analysis, astrology, Tarot, alchemy, Oriental philosophy, yoga, symbolic art, ancient religions, goddess worship, pagan rituals, and literature, poetry, and art. All of these have helped me enormously, but the core of this book comes out of events that befell me personally over a period of twenty years. At the time the psychic door opened to me, I fortunately had already acquired sufficient background not to become overly apprehensive about what was happening. Thus, I was able to accept the experiences and integrate them into my life in a rational manner without undue stress. Not that it was easy—no journey into the unknown is ever easy.

It is my hope that *Your Psychic Potential* will serve as a guide and comfort for all those who need help, who need to know they are not alone. The path of inner freedom is not an easy one to follow, especially today, when we are cut loose from our roots and past traditions have failed to keep pace with the world's accelerated rate of change. As new developments leap forth almost daily, we feel we have lost our moorings. But we cannot return to an earlier, more innocent past for the future presses hard in upon us. Where do we look for stability? *Inside ourselves.* We humans are marvelous beings indeed, we have such powers within us as to provoke awe and wonder, yet these powers are barely acknowledged and as yet largely untested. This book is about those powers and how to use them wisely and well for our personal growth and benefit. In inviting you to share this wonderful world of oneness, to open yourself to its blessings, I have organized the material to approximate a course for psychic development.

At first, as you progress through this book, the ideas and terminology may seem strange to you, and you will see only the broad outline of what is possible inside your psyche. As you work with the techniques and activate your psychic energies, the inner picture will begin to acquire clarity of detail. As your experience with accessing your inner Higher Self increases, you will begin to glow with the realization that you are indeed in possession of a precious talent. You will see yourself for the whole being that you are and begin to apprehend what it means to be psychic—and fully human.

Knowledge Is Power

Part I

Defining and Demystifying the Psychic

The Map of Inner Knowing

The essence of oneself and the essence of the world; these two are one.
—JOSEPH CAMPBELL
The Hero with a Thousand Faces

The words above were written nearly fifty years ago, in the context of the mythological journey of the hero. In ending the paragraph above, Campbell says, "the way...of exile brings the hero to the Self in all."

Many of us, especially workers in the psychic field, have been on our own private hero journeys, and perhaps the long exile is about to be over now that a major change in how people view the "intuitive" is taking place. Recent decades witnessed the emergence of the New Age movement, which is now culminating in a fusion of the metaphysical with the scientific.

The pioneers of the new thinking were not heavily credentialed academics but ordinary people who believed simply that "there has to be a better way." Refusing to accept that the spiritual, mental, and emotional aridity of contemporary life was an unchangeable fact of existence upon this Earth, they experimented with altered states of consciousness, through drugs and through various oriental practices such as Zen Buddhism, yoga, meditation, and other methods of communing with the inner self. The inner states of being they experienced connected them to a sense of the universe being an indivisible whole.

In the wake of their discoveries, and the burgeoning interest in this new thought, the formerly sealed scientific doors began, slowly, to creak open and admit a sliver of light. Although a majority of scientists were shaken when they realized that the basic assumptions upon which they had based their work, their careers, their grants, and even their lives were being called into question, a brave few heeded the call and the rusty hinges of the Establishment door swung open a bit wider.

Albert Einstein himself had proclaimed,

> Everyone who is seriously involved in the pursuit of science becomes convinced that a Spirit is manifest in the Laws of the Universe.

The New Science

In the 1970s, New Agers were saying that we affect our own realities, yet as far back as the early 1900s certain nondenominational religious groups asserted that science and religion were linked through something called "substance," an unseen but very real force upon which our thoughts and intentions acted.

In the wake of MC^2, as theoretical holes began to appear with increasing frequency in the old scientific model, new concepts were put forward, the primary one being that *matter and energy are not two separate entities but rather are intimately and inextricably linked.*

Robert Jahn, in experiments at Princeton University, has determined that,

> ...human consciousness can acquire information inaccessible by any known physical mechanism and can influence the behavior of physical systems or processes.

In the 1980s, Dr. David Bohm, an associate of Einstein's and a physicist on the leading edge of the new science, came to the conclusion that there are two distinct ways in which the universe is ordered.

First, there is the world of ordinary, everyday perception—wherein we are located in geographical space and experience time in a logical sequence, from the past through the present and into the future.

Bohm calls this the explicate, or *unfolded*, order, while Campbell refers to the same phenomenon [of manifested reality] as "the field of time and space."

The second type of order is based upon the idea of an invisible underlying matrix out of which all the visible forms arise; of the universe and all in it deriving from the same source.

Bohm calls this the implicate, or *enfolded,* order. Campbell identifies it as "the timeless world of mythology."

In Hindu mythology, which is rooted in the concept of wholeness, the symbol of the [goddess] Lotus represents this interdependence of the two orders. In *The Art of Indian Asia,* Heinrich Zimmer gives this description:

> Rising from the depths of water and expanding its petals on the surface, the lotus...is the most beautiful evidence offered to the eye of the self-engendering fertility of the bottom. Through its appearance, it gives proof of the life-supporting of the all-nourishing abyss...the infinite ocean of that liquid life-substance out of which all the differentiated elements of the universe arise.

As previously sacrosanct notions about the structure of reality were brought up for discussion, it gradually became clear that how we experience reality is often quite different from reality itself. A new framework began to emerge, taking into consideration heretofore unadmitted observations.

In the words of Cambridge biologist Rupert Sheldrake,

> Life involves both an energy flow, which can be understood as an aspect of the universal energy flux, and a formative principle.

Now, standing on the verge of the twenty-first century, we find ourselves at a stage of a major transformation of consciousness no longer restricted to a few far-thinking scientists and those involved in alternative therapies or lifestyles.

The Intelligent Universe

Today, through one of those wonderful "quantum leaps," which are in reality a series of small, unperceived jumps, we have something called the "Gaia principle," proposed by J. Lovelock in 1979, which states the Earth itself is a living, breathing organism. This idea of an alive, organic Earth is gradually taking hold upon our collective consciousness, radically altering how we perceive our environment and the living creatures within it, including ourselves. For, if Earth is a single organism, its inhabitants are all interconnected cells within it. And it follows that the Universe likewise is an interconnected whole of which our Earth and all on it are an integral part.

In the wake of the discoveries of quantum physics, comes the new view that *matter itself is affected by the field around it, to the effect that both matter and field have the ability to modify each other.*

This concept encompasses the field of the entire universe down through a progression of subfields, from the galaxy to the solar system to the earth, and on to ourselves and all the other inhabitants of the earth, including those which we have preciously considered to be inorganic, like rocks. Down and down we go, like Alice in the rabbit hole, to the basic subatomic particles which constitute our beings.

If we follow this line of reasoning, we are forced to realize that, in the words of physicist John Wheeler,

> The universe does not exist 'out there' independent of us. We are inescapably involved in bringing about that which appears to be happening. We are not only observers. We are participators. In some strange sense this is a *participatory universe.*

And, Dr. David Foster, a cybernetician, postulates the idea of an "information universe" that is constantly transmitting and receiving. He compares the complex structures of life itself to data processing on a grand scale.

In this information universe, we are all connected. Of course, there is an "out there," but it is also "in here," just as the air we breathe is outside us until we take it into our lungs, when we inhale, making it a part of us, and then, upon exhalation, that part of us becomes a part of the "out there," connecting us to others who will in turn breathe in our exhaled breath.

Thus, whether we are aware of it or not, we live in a world much different from what we had previously thought when our notions of reality were based upon the idea of the Universe as nothing but a great machine, running perfectly well but soulless and dead. We now know that the entire cosmos is alive and *interconnected* in some sense of the word, and that there are exciting prospects of interfacing and interrelating with the whole of it through our powers of intuition and psychic perception. That we acknowledge these abilities are within reach of all is the next step in our ascent up the ladder of enlightenment.

What Is "Psychic"?

Intuition has always been a part of human nature. A *natural ability,* one connecting us to nature and the whole cosmos beyond earth, it "comes with the territory" of being human. You arrived in this life with it in perfect working order. And, although all natural abilities are present in different individuals in varying degrees, your intuition is as much a part of you as is your digestive system, your emotions, or your logical mind.

Intuition, which I define as "direct knowing," has long been considered to be the basis of psychic experience. Almost everyone has had some personal contact with their intuitive ability. It may have been a hunch, a gut feeling, a vague sense that something was about to happen, an uneasiness, a prickly sensation, goosebumps, or any other difficult- to-pin-down indication that information was being received from other than the usual sensory channels.

The difference between ordinary, everyday intuition and being psychic is one of degree, just as is the difference between being a member of an amateur string quartet and being a virtuoso violinist. To carry the analogy a step further, it is also a matter of *practice.* You would not expect yourself to play a concert at Carnegie Hall without years of study and daily practice, and you cannot expect yourself to access your own psychic abilities without acknowledging that they exist and then spending time on their development. Equally, just as one musician may be more adept at one instrument rather than another, the forms psychic intuition takes are many.

For many people, the idea of "psychic," or "being psychic," conjures up titillating but suspect images of gypsies reading tea leaves, mysterious veiled women gazing into crystal balls, and astrologers in star-bedizened robes casting horoscopes. To the literal-minded, the entire matter is to be ridiculed or dismissed outright as sheer nonsense ("If I can't see it, hear it, feel it, touch it, or taste it, it doesn't exist."). However, humans, like other animals, have always possessed intuitive powers.

In the long course of human history, in both literate cultures and preliterate ones, people have believed that something existed beyond what could be perceived through the five senses. Something *beyond*—what in metaphysical terms is called "the yonder shore."

Primitive societies believed the world to be inhabited with spirits, that each tree and rock, each bird and bison, each flower and bee harbored a spirit. These spirits were to be recognized and, often, appeased. Shamans, or witch doctors, could contact these spirits and prevail upon them to help heal mental and physical sicknesses. Aware of the interactions between the human and the animal and plant kingdoms, the physical and spiritual realms, they "borrowed" the animal or vegetal powers and brought them to the human sphere.

In ancient civilizations, the Greeks had their famous oracle temples, where priestesses in deep trances produced utterances of great import, and both Greeks and Romans used various methods of divination designed to connect men with their proper destiny, through an inner knowing of what the "gods" wished for them.

In the Asklepieion, a classical sanctuary of healing, the patient was encouraged to bring about the cure from within himself through invoking the "god," usually achieved through dream. Recognizing the necessity of the person's *participation* in his cure, the Greeks created an environment in which a person's innermost depths could be called upon to facilitate healing. Further, the physician was *excluded* from the process.

The idea of inner forces and connectedness to the universe is the common theme, one that stretches around the globe, from the conjuring witch doctor in Africa to the cushioned comfort of the psychiatrist's office in New York. The difference between the primitive and ancient cultures and our own is one of *openness* to the reality of a universe that is radiantly alive, filled with potent if unseen forces. Now, in the span of a few short years, scientists have progressed to an understanding of forces we cannot see, thus confirming their factual existence.

As the scientific intellect with its increasingly sophisticated research methods seeks to grapple with what intuitively seems obvious, what emerges is the information that religion, mysticism, and conscious use of psychic ability all spring from a basic feeling about the universe. This feeling is what Joseph Campbell calls "the sense of wonder."

In that moment of intuitive insight, suddenly transcended, we exclaim, "Ah-ha! So that's how it is!" And, for a brief moment, everything makes sense. It's as if after a lifetime of hearing only static on our inner radios, we suddenly "tune in" to a cosmic clear station, which has been broadcasting all the time only that we didn't have our receivers on the right frequency.

It is clear that, "Civilization cannot evolve further until 'the occult' is taken for granted on the same level as atomic energy," as Colin Wilson states in his fine book *The Occult*.

However we choose to define *psychic* for ourselves, we must do so from a perspective of the whole human being acting in and interacting with a holistic universe where anything is possible. We have only to open our minds and release our fears to summon marvelous genii capable of astounding feats from the depths of our own psyches.

You and the Universe Are One

2

The Magical Tradition

There are no unnatural or supernatural phenomena, only very large gaps in our knowledge of what is natural.
—EDGAR MITCHELL,
Apollo 14 Astronaut

The word "magic" derives from the Persian *magi*, who were priests of the Mithraic religion. This sect was known for its ability to use psychic power to interpret natural phenomena. An example is the three Magi, or wise men, who followed a star to visit upon the birth of Jesus Christ.

Psychic ability has long been connected to the practice of magic, and this connection has led many to denigrate or fear psychic powers. However, magic is actually the *conscious* use of mental powers employed for the purpose of aligning the magician with natural forces. The person who is able to do this is called an *adept* or a *mage*.

Magic was an important component of early religions. All ancient peoples believed in some version of it. As neither the belief nor the practice has ever died out, despite persistent persecution by both Church and science, magic deserves respect.

Based on the belief that unseen forces permeate all of nature and that alignment with those forces allows man to magic control them, magic presumes "higher powers" to exist both in humans and in nature. The actual practice (as opposed to belief) of magic calls upon higher states of consciousness than we generally use. The achievement of these demands greater awareness—the first step in psychic development. A fine-tuning of the sensibilities is required to pick up messages coming from both inward and outward sources.

This super-awareness is akin to religious mysticism. Both magician and mystic seek to transcend the reality of everyday— to go beyond the survival and ego needs of money, temporal power, sexual excitement and conquest, social position, and material possessions—in order to "see" through the obscuring veil masking *true* reality, or the totality of being. This realization comes to most of us as a sudden glimpse in a moment of rare insight.

In a 1931 book, *The Mystic Will*, Howard Brinton describes a revelation given to the seventeenth-century nature mystic, a cobbler named Jacob Boehme:

> It seemed as if he were looking into the very heart of nature
> and beholding its innermost mystery…grass and flowers were
> stirred with strange living forces…the veil of matter grew
> thin and half-revealed the vast struggling life beneath.

The purpose of magic is to render this "lifting of the veil" on command.

Calling nature "God's living garment," Goethe deplored scientists for fragmenting the whole into countless parts. Most magnificent of poet-thinkers, he knew quite well that the mind works holistically, through a series of intuitive leaps. This idea is akin to viewing a late Monet painting. One must stand back and take a long view to see the definition revealed by the shimmering intermixture of colors in the composition. Up close, the painting dissolves into unrecognizable blobs of seemingly undifferentiated color.

The New Scientific Paradigm

Today, leading edge scientists like David Foster and Rupert Sheldrake assert that there are natural, if unseen, forces that possess both intelligence and purpose. This is precisely what the magicians of earlier times believed, and their work tends to support this new scientific argument, rather than the new disproving the old, as is usually the case.

The current theoretical model of the universe is dependent upon the finding of a "sixth quark," which has been called "the God particle." This theory of particle physics, if proved, will explain what is so far a missing link in the universal model of existence. It may very well be that if this elusive particle is found it will substantiate the connection between ourselves and the universe (which practicing psychics already intuitively know exists). The closer we get to the "sixth quark" (which may prove to be adjacent to the sixth sense), the closer we get to the mysterious forces that magic calls into play.

The mage of earlier times believed that it was possible to transcend both time and space. Rather than ridiculing this notion, let us listen to physicist Russell Targ, who says that modern physics is "incomplete and inadequate to describe that kind of activity."

Albert Einstein, who firmly believed in the existence of a wider reality than is presently generally accepted, including telepathy, stated that "Science is in its infancy."

Webster's definition of the psychic is "beyond known physical processes." It's the word *known* we need to pay attention to. There is a lot we don't know, and the only way to find out is to keep an open mind and not to shut ourselves off from our own authentic selves and experiences.

Rather than fault those "magicians" of the past who have made the effort to observe and utilize this wholeness, we can choose to learn from them.

Primitive Magic

We cannot know for sure how primitive peoples experienced their world, but it is fairly certain that they were in touch with extrasensory forces, or what we now refer to as psychic abilities.

The term "sixth sense" is often used to describe psychic gifts, but I believe that there is a range of subtle senses, that we may possess not only sixth sense, but a seventh, eighth, ninth, and tenth as well. The physical senses—sight, touch, seeing, smell, and taste—might be regarded as the "gross" senses, while the *inner* ways of apprehending reality, such as the sixth sense, are governed by our subtle senses of perception. No doubt you are familiar with your own subtle senses—you wake in the night instantly alert, knowing that an unknown someone is in the vicinity; you scare off a prowler and upon reflection realize that you did not actually hear a noise. You certainly did not see, touch, or smell the intruder. What woke you up? Is there some subtle sense whose job it is to alert us to impending danger?

There can be no doubt that primitive peoples possessed such a sense—or range of senses—powers that enabled them to locate hunting sites and allowed telepathic communications. The tribal shamans nurtured these powers and brought them to a high degree of development, passing their knowledge and techniques along to succeeding generations. The trials of a would-be shaman were arduous, for the powers contacted were awesome and to be treated with respect. Magic, in fact, was also an early form of science, used for healing. Typically, the shaman was wise in the lore of herbs and plants, which were known to have healing and other useful properties, and he was able to call upon knowledge of the elements—fire, water, and air.

The Ancient World

A famous quotation, "As above, so below," is attributed to the mythical sage Hermes Trismegistus, known as the "thrice-wise." Called Thoth, god of wisdom, by the Egyptians, Hermes may not represent an actual man but the legend of his attributes stands at the beginning of the civilized world's effort to understand humanity as an integral part of the entire cosmos.

Although Pythagoras, the great Greek thinker, is primarily known to most of us through high school geometry, he was an initiate of the famed Egyptian mysteries, and he believed that the basis of the world was mystical, or magical. Born about 570 B.C., Pythagoras lived during the lifetime of Buddha in India and of Confucius in China. He associated with the Chaldeans, from whom he learned astronomy and astrology, and with the Magi of Persia. It has been suggested that the famous "theorem of Pythagoras" was a product of his education by Egyptian priests, while he was under the aegis of the pharaoh Amasis. He traveled and studied abroad for thirty-four years before returning to Samos, his home, where he attempted to unite numbers, music, magic, astrology, the mysteries, and concepts of the religions of Egypt, Chaldea, Persia, and India into one cohesive body of knowledge. Out of his work evolved the basic principle of the harmonious ordering of matter in accordance with the laws of proportion, a concept which renders the triangle a mystical symbol. The impact of Pythagoras's work on the whole Mediterranean world was immense, and tales were told of his magical powers. The plethora of legend surrounding his powers suggests that he was an exceptionally powerful medium, and it is evident that he was supremely aware of the mystical One as the underlying principle of the universe.

The Hermetic Century

Known as the "Hermetic" century because of the influence upon it of the classical texts, which had been rediscovered during the Renaissance of the previous century, the sixteenth century produced two great occultists.

The first, Cornelius Agrippa, was born in Cologne in 1486. After leaving the university there, he became a wandering scholar, traveling widely, teaching and disseminating information. He learned from the great Jewish mystical tradition of the Kaballah, which possesses many magical doctrines, one of which is the manipulation of numbers. Each letter in the Hebrew language has a numeric equivalent: these number/name components could be used for divination. His major work, *On Occult Philosophy*, written when he was only twenty-four, was published twenty years later. In it, he states,

> The fantasy, or imaginative power, has a ruling power over the passions of the soul…[imagination] does, of its own accord, according to the diversity of the passions, first of all change the physical body with a sensible transmutation, downward, inward, or outward.

This statement, written in 1510, clearly describes the technique of auto-suggestion, used with so much success in the last half of the twentieth century.

The other great occultist, Paracelsus, was seven years younger. His career was somewhat similar in that he, too, was a wandering scholar who performed amazing feats. He was best known for his ability to heal by psychic means, now referred to as thamaturgy.

He wrote that "Magic is a teacher of medicine preferable to all the written books," and by magic he meant "power that comes direct from God," or contact with the whole. He believed that health derived from harmony between the person and nature, that man is a microcosm of the One, the macrocosm. In other words, as above, so below.

Paracelsus, whose writings are full of insights about the relationship between body and mind, says,

> Man is not body. The heart, the spirit, is man...this spirit is an entire star, out of which he is built...first step in the operation of these sciences is this: to beget the spirit from the inner firmament by means of the imagination.

It does not require a great leap of the imagination, nor of faith, to see correspondences between the beliefs of these mages—the basis of whose work was the tenet that man functions in relation to the universe as the human organs function in relation to the body—and the thoroughly modern views of scientists like David Foster. His idea of an "intelligent universe," in which coded information is carried on invisible currents, or waves, is part of the new scientific framework in which Carl Jung's concept of synchronicity can be seen as arising "out of underlying patterns of the universe rather than through a causality of pushes and pulls that we normally associate with events in nature," to quote from F. David Peat's book *Synchronicity*.

And it sounds curiously like what we have heard from these sixteenth-century mages who knew that magic is a natural human faculty and, although we may feel separate from the universe, we are in truth an integral, functional part of it.

Nostradamus, the most famous non-biblical prophet, one whose prophecies are still studied seriously, was another product of the energetic sixteenth century, which was steeped in magical practices.

This remarkable man exemplifies the mage as a knowledgeable practitioner of magic, a savant. Like many of history's prominent mages, he was also a doctor and a scientist. Unlike today, when the straitjacket of academic discipline and rigorous separation of fields of study have been imposed on the inquiring minds of students and professionals alike, in earlier times there was no distinction between magic and science, nor between astronomy and astrology.

Born in St. Remy, France, in 1503 of mixed Christian and Jewish parentage, Nostradamus studied languages, medicine, and astrology, which at that time was considered relevant to both medicine and life in general. As a physician, he proved himself to be a born healer and helped to combat the plague without becoming infected. He understood the importance of antiseptic methods, cleanliness, and fresh air at a time when doctors went from dissecting corpses to delivering babies without washing their hands (a practice that did not cease until the nineteenth century).

After many travels, he settled in Salon in 1547 where he lived quietly and devoted himself to being a mage and prophet, gaining a reputation. In 1555 he published the first of his prophecies, called *Centuries* because they were printed in lots of one hundred. These were all verse-form quatrains of mind-boggling obscurity, but students of the prophecies have concluded that many of them were accurate.

For example, the "Hister" stanzas are believed to have predicted World War II, nearly four hundred years later. Another, which history validated, concerns the escape and capture of Louis XVI and Marie Antoinette, after the French Revolution. Experts believe that the prophecies of Nostradamus concerning the French Revolution and the rise of Napoleon are convincing beyond a reasonable doubt.

Considering their obscure nature and far-flung intent, it is significant that the prophecies were an instant success, bringing the prophet to the attention of Catherine de Medici, the queen of France in 1555, who was deeply interested in the occult. Nostradamus foretold the manner of King Henry II's death (he was pierced in the eye by a lance shard in a celebratory tournament), and he seems to have been equally accurate about the long reign of Catherine. He even foretold his own death.

What keeps us interested in this amazing man to this day is the stanza that says:

Like the great king of the Angolmois
The year 1999, seventh month,
The Great king of terror will descend from the sky,
At this time, Mars will reign for the good cause.

A Modern Prophet

Closer to our own time there is the remarkable example of Edgar Cayce, known as the "sleeping prophet." Cayce (1877–1945) was born on a Kentucky farm and hoped to be a preacher, but the loss of his voice at age twenty-one changed the course of his life.

Put under hypnosis to cure the laryngitis, he informed the hypnotist of what was wrong with him and instructed him how to heal it. The hypnotist then asked Cayce for advice about an ailment of his own, and Cayce, again hypnotized, prescribed a treatment that worked. Soon he had a reputation as a healer, giving diagnoses and suggesting treatments, only a few of which failed. When Cayce would come to from a trance state, he remembered nothing of what he had said.

A devout traditional Christian, Cayce was at first frightened of his powers, thinking them the work of the Devil, especially when he learned that in trance he had told of the theory of reincarnation, claiming it to be factual. As his experience with his abilities grew—and many people asked him for readings—he reconciled his work with his faith. Biographers claim that Cayce's readings for individuals were uncannily accurate; records were kept and still exist. In addition, Cayce predicted the 1929 Wall Street crash, prophesied that two presidents would die in office (Roosevelt and Kennedy), and that the end of World War II would be in 1945. He also prophesied that there would be a period of worldwide disasters from 1958 to 1997, and many think the eruptions of Mt. St. Helens as well as various earthquakes, hurricanes, and firestorms—especially on the West Coast—were foreshadowed by his readings.

Curiously, the end-date of the cataclysmic period predicted by Cayce dovetails with the eerie Nostradamus quatrain quoted above.

The Alchemical Quest

Alchemy was the magic of the seventeenth century, and its practitioners kept their work shrouded in secrecy and encoded their writings in cryptic language. Partly this was a defense against the incursions of the wrath of the Catholic Church, whose Inquisition and witch-burnings were notorious. Perhaps, too, the alchemists remembered the savage attack on alchemists during the Church's early history. After the conversion of the Emperor Constantine, the Christians, catapulted into imperial favor, sacked and burned the great Library of Alexandria, brutally and torturously murdering its well-loved philosopher librarian, Hypatia, known for her beauty and learning. One excuse for this massive destruction of priceless and irreplaceable documents—including Aristotle's personal collection of books—was that the Library's scholars were practicing alchemy, supposedly the art of transforming base metal into gold, but actually an effort to discover the "philosopher's stone," or the secret of eternal life. To protect themselves, the seventeenth-century alchemists not only encoded their researches in arcane terms, they put about the acceptable story that their work was a symbolic attempt at mystical union with Christ.

The pagan world had no aversion to magic; it was an accepted part of everyday life, derived from natural means, and was not associated with evil or the Devil. But Christianity turned magic on its head and assigned it to the devil, literally. Thus, there was real danger in trodding the path of the mage and much need for the resultant secrecy.

Alchemy, like the earlier magic, was the attempt to make contact with the source of all power—*at will.* It's aim was to enable adepts to hook in to that power source on command, just as we access the electrical power station when we turn the light switch. The way was arduous, requiring a complete transformation of the psyche, or personality, a process Jung termed *individuation.* The alchemical idea that there slumbers in nature "a divine secret" is basic to the process of individuation, and to psychic development.

The great Swiss psychologist Carl Jung devoted ten years to the study of alchemy, producing two magnificent volumes as a result of his research. At first, however, he thought it was "stuff and nonsense," but as he perused his studies he came to understand that it was "the historical counterpart of [his] psychology of the unconscious."

The alchemists, he found, were attempting to achieve the same result as he was: to discover the inner workings of the universe, the "secret laws." To do this was to penetrate to the mystery of life itself.

In his autobiographical work, *Memories, Dreams, Reflections,* Jung states that his discovery of alchemy, the central intellectual adventure of his career, was prefigured by a whole series of amazingly precognitive dreams. He could not fail to see the connection between his own inner workings, as revealed by the dreams, and the inner "secret" language of the alchemists.

The secrets of the alchemists, despite the copious writings they left behind, may never be fully known to us, but it is worth noting that Jung considered the Indian yogic idea—that supernatural powers are merely the *natural* result of spiritual transformation—to be analogous to the aim of alchemy.

Women and Witchcraft

From time immemorial women have practiced the magical arts—healing wounds, curing disease, easing the pangs of childbirth—and millions of them paid with their lives for pursuing the ancient traditions and keeping magic alive. Despite persistent efforts by church and state to uproot magic, it refuses to die out—perhaps because it is truth—and the efforts of these countless unknown and unsung women have served to bring the tradition, today known as "wicca," or benign witchcraft, to us in the present day.

An honorable craft and the fastest-growing religion in America today, wicca carries on the great magical continuity—stretching, like a long unbroken thread in the fabric of human history, from prehistoric times to our own. If we can only become sufficiently aware of the interconnectedness of all things, overcoming sloth and preoccupation with the trivial, magic will have a successful and glorious future and take its rightful place among the useful pursuits of humans.

As we study the magical tradition and hear what our leading-edge scientists are saying, we come to the inescapable conclusion that we indeed do live in a "magical" universe, where, beneath the visible forms, an invisible support system of energy connects all to all.

We have said that magic and mysticism have in common the idea that there is an "inner force," and they both attempt to tune in to it. Mysticism, in fact, underlay and inspired the magic of the sixteenth and seventeenth centuries.

Poets and artists, too, have felt this deep truth. After intensively studying the life and work of Vincent van Gogh, I am convinced that this magnificent painter was also a natural mystic able to perceive the basal energies behind the forms of the objects he was inspired to paint and draw. This "lifting of the veil" enabled him to produce incomparable works of art but also contributed to his despair. That he saw what others did not—and that his most profound work was ignored and ridiculed—finally drove him mad. As the fortunate inheritors of his transcendent vision, recorded in the astounding treasure trove he left behind, those with the eyes to see can read the secret language of nature shimmering behind the whorls of paint, gleaming through sunflowers, irises, sunlit fields—even old shoes.

Lest you think it is necessary to be a mystic or a talented artist to contact this underlying realm of energy that upholds all life, try this exercise in focusing, which is based upon the Zen idea that, in meditation, one can focus so intensely upon facets of everyday life that one comes to experience them as having their own transcendence.

Meditation for Transcending the Ordinary

First, choose an object upon which to focus. It can be anything out of your usual environment—something of which you are particularly fond or to which you have a sentimental connection. I find that beginners do well working with plants or flowers, because these are obviously alive. Items from nature such as a seashell or a crystal also work well.

Next, pick a place where you can be comfortable and remain undisturbed for about twenty minutes. Wear loose clothes and eliminate bright lights and noise sources.

Place the object in front of you on a table or the floor (you can also do this outdoors, in a park or on the beach) and allow yourself a few minutes to relax and form a one-on-one relationship with the object you have chosen.

Now, take several deep breaths, exhaling slowly while clearing your mind of random thoughts. Begin to focus closely on the object. You are going to penetrate its essence, become one with it, understand that you and it are of the same essential stuff. As you concentrate your attention on the object, try to sense what it would say to you if it could speak. Imagine the hidden knowledge it contains, which it has learned on its journey through life.

Continuing to focus, really *look* at the object. If it is a plant or flower, examine each leaf or petal, noticing the delicate veins or shadings of color. Look at it as if you had never seen anything like it before. Make experiencing its reality something entirely new, as if it were from another planet.

Take notice of its unique shape and construction and look for small details that set it apart from similar objects. Acknowledge its uniqueness.

Realize that it is made up of the same electrons whirling around the nuclei of atoms as you are and envision these in both the object and in yourself as coming from the same universal source. Recognize that you and the object are one and interrelated. Credit your intuition with having the power to experience this unified life field. Reject the notion of being a separate being in a fragmented world and accept the reality that you are connected to everything in the universe, that your sense of apartness is merely the result of perceptual limitations which you can transcend.

Now, see yourself as able to perceive the true nature of the universe with everything in it as connected to everything else. Imagine what it would be like to live in a world where everyone realized this as the ultimate truth. Envision peace and plenty for all as a result of the world being recognized as a unified whole rather than merely a collection of separate and unrelated parts.

Finish by sending love and harmony to the object and thanking it for existing and gracing your environment.

After you finish this meditation, do something very ordinary—like eating a piece of fruit. Focus on the experience to the exclusion of everything else. Before eating, examine the fruit with care, noticing tiny details. If it is an orange, look closely at the pores in the skin, or try to count the freckles on a banana. Feel the shape in your hands, imagine the tree upon which it grew, the people who planted the tree and harvested the crop.

Continue to imagine the entire chain that brought the piece of fruit to you, from the grower to the supermarket. Literally hundreds of people were involved in the process. Imagine the fruit tree as a small seed and think about the whole life process that transformed that seed into a fruit-bearing tree. Eat the fruit slowly, in tiny bites, savoring each, noticing how you react to the experience of taking in life-sustaining nourishment from the life source. Imagine all the fruit trees in the world as emanating from the same energy and understand that you are incorporating that energy into your own body. Mentally celebrate the joys and benefits of the everyday reality in which you live and have your being. Consider that the flavor of the entire ocean is contained in but a single drop, that the entire mystery of life lies within a seed or an egg.

And then consider the words of the poet-mystic William Blake.

> To See a World in a Grain of Sand,
> And Heaven in a Wild Flower,
> Hold Infinity in the palm of your hand,
> And Eternity in an hour.

You have just experienced your intuition. You now know that it really exists and that you can access it. Having experienced it once, you can experience it again and again.

Imagination Is the Link to the Soul

3

Your Psychic Profile

The need for direct experience—understanding for oneself and doing it oneself—is developing in human beings all over the world.
—MARY ORSER AND RICHARD A. ZARRO,
Changing Your Destiny

Your psychic profile is like no other. Only you can determine who you are and how your inner self operates. There are, however, guidelines for those who are seeking to find the path of intuition and psychic guidance within themselves. It is not an easy task, but with perseverance and practice it can be accomplished. Once you are in tune with your inner guidance system, you will stay on course, or learn to make adjustments to any course you are following at the moment. There is no right or wrong way in these matters. Everything is up to the individual. The only test is that of your own experience.

For some, the psychic experience is ephemeral and hard to pin down. Others experience concrete results, real and specific. Still others want to achieve a high level of precognition. What you want to achieve through your own psychic development is generally what you will get, but it is important for you to assess your *natural* psychic bent.

There are four basic types of psychic experience. You may be a single type, a mixture of two types, or a multiple type. Also, your type may change as you live your life—nothing is carved in stone. Even if you are one definite type, you can develop the qualities of the other types if you want to work in that direction. However, at least in the beginning, it is easier to go with what comes natural- ly, to tune in to your type and work with its energy.

To this end, you are now going to spend some time discov- ering your personal psychic style—you'll uncover what appeals to you and what comes naturally. Once again, there is no right or wrong way. Treat this exercise like a game—have fun with it. Take at least an hour, longer if you wish. There's no time limit, but don't rush through.

You can also do this exercise more than once.

Determining Your Psychic Type

You are going to make a "mind map," using a technique called "clustering." You will need a large sheet of paper and some col- ored markers. Find a quiet place where you can be undisturbed. If you feel that your psychic inclination is changing as you work through the material, do the exercise again. The purpose here is for you to expand your consciousness of your inner capabilities. The more you experience this expansion, the more you will open yourself to various modes of sending and receiving.

Now, take your paper and markers and read the lists of words below. Draw a circle in the center of the sheet of paper. Then, choose one or two words from any category that appeals to you and seems to best express how you think of yourself. and write this word, or words inside the circle. Choose any color marker that appeals to you. This is a right-brain exercise. Try not to think or analyze as you go along. Just let your intuition choose the words and the colors in which to write them. Continue choosing words and group them in little clusters out from the center, using straight lines to connect the outside cir- cles to the center one. You may find that you are consistently choosing the same colors for your words, or that certain words or groups of words seem to belong in a particular color. Just let the process flow from your intuitive self until you feel you have finished. There's no minimum and no maximum. Choose as many or as few words as you like and arrange them spontaneously. Don't try to figure out what goes together, for it all goes together.

Word Lists

ACTIVE	RECEPTIVE
Enthusiasm	Feeling
Expansion	Sensitive
Optimism	Reflective
Generous	Receptive
Generalizing	Emotionally perceptive
Lucky	Sympathetic
Broadening horizons	Nostalgic
Independent	Comfort-loving
Avoiding restraints	Security-oriented
Outdoors	Accumulating
Travel	Moody
Exploring	Maternal
Foreign	Food-oriented
Athletic	Nurturing
Straightforward	Protective
Honorable	Child-loving
Just	Emotional
Ethical	Passive
Spiritual seeking	Changeable
Outgoing	Instinctive
Farsighted	Intuitive
Truth seeking	Subconscious
Prophetic	Cautious
Philosophical	Conservative
Moral	Traditional
Charitable	
Ceremonial	
Positive attitude	
Benevolence	
Goodwill	

ABSTRACT
Innovative
Inventive
Communicative
Independent
Insightful
Original
Unique
Unusual
Sudden
Unexpected
Individualistic
Nontraditional
Awakening
Brainstorming
Free
Breakthrough
Experimental
Open to new ideas
Broadminded
Tolerant
Liberal
Revolutionary
Reformist
Detached
Intellectually intuitive
Mental
Cooperative
Humanitarian
Eccentric
Communicative

FLOWING
Sensitive
Intense
Sympathetic
Compassionate
Benevolent
Fantastic
Creative
Secluded
Idealistic
Subtle
Aesthetic
Artistic
Musical
Inspired
Spiritual
Mystical
Visionary
Interdimensional
Otherworldly
Dreamy
Introverted
Mind-altering
Emotional
Universal love
Movies
Compassion
Dreams
Hidden things

When you have finished your cluster drawing, just sit with it for a while and let it sink into your unconscious. Look at it as you would look at an abstract painting, enjoying the colors and the composition without giving any thought to the meaning. See what it says to you *as a whole*. Does it tell you anything about yourself, perhaps show you some new angle? Maybe you chose one color predominately over the others. Do you see a pattern?

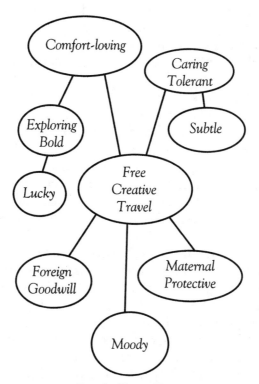

Sample Cluster Drawing

Run your hands over the sheet of paper and see if it gives off any "vibes" that you can feel. Is there a kinesthetic quality to it? Would you like to make it more tactile, perhaps by using textured paper or gluing bits of paper on collage style? Notice your reactions.

Next, read your words out loud, starting at the center and moving outward. How do the words sound to you? Are they pleasant to your ear? How do you react to hearing the words spoken?

Look at your colors. Do you like the colors you chose? Do you feel they harmonize with each other or not? Would you make changes? Do you feel you chose colors you truly like or ones you habitually use? Do you wish you'd been more daring, or more conservative?

After you have experienced your mind map for a few minutes, take a clean sheet of paper and divide it into four sections marked ACTIVE, RECEPTIVE, ABSTRACT, FLOWING.

Count the number of words you selected out of each category and put that number in the appropriate section. Next, count the number of words in all categories in each color you used. Note the number of words in each color at the bottom of your sheet of paper; for example: Blue–10; Green–8.

The *highest* number in your category section is your profile type, which is described below.

If you do not have a single highest number, you are a mixed profile type. Read the descriptions of both types. You may be a "seesaw" mixed type, alternating between one mode and the other, or you may be a blend. Only you can decide. It's also possible for mixed types to have a primary mode and a secondary mode. Usually the two modes are not equally balanced.

If you have three or more numbers that are equal, you are a multiple type. Read all the sections that apply and blend the interpretations. True multiple types are rare, but they do occur. If you are a multiple type, you are probably already very psychically sensitive. On the other hand, you may be confused. The multiple type person tends to be a psychic sponge, soaking up impressions from many sources and not really knowing which apply. A confused multiple type person can concentrate on making a choice of which type to develop and strengthen.

The Active Profile

The psychic energy of the *Active* type is radiant, excitable, enthusiastic. The Active person goes after experiences, welcomes the new and untried. Active people are spontaneous, quick, full of flowing energy. They tend to be senders more than receivers, as they like to initiate contact. They receive information galvanically, in sudden bursts like lightning flashes. High-spirited, they want the freedom to explore their psychic landscapes on their own terms, usually alone. There is a problem with impatience here, and a lack of ability to settle down and concentrate on developing psychic skills. Since the Active person is used to getting information quickly, and acting on it just as quickly, it is hard for this type to spend time in meditation and restful silence. The Active person needs to cultivate these qualities.

The Active person is psychically vibrant and has a vision or a quest to fulfill in life. Inspiration usually comes easily, but the

Active type gets depressed and feels cut off from the inner source when the channel is clogged and there is no flow of inspiration. In order to reconnect at these times, you need to become quiet, meditate, restore the flow. Because you are used to insightful flashes, you don't spend the necessary time in introspection. It is also important for you to verify your hunches and intuitive sparks before taking action. Mostly your intuition functions correctly, but because you rely on it to happen spontaneously you don't take the time to tend the garden of the psychic realm, which can then sprout weeds as well as flowers. If you want to fully develop your psychic gifts, you must learn to be quiet and listen to your inner voice when it whispers. Often, you hear only the shouts.

Persons with an Active profile tend to use psychic experiences to activate them, deriving motivation from their inner intuition pushing them. Often this appears as impulsiveness, but it is a response to an inner drive. Athletes and performers are often Active types, finding a center from where they can move into the physical world with grace and precision.

Active persons are drawn to bright colors, like fire-engine red, orange, lime-green, lemon-yellow, electric blue.

The Receptive Profile

The psychic energy of the *Receptive* type is grounded. This energy is closely related to the physical and emotional planes of existence, and very often Receptive types feel bodily sensations as clues to their psychic experiences. They are apt to get "gut feelings," or to have a particular area of the body respond to incoming psychic information. Some get headaches, tingling sensations, goosebumps, or other physical sensations as clues to the inner process. More receivers than senders, Receptive persons make good healers and counselors. They are patient, thorough, and good listeners. Receptive persons tend to distrust flashes of intuition that are not accompanied by bodily sensations. They are willing to discipline themselves and practice meditation on a regular basis in order to get the results they want. With enormous endurance at their disposal, they persist in their goal no matter how difficult the task. Receptive persons often do very difficult psychic work. Like a miner sifting through tons of ore for gold, the Receptive person keeps an eye on the desired end and doesn't mind the work it takes to get there.

As a Receptive type, you tend to stay with what you already know, in the safe zone. Opening up to different areas of your psychic landscape will give you more variety of experience. Try to go exploring, setting your fears aside. Just because you know what works doesn't mean you shouldn't try something new once in awhile. It's good for you—don't get stuck in a psychic rut. You are capable of sending as well as receiving, and you can receive in more modes than the kinesthetic one. Go slowly at first when exploring the new, but know that you can learn to trust your inner self in all its marvelous variations.

People with Receptive profiles tend to use psychic experience in a practical way, such as making money or being successful at some enterprise. Hotel mogul Conrad Hilton relied heavily on his hunches, and many financial barons and CEOs consult their intuitive selves frequently.

Receptive people prefer muted colors, like rich burgundy, forest green, pumpkin orange, mustard yellow.

The Abstract Profile

The psychic energy of the *Abstract* type is airy and constantly shifting, like the blowing of the winds. The Abstract type can travel very far out on a mental road and usually has no fear of exploring the unknown. In fact, the farther out it is, the less known it is, the more it appeals to the Abstract type. The nonmaterial world is very appealing to the Abstract profile person, who firmly believes in "mind over matter" and uses psychic intuition to build castles in the air. These abstractions seem very real indeed, and they are compellingly fascinating. The Abstract type thrives on ideas of what is possible—likes to imagine "What if…?" and then go inward to find the answer. "What if I could actually feel every cell in my body individually?" "What if I could communicate with celestial intelligences?" No concept is too strange or unfamiliar for the Abstract personality to attempt. Abstract people know that everything on earth existed in the abstract before it became concrete. Their motto is, "We are all an idea in the mind of God." They are unusually good at verbalizing their psychic experiences, although they are somewhat detached because they don't get emotional about what they perceive, finding it all simply intriguing. Like an explorer whose job it is to map new territory, the Abstract type enjoys adventure for its own sake. Often they "see" clairvoyantly, or have visions.

Abstract types can lose themselves in the strangeness of the experience and fail to make concrete connections back to daily life. Like a person using a psychedelic drug, they get their minds blown away by the extravagance of the experience, and then, back on earth, they find it has no relevance to the mundane sphere. They need to connect the two sides of their own reality, test their psychic concepts, and validate them in real time. Excitement resulting from forging ahead into strange and unexplored country is thrilling, but unless one comes back with some useful information, it remains in the abstract.

Those with Abstract profiles tend to be thinkers and scientists. Physicists, the computer proficient, and those concerned with what is new and untried tend to be Abstract. Given to theorizing and conceptualizing, they receive information from their unconscious, which aids them in developing theories and testing them for verification. They often wait long periods for results.

Abstract people favor stark colors, like black and white, or clashing colors, like violet and green, electric blue and tangerine. Whatever is unusual or shocking appeals to their taste.

The Flowing Profile

The psychic energy of the *Flowing* person is intangible. Flowing types are natural psychics. Highly imaginative, they are exquisitely tuned in to feelings, their own and other people's. Flowing types are often "psychic sponges" who soak up impressions from a myriad of different sources and have a hard time sorting it all out. They are very aware of their unconscious processes, even if these seem peculiar to others. Often they feel as if they are "weird," that no one can understand what they feel and experience. Being natural psychics, they both send and receive, and they have intuitive knowing (clairsentience) without knowing where it comes from. However, they trust their inner promptings and act on them, sometimes against good sense. They are the mystics and dreamers among us, the ones who are in touch with the deeper dimensions of life. They flow as water flows, into and out of minute crevices in their own and others' psyches. They are deep, partly invisible, and buffeted by inner currents. Most often they have a problem with verbalizing their psychic experience, and when questioned will reply, "I just *know.*"

The Flowing profile person needs to get a better handle on reality in order to translate transcendent experiences into useable form. Flowing types are mediumistic and can set themselves aside so that other energies can flow through them. They run the danger of getting lost in their own mysterious depths, and therefore they should practice grounding exercises and keep focused in meditation.

As a flowing type, you are the most sensitive of people. You feel everything and absorb the undercurrents of what is going on in those around you. Having the ability to flow into whatever you experience, you are unusually perceptive and imaginative, but you do not "reality-check" your acute perceptions. Though you are often stunningly accurate, you still need to be aware of the source of your information, make sure you are not getting unverifiable signals that may throw you off your track.

People with Flowing profiles tend to be artistic and creative. They are often in the theater or film, and many Flowing types are professional psychics. They also lean toward the helping professions—psychology, healing, and the use of the intuitive arts. They are motivated by compassion and their acute understanding of the sufferings of others.

The Flowing person likes soft pastels like sky blue, powder pink, lilac, banana yellow, moss green, and pale orange.

Your psychic profile shows how you tend to use your psychic energies, which modes (visual, auditory, kinesthetic) you are most attuned to, what you're most in touch with naturally. Your dominant mode will indicate where in the psychic landscape you are most at ease.

Another advantage of knowing your psychic profile is that you can learn a great deal about your natural inner attunement and take the best advantage of developing your psychic abilities. For example, if you are a Receiver you can learn to pay attention to your gut feelings, honor them, and begin to develop trust in them. The more you strengthen your natural mode of psychic perceiving, the more able you will be to develop a range of psychic abilities, and have a broader spectrum of psychic experiences.

Remember also that psychic experience is intensely personal, emanating as it does from an inner symbolic level residing in the substrata of our being. No two people will have identical experiences. Only you can validate and evaluate the information you receive. Others can tell you what has happened to them, but your own experience will be unique.

You can think of your psychic self as a large satellite dish constantly scanning the atmosphere for signals, while at the same time you have a powerful radioscopic receiver always at the ready to receive messages. None of us have both of these in equal proportion. Some are better senders than receivers, some the opposite. And it is possible to switch from being a good sender to being a good receiver. The better you get at one skill, the better you will become at others.

Power, Clarity, and Vision Are Yours

Part II

Opening the Psychic Door

The Psychic Landscape

Avoid the teachings of speculators whose judgments
are not confirmed by experience.
—LEONARDO DA VINCI

The psychic landscape has many vistas, many places to visit, become acquainted with, or take up residence. It is a territory with main highways that are well traveled and familiar; broad avenues where those who trod its daily routes can meet; side streets where vendors of various sorts dwell; back roads known only to those who have ventured far into the domain; little traveled byways familiar to but a few intrepid souls; difficult-to-find paths that lead to enchanted gardens; all-but-invisible tracks with a far-off terminus shrouded in the mists; secret places whose whereabouts are carefully guarded against intrusion by the unwary; trails as yet unblazed; and undiscovered realms waiting for the adventurous—those unafraid to seek greater mansions.

One facet of the psychic landscape with which everyone is familiar is extrasensory perception, generally called ESP, which is a generic term that has been used as a sort of blanket or umbrella shorthand for those experiences and phenomena for which we cannot account by use of the five senses.

You have probably experienced ESP in some form or other. It might have been a hunch that you felt compelled to follow, a sense that something was going to happen, or a sense of urgency to take an action.

For example, I was once in a cab on my way to a business appointment. I was late and rushing, but halfway there I suddenly felt compelled to return to my apartment. Shoving the urge out of my consciousness did not work. I *had* to go back. Cursing myself for a fool for jeopardizing an important contact, I directed the driver to take me home.

The smell of smoke greeted me as I opened my door. I had failed to turn off the gas under the teakettle, which had boiled dry and caught fire. No harm was done, but it could have been a disaster. I thanked my lucky stars for the sense of urgency that brought me back. Missing that meeting was nothing compared to having my apartment—with my cats in it—go up in flames.

Other common ESP experiences include the feeling that you need to telephone someone right away. When you reach that person, he or she tells you that they have been trying to contact you!

If I am correct in asserting that we possess *subtle* senses, in a whole range, rather like a color spectrum, then these subtle senses are what account for extrasensory perception. This theory goes a long way toward demystifying the psychic and allowing us to accept that we all possess these extra or subtle senses.

Just as reading improves skill in comprehension and communication, stretching our mental muscles in the psychic realm leads to acquiring new strength and new capabilities.

Exploring the psychic landscape is a bit like going on safari. You're in a place where wild animals live, but there are well-marked trails and competent guides who know the lay of the land. You can choose to take a tour with a group, or you can strike out on your own. Whichever way you go, you have the possibility of encountering an animal. You may have spent days hoping to spot a tiger and then you see a startlingly beautiful bird you didn't even know existed. Or you may have started out as a bird-watcher and while poised with your eyes on the sky heard the soft fall of a tiger's paws nearby.

If you stay on the known paths, the chances are you will experience what you are anticipating—but not always. I was once working quite steadily to achieve a certain manifestation and quite out of the blue I discovered that I had healing power.

I didn't know where it came from or why I got it; what I could determine was that it occurred in me in response to someone else's need. A client would complain of a headache, and I would feel the sensation overcome me, lay my hands—which became red-hot—on her forehead, and her headache would vanish.

A dramatic incident of the uninvited appearance of this healing power, with potent ramifications, occurred during a trip to Mexico. In the colonial town of Los Alamos, we scheduled dinner at a hotel converted from an eighteenth-century convent. Diners were served communally in an open courtyard under a starlit sky.

A dozen people were seated at the table with my friend at one end and a distinguished-looking gray-haired man at the other. I sat to the left of my friend, and a lady many years his junior sat to the right of the man. Drinks were served and chatter animated the night. After a bit, the man announced to the company that he apologized for his lady's silence, but she had been stricken with laryngitis and could not speak. A general wave of sympathy went up for the dumbstruck woman, and I felt intense pain coming from her direction. After a few moments' hesitation, I told my partner I was going to give her a healing. Walking to the other end of the table, I spoke softly to her, saying I was a healer, and laid my hands on her shoulders. I felt severe constriction in her entire body and my intuition told me that her laryngitis was psychologically based.

Asking her to turn her chair away from the other guests for privacy, I slipped into a meditative state while gently touching her neck and throat with my hands, which had become very hot with the psychic energy. As I held her head between my hands, I realized she was afraid to speak, that she was intimidated by her partner. I sensed an abusive relationship between them with her as the victim. Whispering, I told her she need not be afraid of speaking, that nothing would hurt her, that I would surround her with protective white light. As I spoke, I felt her tears dripping down on my hands. Slowly her body began to release its stored tensions.

In muted and scratchy tones, which only I could hear, she told me her story. Unmarried, she had been the man's secretary and had become his mistress. He had been a member of the U.S. diplomatic service prior to retiring. Though his wife had died and they now traveled together, he had never offered her marriage and constantly berated her, telling her often to "Shut up" or "Keep your stupid mouth shut." Shy and self-effacing, though desperately unhappy at her dependence, she had lacked the courage to speak her mind or defend herself.

I continued to pour energy into her from the deep well of the psyche to which I was connected, and when the heat in my hands began to subside, she spoke in a low but normal voice.

"I'm going to leave him," she said. "I have my own money and I'm not going to be told to shut up anymore."

I squeezed her shoulders gently and returned to my seat. As I left and she turned her chair back toward the table, the man shot me a look of malice and contempt. I could only hope the healing would take and stick.

As I resumed my seat, the first course was served and the man, who was dominating the conversation, gestured preemptorily toward his companion and said, "Eat your soup."

"I won't eat my soup!" she exclaimed in clear, ringing tones. "You know I don't like soup. Why did you order it for me?"

Dumbfounded at her renewed power of speech, the man glared—part malevolence, part astonishment—while the others, collectively paused mid-bite, stared at the unfolding drama. After a few silent, breath-holding moments, she rose, picked up her purse, and left the table, striding out of the courtyard with firm steps, leaving her abuser silent in her wake. As her high heels clicked determinedly across the flagged terrace, he looked after her, apparently too stunned to move I thanked the Higher Power for allowing me to be its instrument.

After some practice, I found I could call up the healing energy, but only erratically. As I could not depend on its occurring, I could not offer a healing service to my clients but only use it when it happened spontaneously. Eventually, I lost the power—or the connection. Probably it was out of disuse, but I had other priorities than developing as a healer, which I knew from association with professional healers was a very specific and arduous path.

So, be prepared for surprises as you scout your psychic landscape, and keep in mind that you will find your own true way, whether it is a clearly marked highway or an opening in the psychic woods that leads you know not where. I often think in this regard of the words of Elizabeth Barrett Browning,

...to the depths and breadths and heights
my soul can reach when reaching out of sight
for the ends of being and ideal grace.

We who trod the psychic landscape are always involved in "reaching out of sight," and though we stand little chance of finding the "ends of being," it is a goal worth pursuing in the hope of glimpsing "ideal grace."

Modes of Receiving Psychic Information

Intuition connects with our conscious mind in the form we most readily accept it. The new science of neurolinguistic programming has shown that there are three basic types of people—auditory, kinesthetic, and visual. Each of us has a primary mode through which we process information coming from the outside world, which is reflected in how we process information coming from the intuitive/psychic realm. Thus, some "hear" a message, others "feel" a sensation in the body, and the rest "envision" a picture.

Auditory forms are common. For example, a research chemist reports that after a long period of concentration and efforts to understand a complex problem, he abandoned the method. Tired, discouraged, hungry, he walked out to find a meal and suddenly, "at a definite spot," the precise description of a new method popped into his head, as if shouted in words.

Visual forms are frequent in children who have not learned sophisticated verbal skills, because children naturally think in images. Artists, especially, will receive visual impressions of psychic messages. An English writer says that he gets "the visualized picture" of a story's central figure or incident "with such force that I am unable to rest...until I have set [it] down on paper."

Kinesthetic forms, which can occur in any part of the body, are often experienced by those who express themselves in a physical manner—the sculptor, the athlete, the active person. The physical sensation may or may not be accompanied by words or images. A New York city detective once told me he always had an "itch" on his right hand when he knew he was about to solve a case. His itchy hand reached for just the right file, or piece of information to fit into the investigative puzzle, almost without his volition.

Although each person will receive psychic messages in the dominant form that is their usual way of perceiving reality, this does not mean that we are restricted to one or the other form exclusively. Some people use all three modes in varying degrees.

For example, before I became a writer I was a graphics artist, which makes me a visual person who is at the same time connected to verbal skills. In using Tarot cards, I call upon images to produce a "field" of information, but when I am reading a horoscope my mind fills with words. Often it is as if I am "reading" them from an already written transcript. The interpretation comes into my mind *whole*, connecting the living person sitting across my table with the symbols upon the sheet of paper I have before me.

However, for many years I had no understanding of what gut feelings were all about, never having had any. Yet I knew people who relied upon them utterly. Only recently have I had kinesthetic experiences, learning that a particular sensation in a specific part of my anatomy always warns me of impending danger. The first time this feeling occurred, I narrowly prevented my cat from falling off a terrace three floors above the ground. A feeling in the groin area shot an adrenaline-like warning to my brain and I acted immediately, without thought or question. Now I know I can rely on that anatomical center's connection to my intuition. Probably you have had similar experiences, especially if the kinesthetic mode is your dominant mode for learning.

In psychic terms, these three modes—auditory, kinesthetic, and visual—are called clairaudient, clairsentient, and clairvoyant, respectively.

Clairaudient, or "clear hearing," according to Webster's, is defined as "the act or the power of hearing something not present to the ear but regarded as having objective reality." The person who is clairaudient "hears" information being received from the intuitive mind.

Clairsentient, literally means "clear thinking" and is defined as "perception of that which isn't normally perceptible [to the senses]." The clairsentient will "feel" psychic information, or "just know" something to be true. The clairsentient functions in the kinesthetic mode.

Clairvoyant, literally "clear seeing," is defined as "the act or the power of discerning objects not present to the senses but regarded as having objective reality; and, clear-sightedness; ability to perceive things out of the range of ordinary perception." The clairvoyant person "sees," or uses the visual mode.

An easy way to determine the mode in which one processes information is to pay attention to how a person responds verbally to questions. For example, if you are pressing a point and the other person says, "I *know* what you're talking about," the kinesthetic mode is being expressed. The auditory mode person will say, "I *hear* what you're saying," while the visual mode person will say, "I *see* what you mean."

Think back to times when you have had hunches. Did you get a feeling in a part of your body? Do mental images come to you when you are intuitively in touch? Does a specific sound, such as a telephone ringing or a doorbell, wake you in the night though it's only a dream?

If you don't already know your dominant mode, here is a meditation exercise you can use to discover what it is.

Dominant Mode Discovery Exercise

Begin by choosing a location where you can be comfortable and undisturbed for twenty minutes. Loosen any tight clothing and eliminate outside distractions such as noise. Nighttime is ideal since the psychic door opens wider during the hours of darkness.

In this exercise, you are going to take a trip into your own unconscious, which is symbolized by an underground chamber. In this underground chamber, you will find three masks—one for the auditory type, one for the visual type, and one for the kinesthetic type. Spend a few minutes imagining what each type might look like. Examine your perception of a person who perceives through seeing, hearing, feeling.

Next, take several deep breaths. Inhale fully and exhale slowly. During exhalation, imagine that all the day's stress is leaving your mind and body. Allow yourself to stay with your breath for a few minutes just concentrating on the inflow and outflow of air. In and out. In and out. In and out.

When you are feeling calm and relaxed, imagine yourself crossing the room and opening a door that leads to a deep underground chamber. Down and down you go until you arrive in the special place where your intuition dwells.

When you reach the bottom of the descent (which may be a stairway, a ramp, a long slope, or even an elevator), you find another door leading to the inner chamber of your psyche, where you will meet your psychic mode, which is waiting to reveal itself to you.

Open the door to the inner chamber and enter it. Look around and notice what you see—if it is small or large, neat or cluttered, attractive or unattractive. Walk around your inner chamber paying attention to the details. Make a note of anything you want to remember or change later on.

At the center of the room there is a table upon which are the three masks, each one representing a different psychic mode. Go over to the table and view the masks and notice your reactions. Allow yourself to become familiar with each one and then choose the one you like best. You may instantly recognize your mode, or you may take some time before deciding which suits you best.

Pick up your mode-mask and hold it over your face. There is a mirror in the chamber. Look into it and gauge your rapport with the mask you have picked. Does it seem just right? Do you like the way it looks? Does it make you feel comfortable? Is it something you'd want others to know about you? If you like, you can try on all three masks before making a decision.

The strength of the pull you feel toward each will be your guide. If only one draws you, you are a dominant-mode person. If two have equal appeal, you are a dual-mode person. If you simply cannot choose among the three, you are a multiple-mode person. No one is right or wrong, better or worse, superior or inferior. What is important is *you*. Remember that whichever mode you identify now is your current mode and can be changed. The more you use your intuition, the more likely you are to expand the modes you can access.

When the psychic message arrives in words, it is usually fairly easy to understand and can ordinarily be expressed to others. Hearing your grandmother call your name is straightforward—though sometimes these verbal messages can be cryptic or seem coded and require deciphering. When this happens, as it often does with dream material, I find it useful to ask intuition to help. I will pose the question "What did that mean?" to my unconscious mind, which always knows the answer even when I am stumped.

However, if the psyche expresses itself in nonverbal modes there can be difficulty communicating with others. "I have this itching in my right hand," might bring on hoots of laughter (as it did with my detective friend's hard-boiled colleagues until he became famous for his itch, which solved cases). Visual images may also prove difficult to communicate, unless one is an artist and can draw what one sees internally.

But we should not place a greater value on one mode of perception over another, accepting our psyche in whichever way it chooses to present itself. Nor should we refuse information in a different medium than the one usually employed, just because it is a variation. The important thing is to be self-aware and openminded.

This openness is, psychologically speaking, a condition of waiting and readiness to receive messages of information and guidance. It is necessary to put aside any fear and trust the intuitive process. You must genuinely accept that the information you receive will be for your benefit, that it will be valid, worthwhile, and deserving of respect.

Trust Your Intuitive Process

5

Variations on the Psychic Theme

We will, by conscious command, evolve cerebral centers which will permit us to use powers that we now are not even capable of imagining.
—Dr. Frederic Tilney

As stated earlier, ESP—also known as psi—is the generic term for psychic experience, but within the psychic landscape there are variations on the general theme.

Here is a broad overview touching on the main varieties of psychic experience. My personal interest is the fusion of psychology—the inner dimension—with the psychic, which might be called the ultra-inner dimension, and the exploration of altered states of consciousness, especially those in the many levels of dreaming, which in turn lead to psychic experiences. You may recognize types of experience you have already had but did not know how to classify.

As you read this book and work through the exercises given, you will begin to recognize your own particular talents or preferences, and you may decide to concentrate your efforts in a specific area of development. Just as a student is attracted to a certain course of study due to innate leanings, we are each drawn to an area of the psychic landscape commensurate with our inner Self. Not everyone needs or wants to explore or master the entire range of possibilities, and this is perfectly all right.

showed that it is possible for subjects to accurately acquire descriptive information about a place unfamiliar to them.

Also, physicist Russell Targ, co-author of *Mind Reach: Scientists Look at Psychic Ability,* who in the 1970s pioneered remote viewing in the United States at Stanford Research Institute, says,

> In the experimental mode, we have extremely strong evidence that people can obtain information about the present and the future that they have not previously experienced. And we can show people how to gain access to and incorporate that kind of information into their lives.

Remote Viewing Exercise

To practice second sight, it is important to be relaxed and comfortable, with no distractions. Because this is an advanced technique, give yourself plenty of time to get into the proper calm state necessary.

Choose a "target" address you wish to visit, a place with which you are totally unfamiliar and have not previously seen pictures of. Now imagine yourself floating gently out of your body and standing beside yourself. Look at your physical self and take note of details—hair, clothing, position. Then imagine your etheric body traveling slowly upward to a place at the top of the building and go out through the roof. Looking down, see the building you have just left, noticing the details. Next, refer to the target address you have chosen to view and imagine yourself being projected to that location. As you travel, look down occasionally and notice details—do you see a park, a bridge, a lake, a river, children playing, clogged traffic?

When you reach the building you want to view, examine it from the outside carefully, noting details. What color is it? Of what material is it constructed? Is it an old building or a new one? What shape are the windows? How many? Is there a fence or railing? Is it set back from the street or close up? Are their balconies or gardens? Look at the front door, examine it carefully. Is there a brass knocker, a doorbell, a handle, a doorknob? Be sure to take your time orienting yourself to the location.

Open the door and step inside. What is it like? Is there an entrance hall, carpet on the floor or tiles? Looking slowing and carefully at all the surroundings, move into the center of the house or building and take a walk around. How many rooms? How many floors? Staircase or elevator? How is it decorated— modern or antique? And in what colors? Is it a harmonious color scheme? Is everything new and clean or shabby and dusty? What sort of people would live or work here?

Continue your tour, always taking note of details. Look at the furniture, the number of pieces, what they are, how they are situated. Are there paintings or other decorations on the walls? Are these painted or covered with wallpaper? Is this a quiet atmosphere or a clamorous one? Do you see any people or animals about? What goes on here? Is there anything out of the ordinary, such as striking art work? Again, take your time. If you begin to feel tired, stop and rest.

When you have immersed yourself in impressions, go back outside and look again at the exterior. Now, begin your return trip back to where you left your body at home. Let yourself settle back into your physical reality slowly, feeling the parts of your body separately—your feet, legs, abdomen, chest, shoulders, arms, hands, head. Breathe deeply a few times before you open your eyes. *Do not get up quickly.* Dizziness could result.

Write down what you have seen or, working with a partner, describe it as you go along and have the other person take the notes. You may want to make a sketch. The best way to do this exercise is either to tape it or have a partner guide you through it. Whichever way you choose, make sure to allow plenty of time between instructions.

Remember, extrasensory ability is merely a channel of information and whatever comes through that channel should be treated with the same respect as any other type of information you receive.

Forecasting

Without doubt, the most commonly asked for psychic service is *forecasting*, or predictions. It does not matter what type of psychic is consulted, most people are eager to know the future—or think it would be a good thing to know. In fact if any of us could absolutely know the future as an unchangeable reality we would quite probably go mad.

What is the reliability factor of psychic predictions? Whether using astrology, Tarot cards, or no medium at all, the psychic practitioner is like a man standing at the intersection of two sidewalks. He has a view of all four directions at once. If he sees you walking toward the corner, and your friend approaching the same corner from another direction, he can safely say that you will meet at the corner—if you both continue your walk at approximately the same pace. However, suppose that you continue walking, but your friend stops to enter a shop and make a purchase. The conditions the psychic observed will have changed. The time your friend spends in the shop will give you time to reach the corner, cross the street, and continue down another block. By the time your friend reaches the corner, you will have missed each other and never know you were both in the vicinity at the same time.

Was the psychic prediction wrong? Yes and no. It was not wrong for the conditions that existed at the time of the prediction. Had they remained in force, you would have met your friend. It was wrong in that you did not meet because one of you exercised choice, or free will, which changed the psychic equation. Thus the difficulty with forecasting is the variables over which we have no control and which may not have been in play at the time the forecast was made.

An experience of mine proved the erratic reliability of forecasting. One summer I was contacted by an editor at a national magazine who told me they were looking for a new astrologer to write the monthly horoscope column. This editor had liked my book *Love Planets*, and she asked if I would write a sample column. If her editorial bosses liked it, I would be hired. Filled with anticipation, I submitted the sample. Two weeks later, the editor called, telling me it was "great." She said she was showing it to her bosses. I thought it was a done deal, but a month passed and no further word came. To reassure myself, I consulted three different telephone psychics, asking the same question: "Will I be chosen to write the column for which I submitted a sample?" All three predicted that I would be hired. One said there would be a delay and one said that she foresaw my going into syndication with a column.

Nonetheless, I had a sinking feeling that something had gone wrong, but I couldn't figure out what—I already knew my contact editor liked my work. Finally, I called her and asked what was going on. She replied that her boss, who had approved my column, had abruptly left over a dispute with the publisher. The replacement managing editor was a personal friend of the astrologer already writing the column, and she planned to keep her friend in the job. My contact apologized, said she was really sorry, but the matter was now out of her hands.

Were the psychics who predicted I'd get the column all wrong? Would I, if I were not professionally involved in the trade, feel I had been duped—those phone calls to psychics can be very expensive—and conclude that psychic predictions are all bunk?

Again the answer is yes and no. I believe that many psychics, especially those who answer the professional psychic lines, like to tell clients what they want to hear. This is a danger for the person who wants to rely on the advice of others. On the other hand, at the time the predictions were made it certainly looked as if I would be hired. As in the example above, had the original conditions remained in place, that is, if the editor had not quit, I would have got the job. But the conditions changed and all bets were off.

Interestingly, my own psychic antennae *knew* something had gone wrong, but instead of relying on my instincts— because I wanted a good outcome—I chose to ask others to predict for me. Had I gone with my own feelings, I would have saved myself weeks of anxiety by telephoning sooner and discovering the real situation.

My advice to the person seeking predictions is to realize that the success rate is, on average, only about 70 percent—and the rate of pure chance is 50 percent. Getting predictions can be fun, but there is the problem of the self-fulfilling prophecy, or that you make something happen because you have been told it will happen. This is especially true of negative predictions. It is definitely unwise to base serious life decisions only upon psychic predictions of specific future events.

What *can* be reliably foretold are trends currently in effect: these have a longer life and therefore are more susceptible to being correct. Perhaps the psychic realizes that you are moving into a new cycle in which you will be more outgoing. After months of being involved in closing out the old cycle, a change is occurring *within you*. This change carries with it great power —for you to shape or reshape your life. Based upon this information it can be predicted that you will be meeting friends more frequently, stepping up your social life, and, quite possibly, having a romantic encounter. This will not be so because the psychic sees "a dark handsome man in your future." *It will happen because you are ready for it to happen.*

The same general principle applies to predictions of negative events, such as accidents. If you are aware that an accident vibe is in the air about you, you can take precautions and the accident need not occur. Thus, such a prediction might be stated, "You are under an influence that causes accidents, especially with sharp tools and motorized vehicles," and suggest taking care. If you interpret "motorized vehicles" as automobiles, buses, and trains, you may avoid commuter transit and hurt yourself on the power lawnmower while staying home to avoid the accident that was predicted. It is as important to use common sense in dealing with predictions as it is in dealing with any other information that is given to you about your life. As we give you the tools to develop your own psychic abilities, you will learn to separate the wheat from the chaff by using the tools of verification.

To practice forecasting for yourself, you will need to become familiar with your personal *timeline*. A timeline is your particular, individual, unique relationship with Time. Just as we experience present time differently under various circumstances— sometimes it flies, sometimes it drags interminably—so too do we experience past and future time in a specific way peculiar to ourselves.

The first step in finding your timeline is to review your relationship with Time: Do you always know what time it is even if you have no clock? Do you wake up a few minutes before the hour for which you have set the alarm? Are you always prompt—or late? Does Time seem vague to you, something on which you can hardly keep a grip? Can an hour pass by without you really being aware of it?

Your personal relationship to Time will affect your ability to make predictions based upon future Time. If you are unspecific about Time, it will be unspecific about you. On the other hand, if you have an intimate relationship to Time naturally, you will get the "feel" of future time more easily.

Finding Your Personal Timeline

To find your timeline, sit comfortably and close your eyes. Now, imagine a cord stretching out from you in two directions, one toward the past, the other toward the future. First travel along the cord to the past and examine Time as you go. What does the past feel like? Does yesterday feel different from last year? How about from five years ago? Ten? When you were a child?

Next, travel along your timeline into the future. What does it feel like? Does tomorrow feel different from next week, next month, next year, five years from now, ten, twenty? Travel out along your future timeline as far as you like and look around. What do you see? Now, return to the present.

Now, decide upon a portion of the Time for which you want predictions. Perhaps you are planning a vacation for next summer and want to know how it will turn out. Travel out along your timeline to the chosen period: look around. What do you see? How does it feel? This is similar to remote viewing except that instead of looking at a location which exists you are looking at a future event which does not exist. Yet the process is the same.

It is best to choose a time fairly close so that your can verify your predictions. Begin by practicing predicting the events of the next day or next week and then expand your repertoire into the more distant future. Think of traveling along your timeline like taking a trip on a train. As you travel, you record the scenes you pass.

If you want a prediction about a specific event, use this method. If you want a prediction about a *nonspecific* event, which has no basis in future time as yet—such as "When will I find a new romance?"—travel out on your timeline and be on the lookout for the future event. Do you see it along the way? When? A good question to pose is, "When is it likely that...?"

Psychokinesis

Psychokinesis is the ability to move objects without touching them. Laboratory tests have proved that certain people can do this, and therefore we can reason that we all are capable of it. During the spiritualist craze that affected the United States and England during the latter part of the nineteenth century, mediums sent tables afloat, hurled chairs through the air, caused musical instruments to emit sounds, snatched hats off people's heads, and produced raps and knocks. Impressive, perhaps, but the craze died out simply because no one had any use for furniture sailing through the air.

Though witnessing psychokinesis can be very impressive, and the possible ramifications are stunning—imagine if you could move the lottery balls around!—the present state of affairs is very limited. However, Robert Jahn of Princeton University, using a computer-controlled random selection technique, has shown that the mind can affect matter on a minute scale, which although insufficient to influence a gaming table, could be important to today's microminiature electronic components. Speculating that mental means could be used to jam electronic circuitry, he continues his experiments in the face of controversy. Jahn's and other laboratory-controlled experiments confirm what magicians have always believed—that mind and matter are interactive.

However, for the ordinary person psychokinesis remains something of a psychic curiosity. If you want to practice psychokinesis, place a small object, such as a pencil, in front of you and concentrate your mind on it, visualizing it moving at the same time.

Mediums

Mediums essentially are stand-ins for itinerant "spirits," presumably emanating from a person once alive. The medium is a person who, in an altered state of consciousness or "trance," appears to receive communications from disembodied entities. Mediums are able to step aside, so to speak, so that the spirit force can enter them and perform. Messages come in various ways—automatic writing, utterances, and physical manifestations such as table tipping, ouija board influencing, raps and knocks.

Serious scholarly attention from men such as Sir Oliver Lodge and Frederic W. H. Myers in England and William James in America led to disciplined investigation of mediums and the phenomena they produced. An outgrowth of this was the founding of the Society for Psychical Research in 1882. The drawback that the researchers faced in attempting to authenticate the work of mediums was that there was no way of determining how much the original information had been altered by the filter of the medium's unconscious mind.

Today, research continues as part of the present effort to discover if there is something on the other side of the curtain we call death. Present-day technologies such as television, videotape, and computers are now involved, and researchers in several countries have compiled communications of "intriguing evidential significance."

Ken Wilber, a writer on the subject of survival after death, suggests that the evidence points toward "an ontological reality which is a continuum from the material at one end of the spectrum to Spirit at the other end."

Perhaps the most famous medium of modern time was Madame Helena Blavatsky, who came to America in 1873 when seances were the rage and spirits regularly made tables go topsy-turvy and furniture sail about the room. During her life, HPB (as she came to be known) manifested many occult powers, some of them suspect. Though she was accused of trickery, it is unlikely that this founder of Theosophy could have maintained the trust and affection of so many disciples by means of fakery alone.

Animals, too, can act as mediums. I had a dramatic example of this with a cat named Phoebe. When I moved in with her owner, I expected to be considered a rival, but she was a sweet-tempered calico who accepted me readily and showed me affection. As I was in the house all day, I became her primary caregiver. Then one day, out of the blue, she hissed at me. When I served her food, she hissed. If I tried to pet her, she hissed. I could not imagine what was wrong, how I had erred or offended her.

For two days she hissed continually at me, and on the third day of hostility her owner unexpectedly announced, "We have to talk." Learning to my utter surprise that he was mad at me, I understood why Phoebe had been hissing at me—she was acting as his surrogate. After we straightened things out, the hissing stopped and she returned to her usual affectionate ways, only now I had a furry barometer to gauge my friend's emotional climate!

Channeling

Channeling is a variation on mediumship, one which has become increasingly popular in the past twenty years.

One of the most famous channels of our time was Jane Roberts, who was able to record the words of a disembodied entity named Seth in a series of books. Roberts was one of the "expert intuitives" used by William Kautz, director of the Center for Applied Intuition in San Francisco, who has been conducting research for testable hypotheses in various fields, which he calls "intuitive consensus."

Working with channels, Kautz collects the intuitive information and then works with it in a systematical manner to produce verifiable new ideas and hypotheses. Kautz says:

> Intuition is the human process of acquiring knowledge directly,
> without recourse to reason or sensual perception, or even
> memory in the usual sense of memory. It is direct knowing. I
> use the term *expert intuitive* to mean someone who has the skill
> of doing that with very high competence.

Kautz believes that information acquired intuitively—without a base of sensory knowledge—can produce both ideas and technical information not available through other means, and which are testable with ordinary scientific methods. In answer to criticism that his use of psychics goes beyond the accepted definition of intuition, Kautz says,

> The underlying process between psychism, clairvoyance,
> telepathy, mediumship and some other types of creative per-
> formance is intuition.

Some channels seem to be spokespersons for so-called entities which exist in other dimensions. A New York channel medium, Robert Johnson, speaks for a group of celestial intelligences he calls *The Tutelage of Alpha Centurion*. Other channels claim to represent a spirit who once lived on earth, many millenia ago.

Unfortunately, stupendous deceptions have been perpetuated by some who have made millions of dollars from the gullible; a few have been sued for fraud. Certainly psychic practitioners have a right to earn a living with their craft, but suspicion will always settle around those who promote spurious phenomena for the purpose of growing rich.

As P. T. Barnum observed a century ago, a fool is born every minute, and alas—there are countless credulous people who are being taken in by moneygrubbers. Although there are many sincere and honest practitioners in the field, many of whom are extraordinarily talented, it is my hope that more people will learn to exercise their powers of discrimination to discern the real from the fake and that they do not need to rely on others. Often, a psychic is "picking up" information about you *from you*. And while it may be impressive for a psychic to say, "Your dog's name is Rover," you already knew that, didn't you?

This is not to say that professional psychic information is invalid. The danger is in relying totally on power other than your own.

All Answers Are Within You

6

Your Latent Psychic Potential

We are explorers…and the most compelling frontier
of our time is human consciousness.
—INSTITUTE OF NOETIC SCIENCES BULLETIN

I n his book *The Occult*, Colin Wilson tells in great detail the
story of St. Joseph of Copertino, the "flying monk," born
Giuseppe Desa in Apulia, Italy, in 1603. According to Wilson,
the brother's "feats are well attested by many witnesses."
Apparently Joseph sailed through the air when in a state of high
excitement, or ecstasy, what the Hindus call *samadhi*. His levitations often took him atop the high altar, amid the burning
candles, but he was agile as a cat and never knocked anything
over. At the end of this fascinating account, Wilson states,

> —Fr. Joseph flew. There can be no possible doubt about
> that…Fr. Joseph's flights undoubtedly proceeded from his
> own powers.

That Fr. Joseph performed his amazing feats under his own
power seems indisputable, but what is in question is whether he did
this consciously, or if his levitations were the result of *unconscious*
energy suddenly projecting itself as a product of his emotional
ecstasy. I would suggest the latter. Probably "the flying monk" was as
surprised by his activities as those who witnessed them.

Wilson goes on to assert that,

> ...the most sensible attitude is to assume that all human beings are potentially capable of flying and performing...other feats.

Difficult as it may be to believe that a man can sail through the air on a current of pure joy, it is not incompatible with the Hindu yogi's ability to levitate, many instances of which are on record. Whether or not we can suspend our own disbelief, would it not be wise, to paraphrase Pascal's famous wager, to at least behave as if it were possible?

Whether Joseph flew or not—and the Catholic Church evidently believed he did having granted him sainthood 104 years later—what is certain is that we humans already possess unused powers, which, if developed, would enable us to live far more productive and happier lives. We do not need to fly through the air (though I think it would be great fun) to begin the process of liberating our unconscious abilities from their imprisonment in disbelief and rational thinking.

Most of us are quite unaware of just how much we are involved unconsciously in the routine phenomena of our daily lives. We accept that our moods can affect others—if I'm feeling blue, my partner gets a dose of depression, or, conversely, when I'm joyously up those around me get an infusion of optimism and positive energy. Why then is it so difficult to accept that our *thoughts* can affect others as well?

A psychic is someone who has discovered, usually by accident, that it is possible to get in tune with his or her inner forces, that being psychic is a matter of uniting the inner and outer worlds, of aligning with the cosmos, and of bringing consciousness into harmony with the unconscious.

Brain researcher Dr. Paul MacLean cautions that it is "important to respect the brain's natural ability...to have information coming from your inside world at the same time as things are coming from the outside"—a concept that echoes the reality of psychic experience.

A Word About Terminology

There is some confusion regarding the use of the terms *unconscious* and *subconscious*.

Sigmund Freud's concept of the unconscious was as a repository for all that the conscious mind rejected. In Freud's view, whatever is unacceptable or considered threatening is buried deep in the psyche where it is totally forgotten, or repressed. For Freud, the unconscious was however a dangerous area, quite prone to spontaneous combustions that adversely affected normal behavior. The only way to defuse its potentially damaging power was through the process of psychoanalysis, which would excavate the unconscious contents from their hidden depths and brings them up into the light of consciousness, where they were subject to being understood and integrated.

Carl Jung, quarreling with his older colleague and friend, insisted that the unconscious was much more than a storage bin for the unwanted elements of life. In time, Jung evolved his theory of the "collective unconscious," as a repository of the building blocks of the psyche, which Jung termed the *archetypes.*

Archetypes are the patterns upon which the individual psyche builds itself, and they are common to all humanity. Thus there is the archetypal Mother, the archetypal Father, the archetypal Woman, the archetypal Man, and so forth. These figures underlie the personal experience of mother, father, woman, man, and reflect them. For example, a motherless child may not have known a real mother, but the concept of Mother still exists within. This image can then be projected outward—either in becoming a mother-figure oneself or seeking a mother-figure in another.

Further, to Jung's mind the unconscious, which was divided into a personal unconscious and the collective unconscious, was a positive force. Once liberated, it would energize the person and promote healing into wholeness. Jung believed that the energies of the psyche tended toward wholeness rather than destructiveness.

In the wake of Freud and Jung a host of therapies have sprung up, some only loosely based on these concepts. The term *subconscious* has come into the vocabulary of professionals and lay people alike. The general popular sense is of a layer above the unconscious. What is subconscious is neither forgotten nor totally repressed—we can bring it into consciousness with relative ease, and we recognize its influence upon us. For example, if you leave your umbrella at the house of a friend you may say, "I guess I subconsciously wanted to go back."

In a different context, which arose out of what is called "scientific Christianity" and was taken up by the early New Agers, the subconscious is the part of us that carries into fruition the intent of our conscious mind. One of the most famous examples of this use of the subconscious is in the power of positive thinking. The idea is that the subconscious has immense power to produce results but no power to discriminate or make decisions. It has the ability to perform whatever tasks you set for it—in other words, it always says yes—and it, willy-nilly, carries out your instructions. If it gets negativity, you get negativity. If it gets mixed messages, you get muddled results.

An example of this is the man who wants a new car but also thinks new cars, being expensive, are hard to get. His negative input confuses the process. The subconscious gets the message, "I need a car but I'll never get a *new* car," and acts accordingly. The man ends up with a cheap used car—new to him but not a new car. In a vicious cycle, because he doesn't get a new car, his belief that new cars are hard to come by is reinforced. It is only by changing his conscious programming of the subconscious that positive results can be achieved.

Thus, when he now says, "I am a person who can get a new car. I see a new car in my future," he leaves the means of achieving the aim to his subconscious. It then kicks into gear and sees to it that he gets the new car, which may arrive as a gift, an inheritance, a prize, or in some other unexpected manner.

Here is an example of how this process functions. A young man, forced to quit his job to care for his ailing mother, is driving on very thin tires. He simply cannot afford to buy a new set, but he knows about instructing the subconscious to provide. He simply acknowledges that he needs new tires and affirms that a solutions to the problem is forthcoming. A couple of weeks later he is invited to visit an old friend he has not seen in years. The mother of his friend asks him what size tires his car uses. He tells her the specifications and she replies that she has a set of new tires that will fit his car. She had mistakenly bought the wrong size for her own car and since they were from a close-out sale they were nonreturnable. He received them as a gift.

In another instance, a woman had moved to the West Coast and was living on limited means. She needed an apartment but could not pay more than $300 monthly. Everyone told her she'd never find something to suit her needs at that price, but she trusted her subconscious process, which is another way of saying she trusted her intuition, and continued on. One day she was walking down a quiet street and saw an elderly woman struggling with heavy bags of groceries. Offering to help, she made the woman's acquaintance and was invited to tea. In conversation, she revealed her plight and told of her search for living space. It turned out that the woman rented an apartment in her house that exactly suited the younger woman's needs. And it was currently vacant. The older woman cared less for the money than for finding the right person to share her environment. The price? Three hundred dollars a month.

Used in this sense, the subconscious hooks us into the psychic network, or information web, of the universe, working in inexplicable ways, all-knowing and all-doing.

You can test this hypothesis for yourself. The important thing is to know the essence of what you want to manifest. Be as specific as possible but do not limit the manner in which what you desire will come to you, which may be in a way different from what you are able to imagine.

For example, for a long time I wanted space for an art studio, but the only way I could imagine getting it was to move to a larger apartment. Various factors precluded moving. When I meditated on the essence of what I needed, I realized I just wanted a place to do artwork. Then a friend offered to give me a small sofa. In rearranging my space to accommodate the new acquisition, I discovered a way to utilize an area I had previously considered unusable. *Voila!* Suddenly I had room for a large table on which could do artwork. The solution had arrived with the sofa!

To work with this technique, ask for something *definite.* Don't, for example, ask for "more money." You may get a dollar. Be specific and have an end use. You may dream of winning millions in the lottery, but finding the essence of what you really need will hurry it to you. Do not be concerned about *how* you will get what you need.

Once you find the *essence* of what you want, ask for it. After you have asked for what you want, release the energy in the subconscious to do the work. Don't worry about *how* the answer will come, just trust that it will come.

A woman painter wanted badly to visit her son, who lived across the country, but her budget could not accommodate air fare, hotel room, meals out, and other expenses such a trip would require. Her son, with a young family, could not help financially. She meditated on the essence of what she wanted. It was for them to have private time together. She posed the statement to her subconscious—"I want to spend time alone with my son."—and then put the matter out of her mind. Weeks later she received a check in the mail from a gallery that had taken some of her paintings on consignment. A painting had been sold and the amount would cover the price of a round-trip ticket from New York to California.

Informing her son of the windfall, she suggested spending the money on a ticket for him, an arrangement actually more satisfactory in terms of the essence of what she wanted, which was for them to have extensive private time. Had she visited him, his time would have been preempted by the demands of his work and family life.

In refuting Freud's theory of the unconscious as a repository for the unwanted, Jung suggested that the unconscious not only contained the past but also the future, which already exists in an embryonic state in us all. It could be considered the *preconscious*, and in theory it should be accessible to the conscious mind.

Today, many make no clear distinction between subconscious and unconscious, using them interchangeably. However, in strict psychological terms unconscious contents are not available to the conscious mind without serious effort to excavate them, while subconscious contents lie just below the surface and can be called up—like remembering a forgotten telephone number or where you put your house keys. In this system, the unconscious becomes a lower level of the subconscious. The idea remains, in both instances, of a sort of mental and emotional basement.

The use of the term *subconscious* to refer to a power level within the self, as given above, is different. This usage can be likened to intuition. When we give instructions to the subconscious, we are accessing our psychic potential, which has the power to provide answers to our questions and solutions to our problems.

In my own experience, I have found it useful to think of *all* these functions as simply *non-conscious*. This term allows us to include the future. My sense of the non-conscious is that it is neither below nor above, but *all around.* Just as we are three-dimensional beings, non-consciousness surrounds us, as does the air in which we live and breathe.

The astrological symbol for the Sun—a circle with a dot in the center—is a perfect analog for my concept of the non-conscious. What is encompassed within the circle, representing the infinite, is the non-conscious realm. The dot at the center represents consciousness, which is totally surrounded by the field of non-consciousness. Alan Oken, author of *Complete Astrology,* says,

> The Sun's glyph signifies the emanation of light, i.e., life giving energy from the unlimited resources of the Divinity. The circle is the symbol for infinity, as it is a perfect shape without beginning or end. The circle is the totality of all matter which comprises the One-Supreme-Atom: the Universe of Universes. The dot is the point of Light which is sent forth as the fount from which the Light comes. The dot is the aperture from which the manifest is born out of the unmanifested.

Thus the "unmanifested," or the future, is *already contained within us,* a part of the circle of the field of the non-conscious, which contains not only everything we have experienced, whether we remember the experience or not, whether we can or cannot actually recall the experience, but also what we will experience in the future.

In addition to storing memories, the non-conscious stores the record of our thoughts, feelings, emotions. It is a grand archive and a source of infinite wisdom. The difficulty lies in our lack of a proper data-retrieval system. As we go along, you will learn how to begin writing your own personal program to access all facets of your non-conscious.

Although in this book I will use the terms *subconscious* and *unconscious* as they are usually thought of, I prefer to think of the entire psychic contents, including the future, not currently in consciousness as the *non-conscious.* When discussing the overall psyche I will apply that term.

Types of Intuition

Intuition, or psychic experience, arises from the deep strata of the non-conscious realm of our being. We take in information, which is stored in the unconscious where it recombines to produce creative solutions to problems. However, we are able to "know" the future through the process—at present a mysterious one—of the future already forming within us, just as a flower bulb holds within its interior the entire blooming cycle, from root to blossom.

Two types of intuition arise from within, *antecedent* and *without antecedent*.

Intuition I: **Antecedent**

Antecedent intuition means that the mind has already been primed with data in an effort to solve a particular problem. Much information has been gathered and stored—and it does not matter *when*. In some cases it could be recent study of a problem; in others, an entire lifetime of concentration on a particular subject.

An example of Intuition I features the famous German chemist Friedrich A. Kekulé, discoverer of the molecular structure of benzene. For many years, he had struggled in vain to solve the problem. According to his own report, one night in 1865 he dozed off in his study before the still-burning fireplace. When he woke, he had the solution. As he tells it:

> Again the atoms were juggling before my eyes...my mind's eye, sharpened by repeated sights of a similar kind, could now distinguish larger structures of different forms and in long chains, many of them close together; everything was moving in a snake-like and twisting manner. Suddenly, what was this? One of the snakes got hold of its own tail and the whole structure was mockingly twisting in front of my eyes. As if struck by lightning, I awoke.

Kekulé's dream realization that the structure of benzene is a closed carbon revolutionized modern chemistry. It was a supreme act of his intuition, which previously had been fed all the available facts and information relevant to the issue.

This was a case of *antecedent intuition*. Much of ordinary problem-solving, however difficult, is handled in this way. The unconscious does the processing in a complex ballet of integration, using its own vast archive of knowledge. When this process is completed, you get the answer.

A few years ago I was working on an outline proposal for a book based on the planet Mercury. It was a complicated piece of work and at one point I got stuck. For days, nothing happened. I couldn't even understand what I had already done, let alone how to finish it. In a state of utter frustration (and frustration, by the way, is a part of the intuitive process that will be discussed later), I occupied myself with nonrelated chores. Then, one night I had this dream.

I was in an art studio working with other people when the telephone rang. Someone answered and said, "It's for you."

When I answered the dream phone, a rough, masculine voice said, "Hey, lady, we can't finish this project until we get the artwork."

I hadn't a clue who it was or what he was talking about.

"Who are you?" I questioned.

"Lady, dis is de Mercury Press and you better get that artwork down here if you want this job finished."

"Where are you?" I asked.

"In the basement."

Like Kekulé, I woke as if struck by lightning. Suddenly everything was clear to me. I had not decided on the illustrations for the Mercury book, and they were an important and integral part of the whole concept. Immediately, I set to work to design the illustrations, which were mythological in content, and as I proceeded the entire project just fell into place, like magic.

That the "worker" was calling from a basement workshop may be seen as lending support to the notion that unconscious processing takes place in an area of the psyche beneath consciousness.

This dream is another example of antecedent intuition. I had been working on the project for some time and I knew that it would be illustrated. I had even chosen an artist to execute the final illustrations. I had gathered and stored a lot of information relative to the illustrations, but what I had not done was to integrate them within the text. It was this omission that had caused me to become blocked.

The writer Robert Louis Stevenson turned his habit of lulling himself to sleep with stories he fabricated into professional writing. His dreams were cooperative partners in this enterprise, and he came to refer to his dream helpers as "the little people."

In cultures in which people believe in magic, the little people refers to a race of fairies or gnomes who emerge from hidden places to do the bidding of humans. These beings are also known as "elementals," or nature spirits, a term derived from the early concept that nature was animated by spirits. There are psychics who can contact these elemental energies and use them in their work, as I have on occasion done.

Stevenson's little people and my own rough-voiced basement worker, whom I envisioned as a troll, seem to me to belong to this elemental dimension.

Immersion in a given subject can trigger intuition to produce the answer to a dilemma. Whether the solution arrives spontaneously—as in my Mercury dream—or whether it is deliberately sought, as in Stevenson's use of his dream workers, a thorough saturation in the matter is characteristic of antecedent intuition.

Intuition II: **Without Antecedent**

The second type of intuition is *without antecedent*. In other words, information suddenly arrives in consciousness, seemingly from nowhere. You haven't been trying to solve a problem, and you aren't feeding your unconscious facts about the matter. It's rather like getting an unexpected telegram in your head. You just *know,* but you don't have the faintest idea *how* you know. A sense of certainty grips you.

This second type of intuition, or direct knowing, I call Intuition II. While many people have little difficulty accepting the workings of Intuition I, the advent of Intuition II into one's life can sometimes be a frightening experience. At the very least, if one is not already experienced in these matters, it is a surprise.

Many people have had the experience of knowing who was calling on the telephone upon hearing it ring. I myself once had a rather startling example of this phenomenon. Having left my hometown, I was residing in New York City. Among the friends left behind was an ex-boyfriend named Jon, with whom I had not had any contact for seven years. One Friday evening, I had bought take-out Chinese food and was preparing to picnic with a friend on the living room rug when the telephone rang. I stared at it, saying aloud, "I wonder why Jon is calling me after all these years?" When I answered the phone, it was indeed Jon, calling to tell me he had moved to another city, wanting to give me his new address. How did I know it was Jon? We had neither spoken on the telephone nor written in the intervening years since I moved to New York. There had been many other boyfriends, and I rarely even thought of him, except that in the back of my mind I knew I could count on him in a pinch, a fact he reiterated during that telephone call.

The only way I can explain this curious incident is that we had formed a close bond that, even when it was no longer romantic, held in place. I believe these bonds, however old, can be information carriers on the psychic network.

Sexual energies cannot be excluded when considering psychic development for the simple reason that the energy produced by human sexual nature is extremely powerful.

Spontaneous psychic phenomena such as poltergeist activity —when bells ring, electricity turns itself on, water faucets start running, and objects hurl through the air—are the outward projection of inner unconscious energies, and, like Fr. Joseph's airborne demonstrations, have been well documented by credible witnesses. Poltergeist phenomena are thought to be the product of repressions, often of a sexual nature, and they mostly seem to occur around teenagers in the throes of hormonal changes.

Some adepts and all yogis consider sexual energy to be of such value that they do not expend it in actual sexual activity or intercourse. Like any other energy, sexual energy can be stored, in the body and in the psyche, and used for other than primary sexual purposes. Dr. Freud called the unconscious diverting of sexual energy to other uses, such as creativity, "sublimation." However, to incorporate sexual energy *consciously* into one's psychic development is a far different matter. Although Hindus believe that refraining from sexual intercourse is the only way to preserve this energy, another point of view holds that proper use of sexual energy in a relationship actually strengthens the energy, increasing reserves. The operative word here is *conscious*. Two people consciously engaged in the use of sexual energy in tandem for purposes of spiritual growth and psychic development can access surprising power.

In one example from my personal experience, my partner and I were able to meet in the out-of-body state and astral travel while actually physically engaged in the act of love. Such results require a reverence for human sexuality and a high degree of awareness of our essentially spiritual nature.

Another, more dramatic, example of Intuition II was one I had in 1981 in Germany, which I have found to be a very psychic country. It was a Sunday afternoon in summer and I was a guest at a garden party in what is Frankfurt's Left Bank. People came and went and almost everyone was speaking German, which I did not. At one point a strikingly attractive woman a few years younger than myself, dressed all in white, entered with a man and a large German Shepherd. I was sitting silently alone when she joined me at the table and introduced herself, speaking perfect English. Gratified to have someone to converse with in English, I talked with her for some time and then suddenly heard myself say, "You don't have to worry about your mother, she's going to be all right."

Instead of expressing surprise at this unwonted remark, she said, "Oh, I'm so glad to hear it! I have been so worried about her since my father died."

"But, my dear," I responded with certainty, "your father isn't dead. You really should get in touch with him and reconcile yourselves before he does die."

"No," she insisted, "my father died three months ago and that's why I've been so worried about my mother."

I persisted with my statement that her father was alive and after a few minutes of this exchange a bemused expression came over her face.

"My God, you're right!" she exclaimed. "It was my *stepfather* who died. He married my mother when I was only three years old and I've always thought of him as my father. I've been estranged from my real father, but talking to you I know that I do love him."

I reiterated that she needed to heal the rift with her living father before it was too late, and, tearfully, she agreed and thanked me for the information. Shortly thereafter she left the party and I never saw her again.

How could I have known these things? In the instance with Jon, there was a previously existing bond but with this woman— nothing. I'd never seen her before. I knew absolutely nothing about her except her first name. Yet I felt inexplicably drawn to her at first sight. Our conversation had been easy and philosophic in nature, and I felt an intellectual rapport with her, but that was all. This is a prime example of psychic intuition with absolutely no antecedent.

My own feeling, which being purely intuitive I cannot prove, is that we humans also have "fields" around us (quite possibly the field which is the aura is involved). I also believe that these human fields are capable of travel and that they can transcend both time and space.

Often what triggers Intuition II is what I call a "psychic crisis," or a spiritual emergency. The root of emergency is *emerge*— a coming out from one state of being into another. When one is ready to emerge, a crisis is precipitated. Like a fever fights infection, the psychic crisis presages healing.

In another instance of Intuition II, which occurred on a visit to Germany, I was the houseguest of a flight attendant who arrived home one evening accompanied by the entire crew from her flight. A schedule change had sent them back to base and though none knew the others before the flight, they had gotten into a party mood and decided to continue their fun. Champagne was uncorked. When the swirl of laughing people settled, I was off in a secluded corner having a serious conversation with the captain, a handsome man in his late thirties.

At this time, I was giving what I called "hand readings." These were not palmistry but a form of psychic communication activated by my holding the person's left hand. The first time I experienced this phenomenon was during a casual dinner with a Corsican man I had met at a wine-tasting he had hosted to promote the products he sold. A successful businessman, he seemed rather prosaic, but I nevertheless accepted his invitation to dine. During the meal, to make a point, I laid my hand on his and immediately felt a terrible sadness emanating from his past. Something must have shown in my face, for he asked in consternation, "What is it?" He knew nothing of my psychic ability.

Gently, I took his hand in mine and as I did I "heard" music—guitar music. His inner pain was somehow connected to the guitar. A large piece of him was missing. I said, "You used to play the guitar and you gave it up. Not having your music is killing you." He looked as if he'd seen a ghost. "You should never have quit," I continued, "because your music gave you life."

He told me the following story. As a boy on the island of Corsica—a rough culture—he had loved the guitar above all else, practicing continually, hoping for a career as a musician. But his parents owned a bar and bordello and he was forced to play for the customers who came for sex. It so disgusted his young and sensitive nature that at the age of sixteen he smashed his guitar and swore never to play again. Splintering that instrument had crushed his soul.

These matters were far from my mind until my friend appeared at my elbow and said, "Read the captain's hand." I wanted to decline, but he had already thrust out his hand and so I took it into mine. As I did so, I "saw" a lush tropical setting—and fire. Hesitant, not quite knowing what I was seeing, I let myself open to the information, and the number 29 came into my mind. Heart pounding with anxiety, for I sensed tragedy, I closed my eyes and slipped into a light trance.

"When you were twenty-nine years old—there was a fire. Not here—it happened in South America. There were children involved—and it changed your life forever."

He went ashen, the gaiety fled. Rapt, he stared at me. His face somber, in a low throbbing voice he told me the story of how he had taken his wife and two children—a girl and a younger boy—along on a flight to Brazil to use his days off as a short family vacation. They had gone to a rustic resort in the mountains in a fairly remote area, and during the night a fire had broken out in the old wooden hotel, which had no sprinkler system. The blaze caught everyone unaware and firefighting equipment was miles away. His baby son had been killed and his daughter badly burned. Though he had risked his life to save his family, in the bitter wake of the tragedy his wife blamed him for what had been circumstantial. And, although they had stayed together, their marriage was ruined and sexless. Her bitterness and blame combined with his own guilt to create a poisonous atmosphere.

Emotionally, he thanked me and said that in his deepest heart he knew that he wasn't at fault, but he had taken on the burden to try and spare his wife her pain.

The time was ripe for him to relieve himself of this unnecessary and painful weight—he was ready to acknowledge to himself that his manhood had not been compromised by his inability to save his son. A potent force chose me as the catalyst to propel him into a new realization that all was not over, that healing could take place.

Some of us accept these inner knowings easily, especially when we are children. Others, sealed off from their natural processes by church, society, science, and the religion of rational thinking, thrust such experiences away from themselves as being "spooky" or "weird." But such intuitions without antecedent are more common than we suspect. They go unreported because people are fearful of being thought peculiar.

The difference between Intuition I and Intuition II is simply one of degree. Intuition II is generally what is called "psychic." It is that sense of just *knowing*, without having any factual information to back it up.

There is, however, nothing to be afraid of. Intuition in any form is a natural process. You only have to come to the realization that you already possess much more intuitive power than you realize. Intuition is rather like a satellite dish constantly scanning the environment, picking up information. Usually we accidentally tune in by a sort of channel surfing of the psyche. But we can learn to receive these inner broadcasts by fine-tuning our psychic receivers, opening up clear channels through which information can come. Just as there are dozens of radio and TV stations broadcasting all the time—of which we are unaware because we are not tuned in—the non-conscious field is always busy gathering and sorting information. It can solve problems, mend the past, and reveal the future. You truly do have magical powers waiting for you to become aware of them. Like the genie in the bottle, they only await release to serve you as their master.

Have the Courage to Discover Yourself

Keys to Psychic Awareness

There is nothing static in the universe in which we dwell. We can change by changing our attitudes and patterns of behavior.
—ISABEL HICKEY, ASTROLOGY,
A Cosmic Science

Keys to psychic awareness are simple and available to all, there for the taking. You can put these keys into use in your life right now. And, like the practice of any skill, the more you use them the more adept you will become. If at first they seem different, or difficult, try the trick of suspending disbelief. That's what you do when you read a novel or see a movie. You allow yourself to *believe* that the characters on the page or the screen are real, and you thereby enter into their lives and experience emotional satisfaction. The keys to psychic awareness are *in you*. They are not concrete objects, but they are nonetheless most effective tools of perception.

Key No. 1: **Attention**

Your mind can be likened to a camera, which is in constant operation, but a very special sort of multi-lens camera that can focus in many different areas simultaneously or focus all together on one area. This mental camera automatically records everything that is going on around it, continuously snapping pictures at random.

These mental images are stored in your unconscious mind, whether you are aware of them at the time or not. For example, in a murder investigation police will ask witnesses to tell them *anything* they saw, no matter if it seems relevant or not. Likewise, they will attempt to probe the "forgotten" images stored in a witness's brain in order to ferret out clues. So prolific are the images taken by our mental cameras, and so rapid the storage of those images, that we often don't even know *what* we saw, or *if* we saw anything. The alert police officer, however, if he can retrieve the witness's images, can integrate them into the investigative puzzle.

Memories come in many different shades of intensity. Some of us can still remember our first day of school—if we were terrified at the thought of separating from mother, or excited at the prospect of a new adventure. For many, however, that memory has faded into nothingness. Why? Usually because there wasn't much emotion attached to the event. Our parents had properly prepared us; we felt secure; perhaps we had already attended nursery school. In any case, there was neither fear nor elation and so the memory was not highly colored by emotion.

Some memories remain poignant for us forever, while others gradually lose their emotional charge unless something activates it once again, such as seeing a movie that seems to replay our own life. Suddenly, memories thought forgotten come flooding to the surface, perhaps with tears of recognition. *That's how it was with me*, we think, no matter if the memory is happy or sad. Later, as the reactivated emotion subsides, the memory slips back into its storage bin in our unconscious.

What happens is that the memory is activated by *attention*. The attention may be accidental, as in seeing a movie, or it can be deliberate, such as when we talk to a therapist about our childhood experiences. The relative strength of the memory will depend on the attention we gave it when it occurred. Obviously, we will forever remember the day we were in a plane crash, while we may forget the details of our first job interview rather soon.

As our mental camera goes about its job of recording our lives—our thoughts, feelings, experiences—we have the choice of letting it remain on automatic, adjusting its focus according to the emotional input of the information or becoming conscious of what we experience.

For example, we may be walking along the street on a lovely spring morning little aware of our surroundings—maybe we are preoccupied with a personal problem—but if we suddenly see a flower cart massed with tulips in brilliant colors, we may be transported—either to our trip to Holland or to a sudden, sharp awareness of the reality of spring, of its glorious *meaning*.

On the other hand, we may be walking along a country road with snow still on the ground, looking intently for crocuses and snowdrops, the first signs of spring. All of our attention is concentrated on the search, for the pleasure it will bring. The calendar has already informed us spring is on the way, but this provocatively tantalizing search for its visible reality—to see one tiny purple head of crocus poking its way up through the snow—will provide an intensely emotional experience that we want to repeat every spring.

As we go about our daily lives, we usually focus our mental cameras only on crises and emergencies. Approaching our front door, key in hand, we are on automatic pilot until we notice with alarm that the door is standing ajar. Our senses go on full alert and we quickly swivel the camera's many lenses into position to survey the scene, noticing if there seems to be a break-in and looking for evidence to report to the police. Our senses, a moment ago ninety percent asleep, now go on red alert, sending out feelers to determine if there is danger. Should we enter the house or go quickly to a neighbor and phone the authorities? Our subconscious mind processes all the information we are receiving with astounding rapidity and accuracy; it will take less time for you to make a decision about what to do than it has taken me to write these words. After absorbing all the necessary information and processing it, your mind tells you what course to pursue, or lists your options.

Suppose for a moment that you lived your entire life at the same state of heightened attention as when you saw the door of your house standing open. Our psychic powers are usually dormant, like your attention when you walk up to the door, focused, if at all, on the evening's programs on TV and what's for dinner. As mostly we are concerned with the routine of our lives we miss the extraordinary, which is all around us all the time. It's like not being home when the phone rings. You never know what you missed.

Most of life is boring because we allow it to be. We are like a first-class racing car in slow traffic. After too much of this, the engine stalls. Sludge collects in the mechanism and our once-powerful instrument is reduced to the performance of any old clunker on the road. It need not be this way. Our psychic powers are there to be developed. They are a completely normal part of the human equipment with which we arrive in this world. The problem is that we have allowed our psychic abilities to be bored almost out of existence.

So much of our everyday life is such a blur of routine that we miss what is going on at the deeper levels of our awareness. I have developed and teach a technique I call *monitoring*, which is a way of consciously focusing on the input of the day, either as it is happening or during brief periods of reflection with a final summation before sleep.

The Monitoring Technique

Learning to monitor seems at first daunting, and it is not easy to keep one's self in an aware state, but the method can be learned with diligence. It is akin to the religious practice of examination of conscious, except that there is no "sin" involved. Instead of examining yourself for faults, you examine yourself for insights and meaning.

To do this, begin *consciously* to store in memory your thoughts, feelings, and reactions to the events of the day. If you have trouble remembering, take brief notes at times during the day that are significant, such as an encounter with a co-worker or a conversation with your spouse. Note the particulars of the situation along with your reactions. A few words will do. The purpose is to give you clues to recall the entire event and its "feeling tone" later.

When thoughts come from your inner self, instead of ignoring them or pushing them aside, record them so that they do not drop into the well of forgetfulness. During the day, whenever you have unoccupied time, review what you have noted, fixing it more firmly in memory for later evaluation.

At the end of the day, set aside time to examine the entire day's input for insights about your inner self. The more you are aware of your inner processes, the easier it will be for you to access your psychic power.

Here's an example from an actual notebook:

> 11 AM: Meeting with Jane. Upset.
>   Not taken seriously. Again! What to do?
>
> NOON: Spoke to John. Doesn't see my side.
>   Made me mad. A turnoff.
>
> 3 PM: Knew Jane was a problem. Could
>   have handled differently. My fault?
>
> 9 PM: Remembered dream about John wearing
>   mask. I don't see the real him?

When we examined her day's input, this client was able to see that she *already knew* that her meeting with her boss, Jane, was going to be a problem, but she ignored this advice from her inner self and repeated an old pattern. After monitoring, she saw that she could have handled the situation differently, to her advantage. She learned to pay attention to her inner messages instead of ignoring them.

Monitoring her relationship let her see that she felt John was hiding behind a mask, dream information she almost allowed herself to forget. Monitoring brought the dream back so that she could access its message. Seeing John wearing a mask allowed her to realize they needed to bring more openness into their relationship in order to improve communications between them.

When I teach this method, a common excuse for not using it is, "I have no time!" However, time can always be found for what is truly important. If you habitually read the newspaper on your commuter trip, or listen to music in the car going to and from work, you can decide to switch your priorities, giving over this time to monitoring. There are many small pockets of time during the day that can be used to advantage, such as standing in line at the bank or grocery, but we usually waste these opportunities in vexation or idle time-wasting devices.

One client, a busy woman who operated her own business, after initially thinking she could never find the time to monitor her inner world, eventually decided it was worth the effort. A well-organized person, she began to carry a small tape recorder, using it whenever she was required to wait to see a client, or a doctor, or for a train or bus. At the end of the day she always had a tape full of thoughts for her evening summation.

ATTENTION, then, is the first key, and it is a most powerful one. In paying attention to what is going on within, we develop our intuitive powers.

Key No. 2: **Acceptance**

You already possess extraordinary abilities. Imagine for a moment that you have been kept in bed since childhood, told you could not walk move around, warned that any activity would be dangerous, maybe even life-threatening. Not only would you refuse to move any more than absolutely necessary, but normal growth would be inhibited and muscles would atrophy. In time, the misinformation would indeed cripple you and you would not be able to walk or move about freely.

Fortunately, the muscles of the mind are resilient and, once attention is paid to the disused—or feared—functions of psychic intuition, full use becomes possible. The problem is our heavily biased, rational-brained society. Like the bedridden child who has been warned never, never to try to walk alone, we believe that learning to use our nonrational mental faculties will in some way harm us, even expose us to some unseen, frightful dangers.

For centuries, the Church practiced a kind of mind control by convincing millions of otherwise quite normal people that their innate and natural abilities were somehow evil and dangerous, thus discouraging, sometimes to the point of extermination, any use of the mind not sanctioned by the higher holy authority. Then, as the power of the Church began to wane from the weight of the overwhelming encrustation of a heinous, Inquisition-ridden medieval past and a new religion, equally tyrannical claimed sovereignty over the territory of the human mind. It was called Science, and its dogma and creed were reason and the rational mind. All other forms of thinking or of information-gathering were outlawed or relegated to the realm of peasant superstition. Triumphant, the new priests declared that humans were to live in and through the pure light of reason. Descartes's "I think, therefore I am," became, "We think rationally, therefore we rule."

So, the second key is ACCEPTANCE. Once you accept that you already possess these marvelous powers, that they are there inside you waiting to serve you and improve your life, you have taken another giant step toward psychic supremacy.

Key No. 3: **Concentration**

People often find it difficult to concentrate upon a task that is unpleasant or unwanted. However, it is easy to concentrate upon that which we desire or in which we are intensely interested. When such is the case, a sort of trance comes over us, a raptness of attention. This kind of concentration conserves, just as great energy reserves are conserved in a seed. It is the opposite of our usual state of mind, which is scattered, diffuse, diluted.

Concentration is not something you have to work at—it comes naturally when you are in the right frame of mind. Think of any activity you enjoy—even daydreaming. Remember how, when occupied with what you truly care about, you seem to drift off into your own inner world? That's how concentration works.

CONCENTRATION, the third key, is vital in the development of psychic abilities because it allows you to eliminate distractions that dilute the flow of intuitive information and weaken the psychic connection.

Key No. 4: **Imagination**

Imagination is the gateway to incredibly marvelous and stimulating worlds within. Too few of us feel free to use our imaginative powers. We look upon imagination as mere fantasy or wish-fulfillment. Once again, we sell ourselves short. Too many people associate imagination with time-wasting (the rational-mind tyrants invented that one), not realizing that they are neglecting a power source within themselves. Imagination is another tool in your psychic repertoire, a tool that can be honed to remarkable precision through careful attention and concentration.

Imagination literally means "the forming of images." It has mostly been associated with *fancy* and *fantasy*, usually in the realm of art, but it is also used as a negative term to denigrate those whose imaginative powers interfere with the rationalists' world view. Moreover, psychological and aesthetic theories have affected the meanings of these terms. In its highest form, however, imagination is an integrative function. It allows us to produce new combinations from elements already experienced and it gives an ability to conceive of ideas unsupported by experience and process these into a complete and integral whole.

Key No. 4, IMAGINATION, is the cornerstone of psychic perception that relies on mental visualizing. It is by making images that we manifest reality. Let us celebrate imagination and release its power within ourselves.

Key No. 5: Optimism

Optimism may not seem to have much to do with learning to use your psychic muscles, but it is a vital key to the process. Put simply, if you believe you can do it, then you can do it. This approach may sound like Pollyanna has taken my place, but new research confirms that "Pollyanna was right," according to science writer Daniel Goldman, in a 1987 *New York Times* article entitled "Research Affirms Power of Positive Thinking." Goldman says,

> Optimism…can pay dividends as wide-ranging as health, longevity, job success, and higher scores…new research is an outgrowth of earlier work on the power of self-fulfilling prophecies…new work looks at people's expectations about their own lives and finds that the power of expectations goes beyond mere achievement to visceral, emotional qualities.

In other words, you need to flex your expectation muscles. Let me give you an example. I was counseling a man whose marriage was troubled by his wife's unresolved and unrealistic relationship with her father. Since she did not believe in counseling, the husband was forced to go it alone, which was like trying to clap with one hand. Without his partner's cooperation, nothing much was happening. Things would get better for a while as he followed what advice I could reasonably give, and then they would slip back to square one. Finally I said that I would try to penetrate her barriers through meditation.

"Well, go ahead, but don't expect to succeed."

I replied that it would be my expectation of success that would bring the desired end, but that if he was convinced she was permanently closed off, then the effort would indeed fail, because it would have to be through his vibrations that hers were contacted.

"Our expectancies not only affect how we see reality but also affect reality itself," says Edward E. Jones, a psychologist at Princeton University, reviewing the new research on expectancy in a recent issue of *Science.*

The practice of optimism, which is the *expectation of positive results,* is illustrated charmingly in this tale from India.

"Stone Soup"

An old woman of the untouchable caste comes into the village square and sets up her cooking pot in the area reserved for the lowest of the low. Since this was a relatively affluent village, which did not itself have a population of untouchables, her arrival attracted the attention of the women at the well drawing water for their homes. Curious, they watched as she set up her cooking pot and, after filling it with water, dragged a heavy stone out of the woods bordering the square, brushed it clean, and plunked it into her pot with a great splash. She then announced for all to hear that soon there would be a wonderful soup.

The women tittered among themselves, wondering where the impoverished old hag would get ingredients for a nourishing soup.

The amused women poked one another in the ribs.

"Old woman," one called derisively, "why have you put that stone in your pot?"

"Ah," she said with satisfaction, giving the rocky broth a stir with her long wooden spoon, "Have you never heard of stone soup? It's a treat." Smacking her lips in anticipation, she called, "I shall share my delicious soup with the whole village when it is ready."

"Stone soup!" they hooted at her. "You can't make soup with a stone."

"Wait and see," she said and went back to her stirring.

Later, when the women came through the square returning from their marketing, she was sniffing appreciatively at her steaming pot as if an enticing aroma arose from it.

"How's your soup coming?" they asked.

She tasted a bit of the brew and proclaimed it delicious.

Her positive demeanor and gleeful anticipation caused the women concern. If the old woman could make soup from a stone she must have magical powers. They debated how to handle the situation. Finally, one, evidently deciding that participation in such powers was the right course, took a bold step. With her basket full of vegetables hanging from her arm, she approached the cook and offered a bunch of onions.

Her action proved contagious, and one by one the other women, not wanting to be outdone by their neighbor, offered produce from their baskets.

"Here, let me add some leeks to your pot," said one. "I'll give a bunch of carrots," offered another. "Take these potatoes," "Here's some celery." The donations continued until the hag had a bountiful supply of vegetables and herbs.

She blessed the donors and invited them to return later to collect soup for their families' dinner.

This story illustrates the principle that we tend to get what we expect, that *intention* somehow sets in motion forces that fulfill our expectations. So, the fifth key, OPTIMISM, is the art of expecting the best.

Key No. 6: **Curiosity**

Curiosity, the sense of wonder, is something we tend to lose as we grow older. In some of us it is already dead by the time we reach high school. This is because our parents, teachers, and other authority figures do not encourage us to remain curious about our world. We are constantly told we are "silly," or we are reminded that "Curiosity killed the cat."

Yet, it need not be so. Our sense of wonder is like one of those odd flowers that appears to be a dried-up and withered corpse—yet when watered springs into vibrant and green life. We can revive our sense of wonder with the water of our attention. One of the reasons curiosity is not more valued for the asset that it is rests with the same sort of bad connotation that imagination has received. Curiosity has been linked with snooping, prying, and being nosy about the affairs of others. "The curious mob had to be held in check by the police."

Curiosity is what makes us discover, and if we have no curiosity about *ourselves*—what's in there anyway?—then we leave a great deal undiscovered. It's like having an attic full of treasures and never bothering to go up and look to see what's there. We all have many undiscovered rooms in the house of the Self. Finding them and examining their contents is one of the most intensely pleasurable experiences I know.

To access the powers of our psychic selves, we must be explorers willing to push into the last frontier of our era, human consciousness. Our quest in achieving our unique psychic heritage can lead us to the discovery of a vision for humanity that integrates science and spirituality. This in turn will reveal to us our innate wholeness and connectedness to one another and to the Earth on which we live—but it will serve most importantly to connect us to our own inner selves.

CURIOSITY the sixth key to this Aladdin's cave of psychic wonders, is worthy of our awe.

Key No. 7: **Purpose**

There is a literary fragment that has stayed with me from high-school days, "The high soul travels the high ways, and the low soul travels the low ways, but the mediocre soul travels the vast and aimless in between." Though I no longer remember who penned those words, they had a profound effect on me at the time and I have never forgotten the message they contain about purpose. It matters not if you are a "high soul" or a "low soul," for you have a path either way. It is only in "the vast and aimless in between"—which sounds like limbo to me—that nothing ever happens.

Unfortunately, most of us get stuck in the "vast and aimless in between," going dully from home to work to routine activities to home to start the same cycle all over next day. It is this repetitiveness that stifles us and makes all life seem "flat, dull, stale, and unprofitable," to quote another poet. What causes this ennui? Not the acts themselves, since we all have to do the boring tasks of life, but the lack of a *sense of purpose*. What could be more uninspiring than taking out garbage? Yet if I am cleaning up my apartment because I am giving a party or expecting a welcome guest, throwing out all that trash is positively exhilarating as I prepare my environment for what I expect will be a pleasurable experience.

It's the same with all the ordinary chores of life—we get bored because there doesn't seem to be any point to it all.

Boredom results from lack of purpose, and with it there comes a falling off of our sensibilities.

Boredom is truly the enemy of our psychic selves. When we are purposeless and bored, we do not bother to reach for our deeper selves. It's too much trouble to expand our consciousness. Rather than make the effort, we turn on the TV and compound the problem. Shaking ourselves out of this lassitude is not climbing Mt. Everest. It only requires a renewal of our life purpose. And if you have never had a sense of purpose, now is the time to get one and use it to rev up your psychic engine. There's nothing like having a good reason to use those latent powers to get them activated and running on all cylinders.

It is my belief that each of us is put here on Earth for a reason, that we individually have a mission in life whether it is grand or humble. And we have the ability to discover our personal mission by going within and contacting our deep source of wisdom. Purpose is not to be confused with goal-setting to achieve success or material rewards. It is the *underlying* reason we do those other things. Purpose permeates life, enlivens and enriches it—and life without purpose is dull and dusty, riddled with meaninglessness.

PURPOSE, then, is our seventh key to achieving psychic awareness. As Michel de Montaigne, the great French essayist, put it, "The great and glorious masterpiece of man is how to live with purpose."

Key No. 8: **Gratitude**

You know how you feel when you've done something for someone and not gotten a *thank you* for your pains. You know you do better on the job or at school when you receive praise for your efforts and accomplishments. So why don't you give praise and thanks for your own inner abilities?

Most of us have simply never thought about this—we take our minds and what they can do very much for granted. Oh, we may have a bit of pride here and there for a task well done, but this is usually expressed in having someone else congratulate us. We seldom thank our own minds for being the sturdy and reliable friends they are to us.

The Unity minister and author, Dr. Catharine Ponder, whose work has been a source of inspiration to me, says,

"Develop an attitude of gratitude." This is good advice to those wanting to delve into the realm of psychic potential. Our subconscious mind is like a robot—it responds to what we tell it. And if we continually nag, rebuke, and criticize, guess what?—it will, too. It's like a mirror that reflects our projected image. If you scowl into your mirror, you see an unhappy face. If you smile, it smiles back. Take your choice.

Gratitude is another powerhouse of a key to psychic awareness. It opens doors that get stuck and allows us to continue even when we feel like stopping. Once you make friends with your psychic elves and get them to do your bidding on a regular basis, you need to thank them for their efforts, praise the results. Even if the results are slow to come, which they can be, you still need to practice an "attitude of gratitude" on a regular basis. You'll be surprised at how much positive response you will get from your psychic friends once you begin to acknowledge their work. You are, of course, acknowledging and thanking yourself and the powers you possess inside you.

GRATITUDE, our eighth psychic key, is of the utmost importance. We Americans annually celebrate a feast of gratitude, appropriately called Thanksgiving—but are we really thankful for what we enjoy? Look around you: no matter what your circumstances, there is always something for which you can be grateful. Right now, sit down and make a list of everything you can think of deserving of your gratitude and you will be on the way to developing an "attitude of gratitude," which can bring joy and bounty into your life.

These keys to psychic awareness are the building blocks with which you will construct your new psychic tower. Use them well and you will build strongly upon a firm foundation.

Fall in Love with Yourself

Your Personal Psychic Journal

There is no reality except the one contained within us.
—HERMAN HESSE

A psychic journal is an adjunct to your efforts to activate your intuition. In it you keep a personal record of life experiences related to your developing intuition. You record your thoughts and feelings, even the physical circumstances in which the psychic experience occurred. In time, you will see meaningful patterns. Your life is not an accidental happening—it has meaning and purpose, and journal-keeping is an excellent method for coming to understand your individual journey on this Earth. In it you will be having the adventure of your life—the discovery of your deepest, most significant Self.

If you already keep a journal, or have ever kept a diary, keeping your personal psychic journal should not pose a problem. If you are new to journal-keeping, you may need some time to acclimate yourself to writing your psychic experiences on a regular basis.

Did you respond to the suggestion of keeping a psychic journal with the common disclaimer, "But when will I find the *time?*" My answer to that question is always the same: "We find the time for whatever we feel is important to us."

You find the time to watch TV, go to the movies, see friends, go on outings, go shopping, and a myriad of other pleasurable activities. Keeping your psychic journal is meant to be another pleasurable activity. If at first it seems a chore, please don't give up on yourself. This is a rewarding and important facet of your psychic development.

Equipment

The form your journal takes is up to you. It should be both organized and portable. You can get a fancy daily journal book from a stationery store; you can use a plain schoolbook-type notebook, either with or without ruled lines. Some people like a stenographer's pad. These items are widely available for a small amount of money.

A psychic journal is not a literary effort. You don't have to spell correctly or even write in sentences. Just jot down whatever you wish in whatever form you like. Go for the spirit of the thing—be playful with it, be creative. Keeping your psychic journal should never become a chore or lose its freshness. Remember that boredom and routine are enemies of psychic development. Some people like to draw or sketch, even doodle, in their journals. You may want to cut pictures or images out of magazines or other sources and paste them in your journal as reminders, or enter quotations you find meaningful. Once you begin to focus on your psychic development and record your experiences, you will find that you become more aware of input from your daily life that is significant, input you had been overlooking.

Journaling and Relaxing

Keeping your psychic journal should be a form of relaxation, another technique for joining your conscious awareness with your non-conscious being. Think of your psychic journal as a friend and companion, one to which you can turn whenever you need a boost or someone to talk to. Most of all, *enjoy* your journal as you would enjoy spending time with any dear friend who is genuinely interested in you, your problems, your daily life, your successes, your dreams, your goals.

Rereading what you have written is also a pleasant way to remind yourself of how much you are progressing. Let your journal-keeping be a gift you give yourself. You might even consider it to be a hobby. Occasionally you may give it more time; frequently, less time. You are following your own intuitive pattern; let the journal "speak" to you when it wants your attention.

Consider the time you spend with your psychic journal as time spent with your Higher Self, or the Source, or God, whichever term fits your personal belief system. Use your journal as a place to give thanks to your intuitive self, as a place to record your intuitive and psychic experiences, or use it for your dreams as well. (If you want to concentrate on dreams, I suggest a separate journal for them.)

When to Write Your Personal Psychic Journal

There is no "right" time for writing in your journal, but I do recommend writing in it as frequently as you can manage, preferably daily. Some of my clients like to use the end of the day, in the quiet period just before bedtime, as the time they turn to their journal. This time of day also leads into sleep, and writing in your journal before going to sleep can influence your dreams. It's also good to combine journal writing with your relaxation and meditation periods.

Some people, especially Active types, like to jot down their experiences immediately. For these, a pocket notebook is a good idea. You can write a few notes while sitting on a bus or train during a commute. Some drivers I know use the time they are stuck in traffic to write in their journals. The time just after waking is excellent—I like to use this time to fit together the experiences of the previous day and the night's dreams.

Conditions for Writing

Like timing, conditions will vary for each person. The ideal situation is to have a quiet, regular spot—whether it is your study or the kitchen table. As with doing relaxations and meditations (and journal-keeping is a form of meditation), using the same place all the time is conducive to the activity. When your mind senses that you are in your writing spot and ready to write, it will shift into the right gear automatically. I sometimes sit at my word processor and simply stare out the window at my garden for a few minutes until the flow begins of itself.

How Much to Write

How long is a piece of string? This is a question that can only be answered by your needs. Write what you want to write. If you feel you have nothing to report, don't write anything. You may write copiously or sparsely, or you may do both on different days. There's no minimum and there's no maximum. Sometimes I write four or five pages; sometimes only four or five lines. For jotter types, those accustomed to taking notes, a few lines in their own brand of shorthand suffices to jog their memories when they want to reread. For others, there is an outpouring of immense detail.

In the Beginning

Some people feel a bit embarrassed looking at a blank page, as if it somehow expects them to perform. Others like to cover every square inch, even writing around the margins. Your journal also becomes a visual tool as you work with it.

If you at first feel shy or have difficulty, don't worry. It's only stage fright and you will get over it. Remember this is your *personal* journal and no one else ever need see it.

To help get yourself started, practice "flow writing." This means you write whatever comes into your head for at least five minutes, even if it seems nonsensical. It's a good idea to do a relaxation exercise before writing, if you feel uptight or restricted. Remind yourself that you are doing this for *you*. It's not schoolwork, a business report, or a test. It is an artwork.

Your Covenant with Your Personal Psychic Journal

Think for a few minutes about why you are doing this and why you are willing to make a commitment to writing regularly in your journal. Then put this into words. Study what you have written for a few minutes and see if you are satisfied with your purpose. You may want to make changes.

Your statement of purpose might go something like this:

I'm keeping my Personal Psychic Journal for the purpose of getting in touch with my Higher Self, my intuition, and with the aim of generating psychic experiences. My goal is to become more aware of messages from my non-conscious and act on this information to improve my life. I believe keeping this journal will aid this process by providing me with a framework in which I can record and reflect upon my experiences and wherein I can chart my progress.

Now, write out a contract that you are making with yourself. It might go something like this:

> Therefore, I make a covenant with myself to pursue this effort on a regular basis. I promise to write in this journal...

Here, you fill in the blanks. You might say "...every day for fifteen minutes," or "...every day," or "...at least twice a week for half an hour," or "...for no less than one hour per week."

You are making this contract and it is up to you to keep to the terms you make. Trust your intuition to keep up its half of the bargain.

Dwell on Your Unbounded Potential

Part III

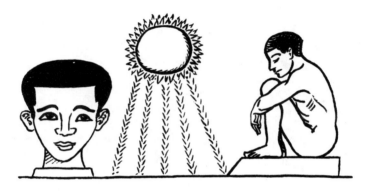

Integrating Mind, Spirit and Body

9

Your Psychic Self

*Our highest, most elegant intellectual capacities lie untapped
and unrecognized in what we call the unconscious.*
—DR. BARBARA BROWN,
Supermind

The unconscious knows everything, literally. It has recorded
your life from the moment of conception to this present day.
It has a complete record of everything you have ever experienced,
thought, felt, dreamed, wished. There is no computer system on
earth that matches the capacity of a single brain with its vast
unconscious reservoir of data. In fact, it would take dozens, maybe
thousands, of computers even to begin to approach the capabilities of your unconscious mind.

Not only does the unconscious (or what I call the non-conscious) have a complete record of the past, it is also already forming your future, which it contains like an acorn contains an oak
tree. Your mind has the power to reach out beyond your physical
environment—both in time and in space—enabling you to travel
far and wide—to the past, to the future, to places you have never
visited and to places that are not yet possible to visit (such as other
planets). If your conscious mind, which is limited, can do all of
these things—think of how much more your non-conscious mind,
which has unlimited potential, can do.

Examples of the astounding workings of our unconscious minds are all about us. Bulgarian scientist Dr. Georgi Lozonov, who has investigated people with extraordinary mental abilities, has reached the conclusion that such powers are a natural human ability anyone can develop. In reporting Lozonov's methods, headlines in Moscow newspapers read, "Hidden Channels of the Mind." What Dr. Lozonov was doing, using a combination of cadenced repetition, music, and relaxation, was teaching people to learn one thousand words a day in a foreign language.

Sheila Ostrander, co-author of Superlearning, who was trained in both music and languages, began translating papers about this new method. She writes:

> In these accounts, writers invariably mentioned a basic con-
> tention of Soviet physiologists: We use barely ten percent of
> our brain capacity, yet we can learn to plug in to the other
> ninety percent; we can...learn to tap the reserves of the
> mind.

Lozonov himself says, "The human mind remembers a colossal quantity of information...the number of buttons on a suit, steps on a staircase, panes in a window, footsteps to the bus stop. These 'unknown perceptions' show us the subconscious has startling powers."

In other words, our brains are like sponges, able to absorb and store information and knowledge continuously. In addition to collecting and retaining information, the unconscious also has the amazing ability to be creative—to come up with new combinations the linear brain could not conceive. The ability to use this capacity constitutes what we call genius.

The brain research of Dr. Wilder Penfield of the Montreal Neurological Institute supports this. Using local anesthesia so that patients remained conscious, Dr. Penfield performed operations using a weak electric current to stimulate brain cells. Like turning on a hidden tape recorder in the mind, patients all experienced verbatim playbacks of old conversations and experiences, including words they had heard spoken *only once*. They remembered childhood experiences such as standing in the rain on a summer morning and smelling the wet earth, heard music once played on a radio, recalled specific incidents from childhood replete with details—such as a birthday party, with all its gifts and decorations, participants, and activities. Such researchers are proving that we can learn to access our hidden resources deliberately to achieve what was formerly considered impossible.

As a result of his work, Dr. Penfield theorizes that every experience is registered and stored by the unconscious, remaining permanently on file. Dr. Lozanov takes Penfield's theory a step further, insisting that we not only constantly record information received through the senses, but that we also record information perceived *intuitively and telepathically*. This forms a vast databank in the unconscious of which we are not aware but which we draw on spontaneously, in dreams or in sudden flashes of insight called the "eureka experience." This refers to a moment of crystal clarity in which the long-sought solution to a problem is revealed. The term *eureka* to describe this phenomenon derives from the experience of the Greek philosopher Archimedes, who, while sitting in his bath, one day suddenly understood the principle of displacement and, shouting *Eureka!* ("I have found it."), rushed out naked into the street to tell the world of his discovery.

Albert Einstein wrote that, "The intellect has little to do on the road to discovery. There comes a leap in consciousness, call it intuition…and the solution comes to you and you don't know how or why."

Not only can we facilitate learning and improve athletic performance, but by being open to the workings of our unconscious minds we are able to solve problems and resolve dilemmas. Dr. Paul MacLean, a neurophysiologist, says, "More often than not if you can plug a question into your noggin and then forget about it, you usually have this eureka experience months later. That's what intuition is all about."

The key to the eureka experience lies in (1) being open to receive information from your unconscious processing center; (2) honoring your intuitive powers and respecting them as a valuable resource; (3) being alert to guidance when it comes.

Dr. Frederick G. Banting (later Sir Banting), the Canadian research physician who shared the 1923 Nobel Prize for the discovery of insulin, is a case in point.

For years, Dr. Banting had worked in vain on the problem of diabetes, a subject in which he was particularly interested. In

1921 there was no cure nor any effective treatment and the ravages of the disease, especially in children, were tragic. Banting worked tirelessly in his laboratory with his assistants—to no avail. Even after exhaustive studies of the pancreas, the answer to its malfunction eluded him. One night, exhausted after spending nearly all night in his laboratory, he went home and fell into a hypnagogic daze. His tired conscious mind had no choice but to turn over the vexing problem to its strongman counterpart, the unconscious. When he came to, the solution was clear. He felt that he had been given "instructions" telling him how to extract the necessary products from the degenerated pancreatic duct of dogs, which became the basis for the formulation of insulin. Not only did Banting's unconscious know what the solution to his problem was, it delivered the information in clear-cut terms.

The non-conscious also has the ability to hook into the web of information that is the universe. It can arrange for us to be in the right place at the right time, a mysterious process Dr. Jung calls synchronicity. In synchronistic experiences, seemingly unrelated events form a pattern that is discernible only later.

For example, at the age of thirty, my life was at a crossroads and I had no clear idea of which direction to follow. I had rather abruptly decided to close my art studio on Madison Avenue and leave a career in the advertising business, the only work I had ever done. The inner prompting for change was strong, but I didn't really know what I was going to do or where my life was going. All I knew was that advertising, which once seemed exciting to me, was now, though lucrative, dull and empty, even ludicrous. A series of "coincidences" ensued, which at the time seemed unrelated but later proved to have put me on the path to my new direction.

First, I required major surgery, and in the wake of the unexpected hospitalization, I had to borrow money. Then, still uncertain about my future but anxious about an immediate income, the idea of becoming a temporary typist hit me as the ideal solution while I sorted things out. Logic and my friends told me this was a ridiculous course of action—that I should be seeking a job commensurate with my skills, experience, and salary expectations. At that time jobs were plentiful. I had already turned down several. There was no rational reason for me to work many notches down at a quarter the salary I could command. Yet I felt an inner imperative—call it a sense of rightness—more compelling than rational consideration of the known facts. I signed with an agency under whose aegis I worked at a number of short jobs quite beneath my capabilities. And though several of these companies, upon discovering I was not what I seemed to be, offered me attractive permanent employment, I refused. Somehow nothing seemed quite right, so I went on more typing jobs.

Finally, the agency sent me out on a job within walking distance of my apartment. My appointment slip said I was a vacation replacement for the secretary to Vaun Gillmor, vice president of the Bollingen Foundation. However, when I arrived I found that the receptionist had confused me with another temporary secretary who had already been assigned to Miss Gillmor. I was instead sent to the editorial department. There I quickly became friendly with an editor who was intrigued by my obvious overqualification. She brought me to the attention of the managing editor, who offered me a permanent position as his assistant. Despite the low salary, I accepted—ostensibly because the slower pace of a nonprofit organization would leave me some mental energy at the end of the day to pursue my own creative endeavors, and for the convenience of being able to walk to work.

Two years later, this low-paying job resulted in my being asked to work with Joseph Campbell, which in turn led to a wonderful collaboration and a long association, the ultimate outcome of which was to set me on an entirely new life path.

Like the man who found the stranded bird on the beach, a beacon was guiding me to where I needed to be. United Church minister Catharine Ponder calls this being "led," and Jung would say it was synchronicity. Surely it was laden with serendipity. The unconscious has these two related qualities in abundance.

My life is so full of such linked occurrences, which I attribute to synchronicity, that I no longer believe in chance at all. In a purposeful, intelligent universe there are no accidents. If you examine your own life carefully you will probably find instances where you experienced synchronicity, where some seemingly chance encounter or event led to something else, or where a set of what appeared to be mere coincidences turned into a meaningful encounter. Take the case of the airline captain previously cited. Here is what had to occur in order for us to meet:

FIRST: I had to be in Germany, and I live in New York.

SECOND: I had to be staying with a particular friend.

THIRD: She and the captain had to be scheduled to be on the same flight—out of literally thousands of possibilities.

FOURTH: She had to get sick or she would never have been on a short-range flight. With seniority, she regularly flew only long-range—to America, South America, India, Asia. But because she was not fit to fly for two weeks due to a flu, she was rescheduled for the balance of her work month on inter-Europe routes. The captain flew only shorter routes as he was not qualified for long-range equipment.

FIFTH: All the other crew members had to be on the same flight for it was their shared chemistry that made the party.

SIXTH: The flight had to be re-scheduled, returning the crew to base without passengers. Had it been a working flight, they would have been too busy to get acquainted.

SEVENTH: The captain had to single me out for conversation in a crowded room.

EIGHTH: My friend's husband had to be out of town on a business trip, or she would not have invited the group home.

While I do not hold that I was the only person in the world who could have served the purpose of opening up the pilot to his recovery, the number of "chance" occurrences is stunning. Can one really write all that off as mere coincidence? To my mind, synchronicity of this ilk seems to be supported by intention and purpose.

In the view of modern science, which is based on a set of unstated assumptions about the nature of the universe, everything is a product of *cause and effect*. You drop a stone, it hits the ground. You throw a ball, it sails through the air. In this paradigm of mechanism and materialism—inherited from Bacon, Descartes, and Newton—there is no room for another system of how things happen or how they are related. However, synchronicity—incidents that are related to each other in a non-linear or acausal way—does occur with startling regularity.

The German philosopher Arthur Schopenhauer, in an essay entitled *On An Apparent Direction in the Life of an Individual*, likens the events of one's life to the plot of a novel. What seems irrelevant at the time can be seen later on to be part of a definite pattern. And, as Dr. Jung has noted, the first occurrence may be ascribed to chance, the second considered as coincidence, but the third shows a pattern. These patterns exist in the non-conscious, and if we align ourselves with them they will provide direction.

How do we allow ourselves to be guided by the wisdom of the deep non-conscious, which always knows what is best for us? The answer, I believe, is in *letting go of control*. It is our attempt, based on deification of the rational mind, always to have the intellect, which shuts off access to the realm of intuition, in control. Letting go of control is achieved through altered states of consciousness. In dreams, this is automatic and everyone experiences it, but we also go through altered states frequently without being aware. For example, the monotony of a long bus or train ride can lull us into a state of reverie where we are not thinking about anything in particular and where we temporarily lose conscious awareness of our physical surroundings. Often we wake from these semi-trance states with a start—a feeling of "where am I?"

Daydreaming is another type of altered state, as is concentration upon a creative effort. We mentally shift onto another plane for a while. The periods just before sleep and just after waking, called *hypnagogic*, are other altered states, neither asleep or awake. Whatever shuts off the chattering of the intellect helps us to achieve an altered state, such as meditation and prayer. Frustration and anxiety can also have this effect. Dr. Banting was exhausted, therefore he stopped trying to control things with his intellect. I was in limbo, what had worked before didn't work anymore. In both instances, the direction received from the unconscious was *non-volitional*—that is, it wasn't consciously asked for. But think of how much more effectively we can use our unconscious powers when we hook them up to our conscious mind. The more we can learn to *consciously* program our infallible unconscious, the greater results we will achieve in time.

Perhaps one of the most dramatic examples of what the unconscious can achieve is that of *psychoimmunology,* which is the effect of the use of specific imaging techniques on the healing processes of the body. You may have heard about some of these experiments, such as the one in which children afflicted with leukemia imagined Pac Man-like creatures eating up the "bad cells." The results were amazing, to say the least. On average, the white blood cell count went from approximately 13,000 to 15,000 after just one week; a week later, the count went up to almost 19,000. Psychologist Howard Hall, who conducted such experiments, says, "For some inexplicable reason, the mind can influence the body by changing the biochemistry of the blood." Mind-boggling? No, mind-using.

Though mainstream science has not caught up to the consciousness revolution now in progress on many fronts, Marilyn Ferguson, editor of *Brain/Mind Bulletin* and author of *The Aquarian Revolution*, observes that,

> Discoveries in brain research, consciousness research, physics, parapsychology, and molecular biology are converging toward a radical, new world-view," [but] "The politics of science is frustrating the most exciting adventure of this century or any other: the search for what it means to be human.

And Colin Wilson has this to say in his book, *The Occult,*

> I believe that the human mind has reached a point in evolution where it is about to develop new powers— powers that would once have been considered magical. Indeed, it has always possessed greater powers than we now realize: of telepathy, premonition of danger, second sight, thaumaturgy [the power to heal]; but these were part of its instinctive, animal inheritance. For the past thousand years or so, humankind has been busy developing another kind of power related to the intellect, and the result is Western civilization. His unconscious powers have not atrophied, but they have

gone underground. Now the wheel has come the full circle; intellect has reached certain limits, and it cannot advance beyond them until it recovers some of the lost powers....It has cut itself off from its source....magical power rises from the subconscious...."

People everywhere, in all cultures, have known that *real power* wells up from the depths of the psyche, from inner sources that are profoundly connected to the wellsprings of life itself. From charismatic healers to charismatic politicians, those who have accomplished great feats have done so because they were able—and unafraid—to tap into the deep underground stream of the unconscious that connects us all with nature and with one another. Most of you can think of at least one experience when you consciously felt you just couldn't do it—maybe it was running a marathon, or writing a paper, or hosting a party. But then your grit and determination kept you going past the obstacle, whether it was fear or fatigue, and you got what runners call a "second wind." Suddenly you felt a great welling up of energy you didn't know you had, and you finished your task with ease, even exhilaration.

You were tapping into your unconscious reserves, which are always available upon demand. It's like switching on a second, more powerful, engine when you need more horsepower. And, if you have done it once, even accidentally, you can do it again—and again. Unfortunately, because we have been convinced by the prevailing scientific and religious world–view that we are limited beings, many of us stumble quite unaware upon our psychic powers, and, not knowing how we got there, don't know how to return. It's a bit like finding a little out-of-the-way bistro late at night in the rain and the dark while in a unfamiliar town. You have a great meal and you want to go back, but you can't remember the path you followed to get there. You weren't paying attention—you were just roaming around looking for a place to eat. You didn't expect anything miraculous.

Now, however, by using the following relaxation and visualization techniques, you can learn to access your deep inner resources and greatly increase your ability to live in a creative, satisfying, and spiritually harmonious manner. Your non-conscious is waiting for you to explore it and use its powers. In times past, these inner mysterious powers were called the gods. We say, "The devil made me do it," or "Her guardian angel was on duty," when we are faced with some unexplained incident. When we tap into our unconscious, we are also tapping into the universal unconscious, where the gods reside. Jung called these inner powers, which are expressed in patterns, *archetypes*, and we can think of them as vibrations to which we resonate at many different levels of our non-conscious beings. When we work with our deep minds, we are tuning into the patterns that suit us best. They are not the same for all, since each person is an individual with individual needs and desires. However, as Alan Oken tells us in his book, *As Above, So Below*:

> It is the same One Force expressing itself in an infinite multitude of forms and intensities. This is often called the process of "Involution" and "Evolution." It is also what we mean, in part, when we refer to the universal law of "As above, so below." Just as an atom is one unto itself, so is Man such a singular organism, so is a nation, so is the Earth, so is the Solar System, so is the Galaxy, so is the ultimate Universe of Universes. In all of creation there appears to be a repetition of the same pattern in all structures from the physical properties of the tiniest atom to the greatest unit of the Cosmos....This is what is meant when it is said that "man was made in the image of God."

Listen to the Silence

10

Twelve Steps to Realizing Psychic Potential

We will eventually discover that all persons have the full range of psychic phenomena as potentialities, all unconsciously understood.
—WILLIS HARMON,
Stanford Research Institute

A ground-breaking change in the way we view our world and our place in it is under way. A major factor in this coming revolution of the mind is our burgeoning ability to direct and control our own inner states of mind and being. This process of utilizing our subtle senses includes the ability to learn how as a specialized skill in itself.

Imagine having the following description apply to you:

All at once it seems as though everything is working. There is no sense of needing to do anything. My actions unfold as they do in a pleasant dream, though my body may be putting out great efforts. I have no thoughts about what I should do or how I should do it. Everything is happening automatically, as though I have tuned myself in on a radio beam that directs my nervous system so that it works in synchronization with everything in and around me. I feel insulated from all distractions. Time disappears, and even though I know the speed of actions taking place around me, I feel I have all the time I need to respond accurately and well. I am so completely involved in the action that there is not even a question of confidence or the lack of it. There are no issues such as worries about failure or feelings of fatigue. Even such feelings as momentary fear appear to serve me, changing automatically into positive forces…I am acutely aware of colors, sounds, the presence of people around me, the feeling of being a source of power and energy in this moment in time. I feel…as though the usual barriers…have been pulled away, and I am completely at one with myself.… It is a wonderful feeling, crisp, full of joy, more *real* than the everyday world, going very deep.

Impossible, you say? Not at all. The above is a synthesis of hundreds of interviews on peak performers done by Dr. Charles A. Garfield, a former astronaut who is now the president of the Performance Sciences Institute in Berkeley, California.

Step One: Learning to Trust

Dr. Georgi Lozanov, the Soviet pioneer mentioned in the previous chapter who originated many of the techniques Dr. Garfield discusses in his book, says that when people begin "tapping the reserves of the mind," they feel as if they have suddenly come into a large legacy.

They see themselves differently. Possibilities open up. They begin to grow into a larger notion of who they are and what they can do.

The person using psychic ability can be likened to someone riding on the top of a speeding train. He can see ahead, behind, to the left, to the right, up above, and down below. The people inside the train can see but a small slice of the landscape as it quickly slides past. They have no idea of what's ahead, not much of what was passed by, nothing of the other side, and it rarely occurs to them to look up. But the person on the train's roof has the best vantage point, better than the train's engineer, who sees what's immediately ahead but cannot see around the bend. The man on the roof, however, has a 360-degree view.

We have the choice of whether we are going to ride on the top of our own lives or take a seat in the enclosed compartment.

Granted, riding on the top of the train is a bit more dangerous than sitting inside, but it can be downright exhilarating to have the wind in your hair and the sense of freedom that comes with not being restricted. When you get your superbrain in gear, there comes a feeling of harmony, of being at one with the world, of taking it all in instead of experiencing only a small, cramped slice of life. It happens when you have that sense of purpose and reach deep inside yourself for the means to bring about the life you deeply desire and know you deserve.

As we limber up our brain and flex our expectation muscles, we begin to feel awfully good about ourselves and our potentialities. We feel smarter—because we *are* smarter. As someone has said, violins are useful instruments; you can use them for doorstops or you can learn to play exquisite music on them. Think of your brain as a violin. It is there waiting for you to learn to play it—it has incredible potential for expressing your total being with clarity and beauty. It can play in harmony with an entire orchestra, or soar into a unique solo performance. The choice is yours.

Overcoming skepticism is the first hurdle you must vault on your path to psychic development. You are here asked to believe in something that you have been taught not to accept as "real." Becoming a psychic person involves going beyond your five physical senses to your subtle senses and developing a sense of trust in yourself and your own inner process. Although you cannot prove logically, or with current scientific technology, that these subtle senses exist, you can learn to trust them.

In his book *Recovering the Soul*, Larry Dossey, M.D., reviews the evidence for a "nonlocal" concept of the human mind, which states that the mind is a force which, although existing in the context of the physical body, is "ultimately independent of the physical brain and body, and that as a correlate it transcends time and space."

The invisible dimension of your being is a place you can visit at will—once you are familiar with it you will want to go there again and again, to receive guidance and access your non-conscious information data bank. Once you experience this higher place within yourself, you go from being an exclusively rational/physical person to being a psychic person in touch with your non-physical self. Below is a special meditation for learning to trust your process. Once you have done this and it has become real for you, a sense of knowing trust will suffuse you. The feeling is like being a so wealthy that you know you can never run out of money, no matter how much you spend. Once you have made contact with your deep inner self, it will always be a part of you, always be available.

Your sanctuary is a place where you can recharge your batteries. It is also a place where you can meet your guides and ask questions or request help in solving problems. Creating your sanctuary is not difficult. Here's how it's done.

Creating Your Sanctuary

Find a time when you can be alone and undisturbed for at least fifteen minutes. Next, breathe deeply and exhale all negative feelings, transmuting them into good as you release them.

Now, create in your mind a picture of a lovely place —it might be a secluded spot in a woods or a cove on a beach. It can be outdoors or indoors. Letting yourself feel relaxed and free, think leisurely about what a sanctuary would mean to you. As this picture emerges (and remember, you don't actually have to *see it*, you only have to *know* it) let yourself be absorbed into its quiet, beauty, and comfort. Know that here good things will happen for you. Let yourself relax totally.

When you have an image in your mind or a feeling about what your sanctuary is like, continue to fill in all the details. Are there pictures on the walls? What are the colors, smells, textures, sounds? Make this picture as complete as you possibly can. Walk around your chosen spot and make it totally yours. You may prefer to go there alone, or you might invite others to share it with you. Only you can make these decisions.

When you feel that you have completely taken possession of your special place, perform a symbolic gesture—such as putting a vase of fresh flowers on a table or writing your name or placing a favorite object there—which will enable you to return to your sanctuary at will. The purpose is to make it easy for you to recall your sanctuary. Once you have done all this, slowly bring yourself back to everyday consciousness by taking several deep breaths.

You have now created your sanctuary. It is yours. You can return anytime you want, and there you can do whatever you choose.

Step Two: Opening to Receive

The doorway to receiving psychic information is the *breath*. Breathing is something we take for granted—most of us are rarely aware of our breathing unless it is impaired by a cold or allergies. However, there is reason to believe that breath is one of the root elements in activating our psychic abilities. Awareness and control of breath allows us to consciously open ourselves to receive psychic information from our extrasensory channels.

Although Western science has largely ignored the benefits and possibilities inherent in the breath, most Eastern philosophies teach that we live in a sea of energy—a bright and vital source that we absorb and activate with our breath. The Hindu yogi tradition calls this energy *prana*, an idea at the core of many systems of thought. Oriental mind-body balancing techniques, such as acupuncture and shiatzu, refer to this as *Chi*. Not only is this subtle energy in the very air we breathe, it circulates through our bodies along specific channels called *meridiens*. When we feel ill or out of sorts, our prana or Chi is blocked. Controlled breathing permits us to extract new prana from the air. The physical body can store this energy in the same way it can store food calories. When the prana is up, you feel exuberant, alive, open. When the prana goes down, you feel tired, uninterested, closed. I notice a lack of prana when my hair goes limp and flat.

This energy is subtle, but it is real. Yogis claim it not only gives vitality to the body, but also nourishes consciousness. A high content of prana in the brain causes the unfolding of mental abilities and psychic powers. In other words, a high level of prana opens us to the experience of receiving psychic output. Prana is there whether we are aware of it or not, like the oxygen in our lungs, but when we make a deliberate effort to increase it, blocked channels of information open. The breath is a powerful tool.

Breathing Exercises

Change your breathing and you will change how you feel. This is quite literally true. Breath *is* life, and how you breathe has a great deal to do with your intuitive and mental abilities. Some people seem to be fearful of deep breathing and deprive themselves of adequate oxygen by taking only shallow breaths, rather like a proper lady sipping tea. If you doubt this, stop now and take a few really deep and full breaths, preferably at an open window, sucking the air deep into your belly. Exhale fully until your lungs are entirely empty, and then do it over again.

What breathing consciously does is to develop a communications link between consciousness and the unconscious, between mind and body, between spirit and psyche. In addition, it helps us to focus by keeping our attention on the interplay between breath (outside) and body (inside). Proper breathing is an asset to concentration.

Rhythmic Breathing

To do this breath exercise, make yourself comfortable in any position you choose, preferably in a darkened room. Loosen or remove tight clothing, including shoes. A warm bath is a good preliminary. Spend a few minutes adjusting your body to a position of maximum comfort. Reclining in a partially sitting-up position works well for many people.

Now, close your eyes and simply pay attention to your breath. Do not attempt to alter the pattern, merely observe it. Breathe in through the nostrils and out through the mouth. Feel the coolness of the in-breath of fresh air coming in; feel the warmth of air leaving your body. Imagine yourself being energized and cleansed by each breath.

Next, listen to any sounds you make while breathing. Do not judge, just listen. Also notice whether you breathe in shallow or deep breaths, where the air goes, into the diaphragm or into the belly. Does your chest rise and fall? Does your abdomen rise and fall?

After observing yourself for a few minutes, gradually begin to slow and deepen your breathing in a rhythmic manner, taking in long, slow breaths and exhaling in a continuous flow. Let yourself do this as long as it feels comfortable.

Breathing with Color

This is a yoga exercise known as "polarization." To do it, lie face up in a comfortable position. Some people like to use the floor. Align your body with the feet pointing south and the head north, to the earth's magnetic field.

Allow your palms to rest face up with the arms stretched out alongside the body. As you begin breathing, slowly and rhythmically breathe in *color.* If you want to energize yourself, breathe in a warm color, such as red, orange, or yellow. Breathe out a cool color, such as blue or green. To calm yourself, do the opposite. Breathe in a *cool* color and breathe out a *warm* color. Think of the incoming breath as a positive current, the outgoing breath as a negative current. By breathing in these two polar opposites, you are balancing your energy state. Imagine these polarized currents circulating through your body, one after the other, cleansing and purifying your inner self. Notice any sensations you feel while you are circulating the breath.

Do each exercise for five to fifteen minutes (longer is better). When you have achieved a state of deep concentration, you are in touch with your intuitive self.

Step Three: Feeling Your Energy

All life is composed of energy. We think that our physical world is solid and substantial, but it is in a constant state of flux and movement. What appears to be a solid object, like a chair or a table, is really a mass of swirling atomic particles held together by their energies. Your body and mind and spirit and emotions all generate energies of different wavelengths. Most of the time you are not aware of your energies. The exercises below will give you methods of contacting deep levels of awareness. It is awareness that is the basic key to developing your psychic potential.

Generating Psychic Energy

You have the ability to generate energy at will. To experience this, sit, recline, or lie down in a comfortable position and close your eyes. Take a few deep breaths, slowly—in and out, in and out—and then picture your dominant hand in your mind. Find your hand mentally and begin sending it energy. Soon your hand will begin to feel warm and alive. It may tingle. This is energy. You can now send energy to other parts of your body at will. Just concentrate on where you want to feel the energy. Send energy until you feel yourself filled with a glowing warmth, emanating from your psychic center. Picture this energy as light cascading through your body. Let the energy build for a few minutes, then see it as a beam of light coming through the top of your head and pouring out into the universe. You can use this energy beam to send information and contact others.

Kundalini Energy Balancing

According to the yogi tradition *kundalini*, there are seven energy centers in the body, called *chakras*. Two subtle energies run along this system, connecting the chakras, one energy is female in nature, the other male in nature. These are called *ida* and *pingala*. The first chakra is located at the base of the spine and represents "sleeping" energy. The second is located at the genital level, representing sexual energy. The third, at the solar plexus, is active energy. The fourth is the heart center, which connects the three lower chakras to the three higher— or spiritual—chakras that are located at the throat, the forehead, and the crown of the head.

The idea here is to activate and release the energies in the lower three chakras in order to allow them to flow through the heart center, or fourth chakra, into the higher ones. It is this energy flow that aids in the realization of psychic potential. As Alain Danielou says in *Yoga: The Method of Reintegration,*

> The Hindu [speaks] indifferently of men or of subtle beings, he intermingles the geography of celestial worlds with that of terrestrial continents, and in this he sees no discontinuity but...a perfect coherence; for, to him, these worlds meet at many common points, and the passage from one to the other is easy for those who have the key."

Learning to locate your seven chakras and allow a smooth flow of energy through them is a good method for achieving a state of centeredness. To center yourself, you find that place where you can go out in all directions and safely return. Some people are naturally more centered than others, but everyone can locate a deep center, like the hub of the turning wheel, where there is calm, like the eye of a storm. It does not matter whether you think these energy centers are real or imaginary. Contacting your kundalini system is a means of releasing your psychic potential.

Opening Your Chakras

To do this exercise, find a quiet place where you can lie comfortably undisturbed for half an hour. Lying on an exercise pad or rug is good. Or if you prefer, you can do the exercise in a sitting position. Close your eyes and breathe slowly and deeply until you feel a state of peace. Mentally shut out the outside world and go inside yourself. Say, "I now integrate my energies," to yourself as you breathe.

Imagine your spinal cord from the base of your spine to the crown of your head, and mentally locate each of the seven chakras described above. Imagine them, one at a time, from the base of your spine to the top of your head, and feel the difference in each energy center. Note the characteristics of each chakra—is the energy light, heavy, flowing, blocked? Allow yourself to investigate each chakra thoroughly, getting acquainted with the energy there. Some chakras may seem to be pulsating with energy, others may seem to be relatively quiet.

Now, imagine two twined cords—rather like a double helix—along your spinal column. One of these is red (the male energy) and the other is blue (the female energy). Starting with the root chakra at the base of the spine, send energy up the red cord through each of the seven chakras, ending with the crown chakra. Then, return the energy along the blue cord back to the base. As you do this, imagine each chakra in turn—see if you experience ease or difficulty in passing the energy through the chakra. Do not be in a hurry. You may need to do this several times before the energy runs smoothly along the path of the spine. As you move the energy, imagine it connecting all of your energy centers in one motion, like the engine of a train pulls the cars.

As you circulate the energy along the spinal cord, imagine that you send out your mind from this central system, like a radio tower sends out signals from a control center. One or another chakra may feel particularly right to you, a sign that you have a natural affinity for the type of energy it produces.

Step Four: Mind-Clearing

Mind-clearing is like housecleaning. You need to dispose of the rubbish that accumulates over the course of time. This means resolutely turning away from what is trivial and unimportant and allowing your intuition to work on what is of most value to you. To do this, you need a clear mind and clarity of purpose.

Single-Flame Technique

This is a simple but effective meditation you can use anytime. Light a candle and fix your attention unwaveringly on the flame. Then, still watching the candle flame, slowly blink your eyes, allowing your thoughts to become still. If thoughts persist in coming, acknowledge them and let them flow through you as you keep your attention on the candle flame. Do this until you feel tired and then close your eyes and feel a relaxed sensation pulsate through your body in waves of warmth and pleasantness. Say to yourself, "I now empty my mind of all unnecessary thought."

Burning the Rubbish in the Mind Technique

This method is favored by Buddhist meditators. After breathing quietly for a few minutes, imagine yourself gathering up all the unwanted material in your mind, just as you would gather up dead leaves and fallen tree limbs to make a bonfire. Now, take all of these old, unnecessary thoughts and pile them up in a place where you can safely start a fire—a fireplace is good. As you collect them, say to yourself, "I now let go outworn thoughts, outworn emotions, outworn attitudes." After you have piled up your mental rubbish, strike a match to the pile and as it goes up in flames say to yourself, "I now return this to the universe for cleansing. I need it no more."

Step Five: Find Your Authentic Self

How you receive psychic impressions, or send them, how you process the entire spectrum of psychic learning and use the experiences, is a product of who you are. Just as no two people will hear a concert in the exact same way, or experience the same emotional response; or view a street scene or remember the details of an accident in the same way, so no two people will have identical psychic experiences.

First of all, you have a unique point of view. Your needs and aims are yours alone. What you want to manifest using your psychic abilities depends on you—not only on your conscious aims, but also on your unconscious self. Remember we said earlier that the psyche tends toward wholeness, and that your unconscious always knows best. Sometimes our conscious desires are in contradiction to our unconscious desires. The unconscious wins out every time.

Conflict occurs because we are consciously programmed by society—parents, teachers, media, authority figures, government—to desire certain things, to hold certain qualities of life dear. The entire thrust of advertising, for example, is homogenization. We are heavily programmed to want a particular soft drink, or a currently trendy type of clothing, or this year's model of an automobile. Not only are material goods set forth as being what is most desirable, but our thoughts are similarly programmed to direct our actions—usually for the benefit or profit of others. Our consciousness gets tuned in to "the thing to do" rather than the thing we truly desire or the mind-set that is best for our personal development.

We must listen to our own individual voices, not be swayed by the monolithic tone of the crowd. A crowd mentality will interfere with the development of psychic intuition because you will be looking for corroboration of an *outside* authority rather than looking to your own *inside* authority for information.

The Secret Door Technique

In this method, you go for a walk in the woods and find a little secret door somewhere. It might be in a tree, or hidden in the grass, or at the entrance to a secret garden. When you open the secret door, you find a passageway leading downward, and you follow it. It may be a stairway, or just a sloping path. All is silent and magical here; you feel safe and comfortable and yet in a state of anticipation. As you go down into the passageway, you leave behind the upper world. At the bottom, you find a secret room that contains your true self. Acknowledge this Self and take some time to get to know him or her. If at first you feel uncomfortable, be patient until you become accustomed to this person, who is you at your best.

Focusing clearly on the issue you want to consult your intuition about is the way to get results. Confusion between what you really want and what you *think* you want, a result of programming by outside influences, will lead to skewed information and poor results.

Focusing Technique

To do this exercise, you will need pen and paper and at least twenty minutes of quiet, undisturbed time. Begin by using one of the breathing exercises following by one of the mind-clearing meditations. When you are clear and relaxed, write three headings on your paper:

1. *What I want to manifest in my life.*
2. *What I like in my life.*
3. *What I want to get rid of in my life.*

Now, list everything you can think of in each column, including not only material goods and physical attributes but also mental and emotional states. You may, for example, want to get rid of depression and manifest happiness; or you may want to get rid of pessimism and manifest a positive consciousness. Recognizing what is already in your life that you like and appreciate also helps you to focus. So often we overlook the good in our own backyards. Being clear and focused about what you want to bring into your life is the key to manifestation. Focusing on what you don't want will keep your energies stuck in the negative, while focusing on what you truly want will activate your inner self to guide you in the right direction.

Once you have made your list, go over it carefully and ask yourself if you truly want to be rid of the things on your list; if you are truly glad to keep the things you chose; and if you truly want the things you are asking your subconscious to manifest. Having done this, put the list away for a week and then return to it and evaluate it again. Do this weekly over a period of a month *without discussing it with anyone.* This must become a reflection of your authentic self, not a mirror image of others' wants for you. Be as honest as you possible can, reworking your list until you are completely satisfied.

Next, take the items in column one and three and arrange them according to the following priorities. Give each an A, B, C, or Z code. A is for *Absolute Must.* B is for *Better with than Without.* C is for *Can Do Without.* And Z is for *Zilch*—you know this isn't important. If you have more than three items in A, B, and C, reduce them to three and re-prioritize those three. Now reconsider once more, until you have two or three A items in both the "get rid of" and the "want to manifest" lists. This is your focus on your authentic self.

I have found this method to be especially helpful for people who are unclear about what they want from their psychic abilities. They know they want to improve their lives somehow, but there is confusion about what is important and what is simply an old mind-set. Really focusing in a sharp and clear manner, and writing it all down, seems to activate the psyche to provide solutions to everyday problems.

Step Six: **Relaxation**

Getting into a relaxed state prior to asking intuition for information is vital. The more relaxed you are, the easier it is for your intuition to operate freely. Learn different modes of relaxation and see what works best for you. Also, learn to relax in different situations, not just in the safety and comfort of your favorite chair or in bed. Once you have practiced a technique and mastered it, you can return to it anytime you like, usually under any circumstances. But at first it is best to practice under ideal conditions of quiet and non-disturbance. Once you have programmed the technique into your non-conscious, you will be able to access it anywhere, even in hectic or noisy circumstances.

The first step is to relax your mind into what is called an *alpha-theta* state. There are four brain wave patterns that we know about, though I suspect that others will one day be discovered. These are:

Delta - 0 to 4 cycles per second (cps), the slowest, evident during the deepest sleep.

Theta - 4 to 8 cps, evident during periods of daydreaming or deep reverie, what used to be called "a brown study." In the theta state, we are neither awake nor asleep.

Alpha - 8 to 13 cps, fully relaxed, yet still aware of our surroundings, with eyes open or closed. The sort of somnolent state we go into on a long train ride when we have been staring out the window at a monotonous landscape for hours.

Beta - 13 to 26 cps, which is the "normal" state of waking consciousness, where you are when you are working or socializing actively.

None of these states of consciousness are foreign to us. We cycle through all four of them during the course of our day/night. We slip into and out of them, mostly without noticing. During beta, for example, we might drift off into reverie and find ourselves in an alpha state, daydreaming about tonight's date, and then suddenly snap back into beta when the phone on the desk shrills.

We could be driving our car along a monotonous route with little to claim our attention and slip for a few moments into theta and then back into beta as we see a sharp curve coming up ahead. And everyone is aware of the phenomenon of "dropping off" to sleep for just a second or two during ordinary activities.

The techniques that follow make use of these brain wave states, although you already use them naturally every day and night. When you awaken, but are not fully awake, still half in your dreamworld, you are in the alpha-theta state called hypnagogic. The same is true of the period between going to bed fully awake and finally falling asleep. There is a twilight zone where you are neither awake nor asleep, yet alert to slight disturbances. I find that I slip into alpha-theta states easily when attending concerts of classical music, especially if I know the music well. I feel totally relaxed and "into" the music, but my mind drifts off someplace else and I barely hear the music until the clash of the tympani arouses me. I do some of my best work and get many significant insights while attending concerts. You may want to accompany your relaxation exercises with soft, soothing music.

Pay attention as you go about your daily rounds and watch for those moments that you slip into alpha-theta states. You might be mesmerized by a display in a shop window and lose yourself in admiration for the objects there. A sunset might catch your imagination, taking you back to some previous time. A haunting tune might show up in your mind, pulling you to reexperience an old emotion. You might be concentrating on some routine task and slip away into reverie, hardly aware of what your hands are doing. Some men, for example, can't remember if they have shaved without touching their faces. These states are actually self-hypnotic and can be induced deliberately.

The first step in programming yourself with relaxation techniques that lead to the alpha–theta state is to learn how to make

the body, mind, and emotions receptive—to whatever questions you wish to pose to your intuition or to solutions to problems you are facing at the moment.

The following techniques, though they may seem to be a bit
daunting in print, are easily learned and actually take only a few
minutes. Practice at least twice a day, preferably in the morning
when you awake and again at night before you sleep. It is also
good to use these techniques as "coffee breaks" during the day
when you need refreshment. Frequency is of more value than
length of time spent on any one session. It's better to spend fifteen minutes a session three times a day than to spend an hour
once a day. Each person is an individual, however, a point much
stressed in this book, and you may find that longer sessions work
best for you. Active profile types will likely respond best to short
sessions, while Flowing profile types may enjoy longer sessions.

There is no precise time table for learning these exercises, but
it usually takes about two weeks. You will come to recognize the
inner shift that occurs when you enter the alpha-theta stage. Once
you know how, it comes automatically.

Physical Relaxation

Physical relaxation helps almost everyone to connect with the
intuitive part of their being. Although not a new idea—yogis in
India have been doing it for centuries—Western thought has
only recently discovered the many benefits of relaxation, from
psychotherapeutic use to painless childbirth and the treatment
of tension-related diseases, such as high blood pressure and
ulcers. The following technique is especially helpful to those
who are prone to a buildup of physical tension resulting in tight
and sometimes painful muscles. To perform this technique, you
will need about ten minutes, but up to thirty minutes is fine if
you want to spend longer with the method.

Tense-and-Relax Technique

Find a place where you can sit, recline, or lie down
comfortably, where you will not be disturbed. Start at
your toes and work your way upward through all the
muscle groups of your body, first tensing them and then

relaxing them. After you progress from your toes to your head, reverse the procedure and tense-and-relax from your head to your toes. This is known as progressive relaxation.

At each stage of the way, take a deep breath, let it out, and then tense the muscles, holding for the beat of a breath, then again breathing deeply and releasing the tension on the out-breath. Begin with your feet, tensing and relaxing them; move to the calves, tensing and relaxing them; then on up to the thighs, continuing to tense-and-relax each muscle group while leaving the previous group in a relaxed state. From the thighs, move to the buttocks, then to the abdomen, lower and upper. Next, the chest, arms, and hands. Progressively let yourself go limp as you finish the tense-and-relax procedure. Finally, move to the muscles of the neck, shoulders, head, and face. Make a "lion face," as if you were snarling or trying to scare someone. Repeat each tense-and-relax three times before going on to the next group of muscles. When you reach the head, reverse and go back down the body to the feet. You should now be totally relaxed with all bodily tension released.

At this stage, you are ready to program your intuition to give you the information you want or to solve problems. This is also the time to program yourself for changes you want to make or experiences you want to happen.

Self-Hypnosis

The Greek god Hypnos, also identified as Somnus, from where we derive the word *somnolent,* was a god of sleep, as was Morpheus, from which we get *morphine.* Hypnosis, however, is not the same as sleep although it mimics it. In the hypnotic state, we are in a condition of deep relaxation and especially subject to suggestion.

Many years ago, before the invention of anesthetics, hypnosis was used to perform surgical operations without pain. The patient was hypnotized and then told he or she would feel no pain. The treatment was remarkably successful and is still used today, although not very widely.

When hypnosis went out of fashion in the medical establishment, it was the psychiatrist Dr. Milton Erickson who revived its reputation. To a great extent he is responsible for the AMA re–recognizing it as having therapeutic value. Today, hypnotherapists abound. Much of the renewed interest is due to the work of Dr. John Grinder and Richard Bandler, founders of Neuro-Linguistic Programming, who have extended Erickson's work into the popular consciousness, making this potent tool of self-transformation available to all.

In the January 1983 issue of *Esquire*, Thomas Morgan told about how he had succeeded in removing his writer's block through self-hypnosis:

> How shall I describe self-hypnosis? I don't want to exaggerate. For one thing, it is a temporary, self-managed altered state of consciousness that can make the resources of your brain and body and persona more responsive to your needs. Looked at another way, self- hypnosis is a natural phenomenon that helps you follow your own suggestions, listen to your own admonitions, and submit to your own commands.
>
> In hypnosis, you are wide-awake but focused within yourself. It is not a waking dream—a *working* dream would be more like it, a kind of businesslike hyper-consciousness that lets you concentrate, really concentrate, on a matter of importance without mumbo jumbo at the beginning or rigmarole at the end, and all under *your* control.
>
> That is the point. Psychiatrists like to describe the event in hypnosis as a trance. I accept the word, but it is misleading, because it describes the event only from the observer's viewpoint. To most people, *trance* probably suggests a spaced-out person dropping out or away from reality, letting go, tending toward zero—whereas to you, in your trance, inside *your* head, you are in a vivid state of concentrated awareness. You are still in the real world working on a real problem. You are in charge.
>
> In general usage, the word *trance* misses that sense of direction. It suggests *less* control when…it may mean that you have more command over your life than ever before. It can, I believe, connect your unconscious to your problems…If within the trance or soon after, you find new ideas, new combinations of old ideas, unexpected twists of thought, or simply more courage to go on, you will know [it is] working.

You can induce a state of self-hypnosis with the following advanced relaxation techniques. This is a commonly used technique to deepen your relaxation and get you in touch with your deep inner self. You can use this technique after any of the breathing methods in order to become even more relaxed while remaining in an aware state.

The Elevator Technique

Imagine that you are standing in front of an elevator. The door is closed. You press the *Down* button and the smooth, shiny doors slide open, inviting you into a pleasantly lighted interior space. You get in and the elevator begins slowly to descend. As it does, you watch the numbers light up. Counting slowly, beginning at 100, allow the elevator to descend floor by floor in batches of ten numbers. You reach 90, then 80, then 70, then 60, then 50, and with each number you feel more and more relaxed, knowing that you are actually going deeper and deeper into your inner self where magical things happen. You feel comfortable and safe and you are looking forward to the bottom level. At last, you step off the elevator when it reaches 0. You find yourself in a beautiful room where you are ready to contact your intuition.

The Stair-Case Technique

Some people don't like the image of an elevator. If you are one of them, you might try the method of descending a staircase, one step at a time, counting backward from 100 until you reach the bottom. In this visualization, you imagine a door that leads to the staircase. You walk to the door, open it, and begin to go down, counting as you go, descending ever deeper. This is one of my own favorites, and I always imagine a circular staircase carpeted with rich red plush, such as one might find in an old castle. You can decorate your stairway as you choose.

The Parachute Technique

If neither elevator nor staircase appeal to you, you might want to try the parachute technique. In this method, you imagine yourself soaring very high into the sky and then jumping out of the plane and slowly descending, supported by your parachute, counting slowly backward from 100 until you reach the ground.

You can also, develop your own relaxation techniques, and I encourage you to do so. You know what works best for you. These techniques have worked for others, but they are given only to get you started on learning what works for you.

Step Seven: **Visualization**

Our ability to program—or reprogram—our deep inner minds with images during the alpha-theta, or self-hypnotic, state connects our conscious minds with our unconscious, or intuitive, selves. Remember that the right brain, which rules intuition, thinks in pictures or images. The left brain is the verbal, word-oriented side.

The mind is a marvelous mechanism. It can do almost anything. It can make you sick or make you well. One of the most interesting things about our minds is their *power to make images.* Images are themselves fascinating—symbolic images arise from the deepest unconscious levels of our beings and carry with them great power to affect our emotions.

The power of symbols is undoubted, and the good news is that we can create our own inner symbolic language as a sort of shorthand for the intuitive psyche to work its magic on. We call this *imaging.* We don't really know *how* it works, but we do know that it does work. Imaging seems to connect with an inner switch, to power our intuition.

The body, not knowing the difference, accepts what the mind sends it—if you signal fear, it responds with increased adrenaline. If you signal happy anticipation, it responds with increased blood flow.

Try a simple experiment. Tell yourself that you are tired, very tired, imaging what it feels like to be really exhausted. Do this for five minutes. Soon you will begin to yawn, get sleepy, or lose the power to concentrate. Now, tell yourself that it was all a lie, that you aren't tired at all, that you are wide awake, feeling alert, and ready to work. Do this for five minutes. Soon, your feeling of tiredness will vanish and you will be back to normal.

Now, imagine that you are being sued by an angry litigant, that all you possess may be taken away from you. Anxiety will come: you may feel anger. As you get into the fantasy, your body will react as if there were a real threat. Your palms may get sweaty, your heart rate will increase, your blood chemistry will change. But, if you now switch off that image and replace it with one of peace and calm—perhaps imagining that you have just come into a lot of money—your heartbeat will slow, your pulse will return to normal, your biochemistry will subside.

That's how imaging works.

Practitioners of magic have always believed that they could project an image outward into manifestation, and there is some evidence that this is indeed possible. Magic aside, we ourselves can use our power to make images in order to change and better our lives.

❦ When you allow a thought-image to sink into your unconscious during a relaxed state, you open the psychic door wide. The use of visualization for contacting your inner psyche is an excellent tool. What we can visualize, we can make happen. However, you do not actually have to make "pictures" in order to visualize. You can *think* an image, or *feel* one. How you visualize will depend on what mode of perception is easiest for you—visual, kinesthetic, or auditory—and what your psychic profile type is.

Treasure-Map Technique

An excellent aid to visualization and imaging is the making of so-called "treasure maps." To utilize this method, you will need a large piece of poster board, glue or tape, and images that apply to the issue at hand. If, for example, you want intuition to help you find the right place to live, collect pictures from magazines and other sources that represent what you want. Be creative with the technique—make it into a game. Be specific, and add as many details as you can.

When you have collected a sufficient number of pictures representing your wishes, paste them on the poster board in any manner that appeals to you, using an image of particular significance at the center. Some people like to use a religious symbol; some use a photograph of themselves. Once you have made your treasure map, put it where you can view it often. A good idea is to view it just before sleep and just after waking, when you are already relaxed. You can also get into a relaxed state at other times and allow the images you have created to sink into your non-conscious. When you feel you have absorbed the images sufficiently, put the treasure map out of sight and let your psychic mind do the rest. Be alert for information coming in about the subject.

Step Eight: Use Your Imagination

When using imaging, let your imagination roam freely. Visualization works best when it is accompanied by sensory elements—if you imagine a luscious piece of richly frosted cake, your saliva will begin to flow. If you imagine yourself engaged in exciting sex, your body will show signs of arousal. When we imagine something in detail, the act sets up what Dr. Karl Pribram,— known for his findings about how the mind forms pictures—calls a "neurological template," or a set of instructions we give to ourselves. By using our brain to create richly imagined images, we affect the brain itself, although just how is not clearly understood.

The human faculty for image-making is unique—furthermore, we have the ability to manipulate images inside our brains, and those changing images in turn affect our brains. You already do this all the time without being aware of it—when you replay last night's party in your head, remembering all the things you wish you'd done or said differently, for example. Or when, after a confrontation with your boss, you go over what was said and done in an effort to sort out the experience. Though you may not be able to change the bare facts of a situation, you *can* change your response and feeling about the situation by using active imagination.

Active Imagination Technique

In this technique, you take the picture of the event and put it in an imaginary frame. Then you stand back and take a good look, deciding what you want to change. You look at it this way and that, perhaps alter-ing the lighting or moving elements about. When you do this you manipulate images to get particular effects. like a creative director or a filmmaker.

For example, suppose you were denied a promotion you thought you deserved. Look at the image of your-self feeling rejected and betrayed. Step closer to the image and then back away. Notice the difference in how you feel. See the image in full color, then switch it to black and white. Notice the difference in the inten-sity of your feelings. Turn up the audio, and then switch it off entirely and view the scene like a silent movie. Now, mentally rearrange the image, changing it any way you like.

Next create an image of something pleasant—per-haps a wonderful vacation in an exotic locale. Use your active imagination to furnish the event in full detail. Imagine going to the travel agency and getting brochures for interesting destinations—Hawaii, the South Seas, South America, the Orient. Now, choose an itinerary, deciding just which cities you will visit, how long you will stay, what hotels you will occupy, where you will dine, what side trips you will take. Perhaps you choose an island vacation. Smell the sea, hear the waves, imagine walking barefoot in warm sand under a clear blue sky. Hear bird calls, see the flash of tropical fish. Imagine your feelings of pleasure and relaxation. See yourself in the new clothes you bought for the trip. Fill in all the details. When the entire pic-ture is so complete that you can recall it whole easily, sink it into your deep non–conscious mind.

When you release your imagination into your non–conscious you connect with power. If you are looking for the answer to a ques-tion, or the solution to a problem, imagine the possibilities. Then, let your intuition choose for you. You can use active imagination at any time. You need no special equipment or environment. You only have to let yourself drift into the alpha-theta relaxed state and let your mind create images. Through imagination, you set up commu-nications links with the non–conscious to tap into the deep reserves of your psychic potential. Making mental movies can help in every area of your life.

Step Nine: **Letting Go**

Letting go and letting the psyche do its work is the next step. Once you have sunk the question into your deep inner mind, forget about it. Know that a solution will be forthcoming.

The non–conscious works on its own time schedule. Once you have asked your question, be patient and allow your inner process to work through the matter at its own pace. Sometimes you will get an answer right away, sometimes much later. Not all fruits ripen at the same time. Your intuition is eager to cooperate with you, but it needs to be left alone to do the job.

Affirm to yourself that your non–conscious is all-knowing and will direct you correctly. Create a zone in your mind where you believe that you possess unlimited powers. Tell yourself this truth: *If you can conceive it, you can manifest it.* It does not matter whether you are asking your psyche about a mental or material issue. Letting go means letting go of any idea of limitation. It also means releasing any doubts, fears, judgments, or negativity. Remember the man who asked for a new car but then told himself that he'd never get one? Don't confuse your psychic mind with mixed messages. Determine precisely what you want, or want to know, and then release the energy into the unconscious.

Allow yourself to become comfortable with the idea that your inner feelings—such as hunches or a sense of urgency—are valid guidance. We call prayer "talking to God," but when we get answers we often disregard them as mere fantasy. Don't do this. Be alert for what comes and honor your psychic abilities. When you become at ease with them, you will come to know them as helpful guides from the non-physical, invisible world.

Releasing Technique

Get comfortable, do some breathing, relax yourself. Now, get ready to release. Take whatever problem or question you have and give it a form—make a mental picture of it or your feelings about it. Then, purse your lips as if you were going to whistle, and gently blow a huge pink bubble around the form you have created.

Totally enclose it with this shimmering pink bubble—like the one Glenda the Good Witch floats down to Oz in—and then release the bubble and let it drift up, up, and away. Watch it go. Let it sail off into the distance. See it becoming smaller and smaller until it vanishes from sight. Say, "I now release you to universal intelligence."

Once you have practiced releasing, if you find yourself worrying and wondering, do the releasing technique again. Train yourself to forget about outcomes and wait patiently for a signal from within. This is becoming mindful—a state of mental alertness just below consciousness, calm and free of anxiety yet ready to respond—like a sleeping cat.

Step Ten: Verification

Take the time to verify your hunches, if at all possible. Sometimes, we cannot verify: if, for example, you feel a definite sense not to take a particular flight and act on your intuition, and then find that nothing went amiss with the flight, you will never know whether you were given accurate information. You may have avoided a road accident on the way to the airport, or something else. However, you can set yourself small verifiable experiments with which to test your intuitive perceptions. Remember, this is a whole-brain activity; make your rational consciousness part of the process.

Verification Exercise

For one entire day, write down everything you experience which is nonsensory—beyond the senses of sight, hearing, smell, touch, and taste. Keep an accurate record in your personal psychic journal, minute-by-minute if you can, and note the thoughts, feelings, insights, urges, anxieties, premonitions, and so forth. Especially note any hunches or other psychic phenomena. Check each one out carefully. If, for example, you find yourself thinking strongly of a certain person, contact that person. Was he or she also thinking of you? That's telepathy. If you get a feeling to go a particular place, follow that urge and watch for developments. Make notes of any intuitive leads that produced results. Also note those that seemed empty, since verification may come later.

Not all psychic messages give precise information. It's important to recognize that urgent feelings, hunches, unexplained anxieties, and the like are channels of communication. Once I had a strong urge to go for a walk late at night , for no particular purpose. Thinking just to spin round the block, I went out, but the mood to walk endured and I dawdled away most of an hour. Upon returning home, I had an especially pleasant sleep full of sweet dreams, which I attributed to my nocturnal ramble. The next day, I received a phone call from an unpleasant person I was avoiding, complaining about my absence the night before. This disgruntled friend had come to call—and had waited for three-quarters of an hour! Her purpose had been to regale me with an angry tirade about a mutual friend with whom she was quarreling. Not finding me home, she had gone off to locate another unlucky victim and I was spared.

Her visit would have polluted my atmosphere and robbed me of a sweet sleep, since I am very susceptible to unexpected negativity, especially at night. Fortunately, my psychic antennae picked up the impending event and sounded a warning bell. Since the signal was not explicit—it didn't say, "Get out of the house: you are going to receive an unwanted visitor" I might have missed it had I not been responsive to the urge to take the unplanned walk. Had my caller not telephoned to vent her irritation at not being able to use me for an emotional garbage can, I would not have known what I had missed.

Step Eleven: Thankfulness

Develop an "attitude of gratitude" toward your inner self and what psychic intuition does for you, including the manifestation of material goods. Remember that all you have, do, and think is a product of your deep inner mind. If at first thanking yourself seems strange to you, do it anyway.

I make it a habit to offer praise and thanksgiving on a daily basis, or more often. This simple act will produce surprising results. One woman I know was attempting to bring love into her life through using psychic power, but it did not seem to be working. Finally, I told her about the benefits of thankfulness and she began daily to praise and give thanks for love she did have, which turned out to be more than she had realized. Once she developed an appreciation for what was already hers, she was able to manifest more good for herself.

An opposite example is the case of a trim woman in her forties, who was struggling to make ends meet in the wake of a divorce. She badly needed clothes to go out on job interviews. I helped her to focus, ask, and release her need and soon she was given an entire winter wardrobe by a woman her size who was moving to a warm climate. Of exceptional quality, for the woman was well-off and had excellent taste, the clothes were of the timeless style of simple tailoring and made of beautiful, fine fabrics.

Instead of being delighted at her windfall, which solved her wardrobe problems, this woman fussed and fretted as she tried on the perfectly fitting garments in front of my full-length mirror.

"I don't know," she said over and over. "Are they wearing clothes like this now? What's everyone wearing this year? I can't wear these if no one's wearing this style."

Rather than appreciating her fortunate legacy, she spoiled her own good fortune (and perhaps the answer to her prayer) with overconcern for what was "in."

Meditation on Thankfulness

Go back to the list you made in Step Five of the things you were glad to have in your life. Review your list and begin to expand it to include what your intuitive mind does for you. A state of thankfulness will not only purify your emotional system, it will activate your non–conscious to bring more and more good into your life. List absolutely everything you can think of for which you are grateful, both mentally and materially.

Write out your list and keep it in your journal. Review it on a daily basis. Add anything that comes to you as a benefit you receive from your interior self. List your mental, physical, emotional, and spiritual attributes—and praise and give thanks for each and every one. Ask three friends each to tell you three things about your mind or spirit that they find appealing, and add these to your list. You may have qualities of which others are aware but that you fail to appreciate. My own realization of this blind spot in all of us came one night when I was having dinner with a colleague. In the middle of a lively conversation, she suddenly said, "You are the most *interesting* person I know!" This was not my idea of praise—it seemed I was always being asked to sing for my supper, and I said so. Laughing, she said, "Would you rather I had said you were the most *boring* person I know?" Since that day I have given thanks to my Higher Self for what I had previously considered a burden.

Keeping your list beside your bed and going over it prior to sleep will put you in the right frame of mind. Meditate on thankfulness often, quietly going within and discovering that infinite invisible intelligence is always there for you. It's a bit like phoning a friend just to say, "Hi, how are you?" Being thankful keeps us in touch with our higher selves. We all like to know that someone is thinking kindly of us, and your intuition will respond to being praised and acknowledged for its work on your behalf.

Step Twelve: **Practice**

"How do I get to Carnegie Hall?" asks the tourist.

"Practice, practice, practice!" intones the venerable elder.

The same holds true for your psychic development. Practice, particularly if you are unfamiliar with or have been neglecting your intuition, must be done on a regular basis. As with any new skill, learning how to most effectively access your intuition requires both technique and knowledge. At first your efforts may seem clumsy and unrewarding, but persistence pays off. Gradually, through practice, you create communication links between the conscious and non-conscious enabling you to tap the reserves of the mind. With repetition, conscious control of the psychic process is strengthened. Practice with relaxation allows the release of stress to become automatic.

Make a firm commitment to yourself regarding how much time you are willing to devote to practice. This is important. The more time you have to practice, the greater will be your results. But even the person with limited time can achieve results with consistent practice. My recommendation to the serious minded is a minimum of one hour a day. Two is better; three, optimum. Divide the time into two or three sessions: one in the morning just after waking, a second during the afternoon or evening, and a third just before sleep. The morning period is especially fruitful, for you are naturally relaxed and still close to the alpha-theta wave of the dream state. When I was first learning to read the Tarot cards, I always spent the first hour of my day alone with the cards, letting the images sink deep into my unconscious mind and "speak" to me. Only afterward did I open the blinds and do the usual morning activities. And, no matter what the day brought, I felt close to the psychic realm all day long, with a sense of comfortableness such as one feels after a nourishing meal and a warm bath.

For the person whose schedule is tight or who has difficulty portioning off that much solitary time, I would suggest two half-hour sessions, morning and night, with a third in the evening if possible. Regularity and consistency will bring more desirable results than long periods of work done unevenly or spasmodically.

Suggested Practice Program

Let us assume you have decided upon the two-hour per day option. You can allot one half-hour in the morning, just after you wake, a half-hour during midday or evening, and an hour before you go to sleep. Or, one hour each morning and night. Your morning session will set the tone for your daily practice.

Although the Steps have been listed in a specific order, it does not have to be followed rigidly. However, it is advisable to follow the order given at least once through. You may wish to concentrate on some Steps more than others. You may not have trouble with focus, but you may have difficulties with relaxation. In the beginning choose one or two Steps and practice them regularly. When you have become accustomed to the routine, add other Steps, or replace the earlier ones. Mainly, *do not hurry yourself,* and work slowly through the twelve Steps. As you become familiar with the process, you can design your practice program to suit yourself. Be sure to keep an accurate record in your personal psychic journal.

Before starting your program, take some time to think about how you want to proceed. There is nothing rigid about this part of the scheme. You have already been given the basic tools, and now you are going to use them to shape your future. In a calm and rested state jot down what you want to get out of your psychic Self. What areas of intuition do you want to develop? You can choose one now, and later on switch if you like. It is best to concentrate on a single area at a time, in order not to dilute your effort. As you practice and gain skill in contacting your intuition and verifying the information you get, you can branch out.

Either memorize the Steps or tape yourself reading them aloud, as a guide. A tape is especially good; you can use it during quiet periods of the day, such as while commuting. Work through the Steps until you feel comfortable with the techniques. For example, in Step One you create your sanctuary. Once you have done this meditation to the point where you can recall your sanctuary just by taking a few deep breaths, you have implanted it permanently and all you need do in the future to recall it is to close your eyes, breathe deeply, and you will be there. This applies as well to the relaxation techniques, visualizing, and other meditations given throughout this book.

At night, begin with either a sanctuary meditation, a mind-calming exercise, or a relaxation exercise, or any combination thereof. Night is an especially good time to practice deep relaxation exercises and visualizations. During your night practice, go through the entire set of Steps you are working with at that time. Once you have mastered several Steps, you need only review them briefly, just as you might have a checklist for something you already know how to do. As you master each Step, it will be programmed into your psyche automatically, and you can always access the technique easily by deep breathing.

After you have learned all the Steps, you can proceed to any special site on the psychic landscape on which you want to concentrate, such as precognition. Just add the appropriate meditation to each session. Implant whatever words or images you have chosen into your intuitive soil. You might say, "How can I best view my future today?" Then, while in the relaxed state, return to your screening room and "view" the answer. Take whatever information comes. If you get a blank, return later.

Or, if a particularly important consideration comes up on which you want your intuition to work, you can concentrate on that issue, setting aside some extra time to do so. In the beginning, try not to ask too much of yourself. Be patient and keep working. Be gentle with yourself, knowing that you cannot fail because this is a natural talent we all possess.

Be playful and avoid boredom. If your practice becomes monotonous, change the setting or practice another skill for a while. ESP does not flourish under conditions of boredom. Make up games to play. If you are concentrating on precognition, you can try guessing tonight's lottery numbers (you don't have to bet), or get a racing sheet and pick horses. It's only practice.

How long will it take? That's up to you. Each person is an individual and results will vary. One medium I know spent five years in steady meditation before a channel opened for him. Others achieve quicker results. Much depends on your personal goals, the quality and length of time you invest, individual aptitude, and factors as yet unknown. I urge you to be patient with yourself until you reach your goal. Sometimes people work diligently for a long time and nothing seems to be happening and then, *bingo!*—what is called a "gateway" intuition occurs. It's like walking along a dull, dreary street and suddenly going through a gate into a beautiful, flower-filled courtyard hidden behind the façade of a building. This feeling is exemplified for me in *The Wizard of Oz* when Dorothy steps out of her house into the land of the Munchkins—and the black-and-white film turns into glorious Technicolor. When you have had a gateway intuition, you'll know for sure you aren't in Kansas anymore. This is also known as the "ah-ha!" experience," a moment of clear understanding of what before was murky.

These practice examples are only guidelines to get you started on your personal journey into the psychic landscape. It is your journey, and the experiences you have there are yours alone. Although I can tell you what I experienced on a trip to San Francisco, inspiring you to make the trip yourself in search of the same or a similar experience, no matter how precisely I describe what I did and saw, and my impressions of the event, yours will be entirely different. We both see the Golden Gate Bridge, but our emotional responses are not the same. I may have seen it at dawn; you may see it at sunset. I may have visited in June; you visit in October. The locale is the same; the person is different.

Thus, it is not possible to give rigid definitions or to define precise methodologies. Psychic intuition doesn't work that way. It's part and parcel of you—your moods, your intelligence, your education, the "furniture of the mind," your energies, your past experiences, your future aims, your ability to be open to the experiences you will encounter. Bear in mind that this is a *process*, not a course of study, like engineering. If you are not used to processing in an aware manner, it may take a bit of time for you to get used to doing so. The important thing is to make a commitment to yourself and follow through on it. Don't expect immediate success (but don't rule it out, either). In the end, as you learn to trust your psychic responses and let them operate on their own success becomes automatic.

Remember, using intuition is not a logical/rational activity. If you are accustomed to being mostly left-brained (as most of us are), it may at first seem a bit strange. You may experience odd sensations, such as a mild pulsing in the forehead, or a kaleidoscopic effect. You might even chance to float out of your body, but don't worry, you'll get back in. Your intuition cannot hurt you. However, if at any time you feel uncomfortable, stop and try again later, and if you encounter any negative information, it is wise to treat this as what it is—*information*—and proceed accordingly. Psychic information is like a weather forecast. If we know the weather is going to be stormy, we can take sensible precautions. Sometimes psychic "warnings" allow us to avoid a difficult situation.

Using intuition uses all of you. It is precisely the holistic nature of intuition that gives it its power. In your unconscious you have a huge data bank of experiences upon which to draw, most of which you are not aware. You know much more than you think you know, and your psychic intuition has the ability to come up with new and creative combinations of knowledge to produce solutions to problems. It is an innovator with great creative ability. Its products may amaze you.

Practice the Art of the Possible

11

Developing Positive Consciousness

Images the mind makes work into life.
—EURIPIDES
Medea

There are many ways to discover your own inner dimensions. One of the best of these is the contemplation and meditation upon symbols that are meaningful to *you*. Experience has shown that the use of symbols to which we do *not* readily relate is less effective than those to which we do relate. The symbols produced by your unconscious mind are truly yours. Like dream symbols, they are unique to you and can reveal you to yourself. Working with your inner imagery, using active imagination to change what you don't like or wish to improve, can make you more confident. Nothing negative that has been said to you or about you need be accepted as a truth. We can remove obstacles from our paths, many of them put there by others when we were children. We can be better than we suppose we are.

Think of yourself as a tower you built as a child. Whatever structure you built, you used the building materials available to you at the time. You did the best you could.

You may have kept many of the limiting beliefs about yourself that you constructed in childhood and when you were younger, and still be hampered by an outmoded sense of who you are and what you can do.

Developing your intuitive process gives you the opportunity to take apart and reassemble your old structure, perhaps using new materials as well as rearranging the old materials. Each one of those materials represents your feelings, emotions, thoughts, attitudes, and conceptions about reality. Nothing has been carved in marble. You are free to redesign your house of the Self as you wish, according to your present-day needs.

One of the joys of using psychic abilities is that it makes life much richer and more interesting. You get the sense of being on a roll. When you are truly tuned in, you feel you cannot fail and you have a wonderful feeling that everything's going your way.

There is inside you—*right now*—a marvelous, confident, successful personality, just waiting to be released from your self-imposed restrictions. This unobstructed personality can do *anything,* and you secretly already know that. Don't, however, start blaming yourself for having negative self–images. When you were younger, you needed them. In some way they protected you during vulnerable periods of your life. When you start to work with your infallible unconscious and begin to tap into your unlimited potentials, you'll discover that they are no longer needed. You'll be able to let them go.

As you replace negative images with positive ones, you will seem to be plugged into a wider consciousness that knows how to accomplish almost anything. At first, of course, you may have doubts, and success is not always instantaneous. Starting small, you build on each success until the process becomes automatic.

As you develop positive consciousness, many previous difficulties will drop away as if by magic. You'll know you are on the right track because you will feel good—about yourself and about others. This isn't magic—it will just seem like it. For a minute, imagine yourself as absolutely free of fear and absolutely certain it will never return. Doesn't that feel good?

The following guided meditation will help you to get in touch with those areas of your life that can benefit from the development of a positive consciousness. By using the powers of your unconscious mind to generate specific and meaningful symbols, you give yourself the power to *change* negative images into positive ones. Not to be confused with ordinary positive thinking, which tries to replace a negative *thought* with a positive one, the difference here is that you are working with the images your own unconscious mind has produced. By use of your conscious imagination you can change them permanently. When you have replaced a negative image with a positive one, the new image sinks deep into your very being and becomes your truth. Remember, the negative is *never true*. It is always a product of faulty construction.

A Journey into the Self

A simple and enjoyable guided meditation to put you in touch with your inner symbolic dimension is given below. Each of the experiences you encounter in this exercise has a specific correspondence to how you truly feel about the different areas of your life, which will be revealed after you have finished. It is easier to do this with a friend, asking the other person to guide you through the steps. However, if you prefer to do it alone, you can memorize the steps or tape them. If at any time during the exercise you feel uncomfortable, stop. You are in total control.

Read the following outline carefully. It tells you exactly how you will proceed through the meditation.

FIRST— Get into a comfortable position where you can remain still for about thirty minutes. It can be sitting, reclining, or lying down. Make sure you are totally comfortable physically and that you will not be interrupted. (If you are interrupted, you can always start over another time.) Eliminate all outside distractions, such as noise, before you start.

SECOND— Using one of the breathing techniques already given, relax your mind and body. Gradually, let your breathing become slower and deeper. If you are doing this with a partner, arrange a hand signal to show when you feel ready to begin. Also, arrange a hand signal in case you decide you want to stop.

THIRD— Know that in this exercise whatever imagery you produce and your response to it is perfectly all right. Nothing is right or wrong. This is about you. Approach the entire episode in a playful mode. You are going to have a fantastic adventure.

FOURTH— When you have reached a state of deep relaxation, either signal your partner to begin reading the exercise or start your tape.

FIFTH— When the exercise is over, return slowly to full waking consciousness and describe your experiences to your partner, while making notes for your own later use, or remember the experiences and write them down later.

SIXTH— Compare your experiences with the symbolic meanings of the imagery given at the end of this section.

Important: Do not peek. It is important that you complete the fantasy without knowing the symbolic interpretations in order to assure that you get a spontaneous reading of your own inner landscape.

The Adventure Trip

1: Your Special Place

Allow three minutes.
You are going to find a wonderful, special, secret place. It can be anywhere you choose—a beach, a woods, a park, a forest. It is a place you like to be, where you feel comfortable and safe. If at any time during the exercise you feel uncomfortable, you can instantly return to this place. When you have found your place, spend a few moments experiencing it. Notice how it looks, feels, smells. Are there trees, birds, flowers, water? Smell the air, pick a flower, listen to a bird singing, hear the rush of the ocean waves or the rippling of a stream. Maybe there isn't any water. Maybe you have chosen the desert, or a hidden-away garden.

2: Your Personal Path

Allow two minutes.
Now that you have found your secret place and feel comfortable and familiar there, look about you for a path. There will be a path somewhere. It might be right in front of you or it might take a little poking about to find. Take your time. The path is there and it is the right path.

Once you have found the path, describe it to yourself. Notice everything about it. Is it broad or narrow, smooth or rough, paved or dirt, straight or crooked, open or obstructed. Are there any people or animals on the path? If so, feel free to interact with them and remember the experiences. If not, go on alone. Notice how you feel about the path—is it nice, or is it difficult? Do you like walking there or would you prefer to be elsewhere? Do not analyze your response, merely notice it.

3: Finding Water

Allow two minutes.
As you proceed along your path, noticing the entire environment, you will encounter a body of water. Describe the water to yourself. It might be a placid lake, a burbling stream, a rushing river, the crashing ocean, or a fresh spring. You may or may not be able to see the water. It doesn't matter. If you like, spend some time with the water. Get in it, go wading, splash around, or gaze into its depths. Again, if you meet any people or animals—perhaps see fish swimming—take note.

4: Finding the Key

Allow two minutes.
Leaving the water when you are ready, continue once more along your path. Find a key. Describe the key. Is it large or small, plain or ornate? What kind of metal is it made of? How do you feel about it? Where was it, in the open or hidden? Put the key in your pocket and continue along your path.

5: Finding the Chest

Allow two minutes.
As you walk along your path, continue to notice the details—sights, sounds, smells, other creatures. Now you find a chest. Describe the chest. Is it wood or metal, large or small, open or locked? Does the key fit the chest? Examine the contents of the chest and see how you feel about the chest and what it contains. If you like, you can take something from the chest along with you on your inner journey.

6: Finding the Cup

Allow two minutes.
Continue to proceed along your path, noticing if there are any changes. If the path started broad does it now narrow, or vice versa? If it was smooth, is it now rocky? Continue to be aware of

your surroundings as you stroll. Now, you find a cup. Examine the cup. What is it made of? Is there anything in it? What? How do you feel about the cup? Is it pretty, or dirty and damaged? Is it something you'd like to keep or leave behind? Describe it.

7: Encountering a Bear

Allow two minutes.
Continue along your path, keeping aware of what is around you and how you feel about it. Now, you encounter a bear. Describe the bear. Is it on the path coming toward you, or off in the woods going away from you? Is it a large bear or a small one? What color? Does it notice you or is it intent on its own business? Do you feel threatened by the bear? How do you react to finding a bear on your path? Remember the details. Does the bear smell? Does it make any sounds? Do you make eye contact with the bear?

8: Reaching a House

Allow three minutes.
Leave the magical being and go on along your path. Soon you will see in the distance a house. Describe the house, what it looks like, what it is made of, how you feel about it. Is it large or small, wood or brick, old or new, empty or inhabited? What about the grounds? Landscaped or overgrown, spacious or cramped, inviting or dismal?

When you reach the house, check to see if the door is open or closed. If locked, see if your key fits the lock. Describe your reaction to the house. Enter the house and look around. How many rooms? How furnished? Any people? Is there an upstairs level, a basement? Go exploring.

9: Finding the Vase

Allow one minute.
As you explore the house, you will find a vase. Describe the vase. What is it made of? Large or small? Beautiful or plain? Ornate or serviceable? Is there anything in it? How do you feel about it?

10: Seeing the Fence

Allow one minute.

Go to the back of the house and look out the window. You will see a fence. Describe the fence. High or low? Wood or rock? New or old? Well kept or run down? What is your reaction to this fence? How does it make you feel?

Now that you have taken this inner journey, read through the symbol correspondences below. Remember, there are no right or wrong interpretations. This exercise is to give you information about yourself and your perceptions of various areas of your life where negativity may reside. If there is anything you do not like, remember that you can always change it. Life is not static, it is always in flux. You are in a continual process of growth and change, even when you are not aware of this. Once you have done this meditation, you can re–enter the experiences you encountered and make any changes–you desire. It is our ability to change the images we produce that gives us the power to revamp our lives..

This exercise is a powerful guidance tool to show you where you are in your attitudes at any time. You can repeat the exercise as often as you like. Once you have learned the steps, you can activate your symbol-making faculty to tune in to your current inner state of affairs, changing anything you want. That's the beauty of the unconscious—it's there to help us. Its power to create images allows us to reprogram ourselves by changing images that are not right for us. While you cannot change your past experiences, you can rearrange how you feel about them, thereby releasing feelings that may inhibit you from becoming the person you were always meant to be.

Interpreting the Symbols

1. The Starting Place

The starting place represents the environment to which you naturally resonate. This is important information. If your starting place gave you any discomfort, you may fear beginning adventure. If the experience was unpleasant in any way, or unexpected, you may feel timid about embarking on a new course of action in your life.

If your starting place was comfortable and felt good and safe to you, you are already on your way to accepting the great adventure of exploring your psychic landscape.

2. The Path

The path represents your life's path as you currently view it. If your path was open, broad, smooth, and free of obstacles, you view your life as proceeding along quite well.

If your path was narrow, difficult, hilly, rocky, or otherwise difficult to transverse, you are generally unhappy about your life as it is now unfolding and may want to make some changes.

One client's image of her path was a deep rut in which she was walking two feet below the surface of the surrounding ground. The message was unmistakable: she felt she was in a rut—and she was. This information, revealed by her psychic depths, enabled her to face a reality that she had been refusing to acknowledge.

At a time of transition in my own life, I entered this meditation. My path was a level bricked walkway, very pleasant and smooth. On one side it was landscaped like an English garden, with neatly clipped hedges and well-tended flower beds. Tame and civilized. But the other side of the path was bordered by a virgin forest, dense, dark, unknown, wild. The garden side held no charm nor challenge, but the wild side pulled me to want to know what was beyond the safe, neat path. I could hear rushing water in the distance, deep within the forest, and I imagined a swift-running, deep, clear river of great power.

The imagery told me that I had a choice between continuing on a safe and orderly but unchallenging way or risking the adventure of going off into the unknown, uncharted region of myself, which promised exhilaration as well as hinted of possible dangers. I chose the forest of the psychic life and found it full of exotic flora and fauna and peopled with magical beings.

The image of the path is an important one. It can reveal a great deal about how you approach the journey that is your life. Examine your feelings about your path. Did you enjoy being on it? Would you like to continue on this path? Did you feel good about it? What would you like to change?

3. The Water

The water represents sex, how you feel about it, how you experience it in your life. As mentioned previously, sexual energy is closely linked to psychic ability. (This does not refer to the sexual *act* but to the basic human energy residing in the sexual center of the body/mind/psyche.) Attitudes and feelings about sexuality are deep and far-reaching. They can cause conflicts and inhibitions. There can be compulsions, obsessions, fear, or lack of interest. Again, nothing is right or wrong. This is all information to enable you to release blocks so that you can become the person you truly want to be.

Water that is calm and placid, such as a quiet lake, represents a passive sexual nature, one that is not easily aroused but that gives little trouble. Or, it might represent a temporary period of quiescence or abstinence when sex is not an issue for you. A rushing river, deep and dark, can mean a turbulent sexual nature, exciting but at the same time frightening. The ceaseless ocean indicates a restless sexual nature that makes it difficult for the person to settle into a monogamous relationship. A country pond bordered with flowers, with ducks swimming on it, suggests a person who is either sexually content or not sexually adventurous. A fog-shrouded bay indicates someone for whom sex seems mysterious or unobtainable. A stagnant pool, where nothing grows, implies being cut off from spontaneous sexual feelings. A cascading waterfall represents abundant sexual energies that need to be appropriately channeled.

Your image must be interpreted by you. Sexuality is a vital and intimately personal element in our makeup. No two people are alike in their inner sexual beings. Like every other human energy, sexuality ebbs and flows—with the years, with the seasons, with the months, with the days. How we use our sexual energy is up to us, but it is important to realize that this is a power source within, never to be misused or taken lightly. Rising out of the second chakra, sexual energy fuels the sixth chakra, the energy center where we contact the Higher Self. It is worth pondering the image your unconscious gives you for the water. Ask yourself how you felt about the image, whether you liked it, if you wanted to immerse yourself in it, if you wanted to leave or linger. Were you comfortable, did you enjoy the experience? Was there anything about the water you'd like to change?

4. The Key

The Key represents self-esteem. The image you received tells how you feel about yourself, way deep down. It is not the description of the key that matters, but how you feel about what you find inside yourself.

For example, one woman found a key that was ornate and beautiful, but she didn't like it because it seemed useless. A "trophy wife,"—beautiful and decorative to her rich older husband—she felt herself of no use in any significant way.

A man found an ordinary-looking house key. It seemed uninteresting—merely utilitarian. But upon examination it proved to be a master key capable of opening all locks. Because he considered himself to be just a plain and simple guy, his self image was poor. His unconscious knew better, showing him that he was a master in his own right, possessing many talents—ignored because they were not fancy. After doing the meditation, he began to appreciate himself more.

An artist who felt that her talent was limited in comparison to what she wished to achieve found a small key, which was, however, beautifully worked and made of solid gold. This image allowed her to acknowledge that her talent was, if not commercial, genuine and valuable.

Consider your key carefully. What feelings does it call up in you? Are you happy to be the possessor of such a key? Would you be upset if you lost it? Or, does the key generate negative feelings in you? Do you dislike it? What would you change about it? Would you prefer a substitute?

5. The Chest

The Chest represents the value we put on our mind/brain and the knowledge it has gathered to date. An open chest signifies that we feel we can access and use our brains freely while a locked one indicates we do not feel that our mental faculties are readily available. The contents of the chest give clues about what we think we possess in the way of mental products and about how we value those products, such as knowledge and experience and our intelligence.

When the key fits the lock, it is an indication that we are in possession of the key to our own minds. If the chest is locked, it tell us we feel locked away from our own inner resources.

The size and shape of the chest are also indicators of our attitude toward the mind and its abilities. The chest can be old or new, large or small, plain or fancy, open or closed, full or empty. You must interpret the symbol your unconscious gives you in the light of your own self-knowledge. An empty chest need not be a negative—it might just be waiting to be filled up. An overflowing chest may indicate a cluttered mind, or one filled with inappropriate knowledge. No one but you can say what your chest means to you, but here are some examples.

One client's chest was locked tight and bound with iron. Her sweet little key, the kind a young girl has for her diary, did not fit the rusty lock. As she had never been good at left-brain, rational-type schooling, this woman felt her brain was of no use to her at all. Although she had artistic leanings, she had never bothered to try to discover or develop any talents she might possess for fear of failing. Her parents had made her feel small and childish (the tiny child's key), even in adulthood. At age forty-two, she did not feel like a grown-up. Once she saw what was blocking her, she was able to access her intuition and her artistic abilities flowered. She's now a well-paid illustrator of children's books—she kept the childlike attributes represented by the key but turned them to her advantage.

Another client, an accomplished intellectual, not surprisingly encountered a chest both open and well stocked with books. What was surprising was that this man found the book-filled chest a burden and kicked it off his path. I instructed him to dump out all the books and see if there was anything else at the bottom. There was—a music score. Jim was a frustrated composer who had been forced into an academic career by his professor father. He'd lost touch with his right-brained, musical, intuitive self but though it was buried under the book-learning, his unconscious showed him it was still there! He now plays in an amateur string quartet and writes music on weekends.

6. The Cup

The cup represents our attitude toward the positive/negative polarity of life. Was your cup half-full or half-empty? Was it a sturdy mug, fragile china, throw-away paper cup? Did it contain something lovely to drink, like fragrant tea? The cup is how we feel about the hand life dealt us, and the experiences we have sustained. Remember, whether your cup was full or empty, beautiful or ugly, you have the power to change the feeling it represents by changing the image that has been programmed into your unconscious by your attitude toward your life.

As with all of these symbolic representations, you are the best interpreter. You are already the world's expert on yourself. Meditating upon the images you receive will clarify their meaning for you. What is "good" for one person may be negative for another, and vice versa.

For example, one woman's cup was a lovely piece of Limoges porcelain, of great value. It was a delicate teacup. A nice image, isn't it? She hated it because it represented her restricting lady-like life as the idle wife of a rich man. Holder of a master's degree in economics, she was reduced to giving tea parties and caring for a large, expensively furnished house. She was slowly dying of *things*. In a return to the meditation, I encouraged her to smash the lovely Limoges cup—to break out of her restraints. Now she has a job and a sturdy ceramic coffee mug for her desk.

A young man who thought life had given him a raw deal found a discarded styrofoam cup that had held coffee. A cigarette had been crushed out in it leaving a disgusting-looking mess at the bottom. He was revolted by what he saw. His life was a mess, or so he thought, and he just wanted to throw it all away. In a return meditation, he decided upon a brand-new cup, one he could now fill to the brim with optimism. By contacting the feeling that his life was fit only to be discarded, he found the strength to make changes.

7. The Bear

The bear represents the outside world and our feelings toward it. It also stands for authority of all kinds imposed upon us by the world. Some bears are cuddly teddy bears, while others are fierce and scary. If your bear was a mean one—well, just remember he is your bear and you can change him at will. Sometimes we don't actually meet the bear—he is off in the woods somewhere and we only hear him crashing around. Again, the important thing is not the bear himself, but how we feel about him.

A talented singer who had run aground in the commercialized music-making industry had retreated to the safety of giving music lessons. In her fantasy she dressed as a little girl, scampering up a tree when she saw the big scary bear coming. Hidden upon her safe perch, she watched as he went his way. Later, we returned to the meditation so that she could confront her fear. This time, she offered him a jewel she'd taken from her chest, which he ate with relish and then gave her a hug.

Her talent—represented by the jewel from her chest—served to neutralize the bear, who appreciated having it for a snack and treated her with affection. She realized that withholding her talent from the world was causing the hostility she felt coming from it. Back on track now with her music career, she uses her newly found intuitive powers daily to guide her.

An actor, in a constant and unsuccessful struggle to get good parts, saw his bear as an adversary whose intention was to block his path. This bear made him very angry. He wanted to kill it, but he realized he was not strong enough, which engendered a high level of frustration. On a return trip, he took the bear a large pot of honey and made friends with him. The experience allowed him to accept that the world was not against him, that struggle is part of life. It is our attitude toward adversity that either gives or removes its sting. Though he doesn't always get the parts he wants, he now knows he doesn't have to fight the whole world.

8. The House

The house represents your unconscious goals in life. You may be surprised at the difference between the image your unconscious presents to you and the conscious image you have of your aims in life. Remember, the unconscious gives you the true picture.

One man, a Washington, D.C. lawyer, saw his life goals as becoming politically powerful and being able to help other people. He considered himself an altruist, interested only in the "welfare of the people." However, the image his unconscious presented to him told a different story. His house was an old stone hut, almost primitive, in a remote place where there were no people at all. The territory was rugged and demanding, the place for a loner who wanted to seclude himself away from all humanity. He became a lawyer to please his parents and devoted himself to *their* code of altruism, donning a cloak to hide his true self from himself.

Your house may have one or many rooms, be a cottage or a mansion. It may be full of laughing people having a party or be totally uninhabited, waiting for you to fill in the spaces. It may be cozily furnished with everything to make you comfortable or barren and bare. What is important about this image is what you make of it, how you react.

One client found a house full of partying people and was dismayed—she wanted to be left alone to do her painting, or so she thought. The fact was that she had retreated into her artwork to avoid the pain of shyness and difficulty making friends. She longed to have a house full of friends all having a good time. Yet, the image distressed her. We later returned to the house and she sent all the people home, telling them she would invite them in later, in small groups, when she felt more settled.

Whatever your image of your house is, it is a vital component of who you are and where you are going. If your conscious goals conflict with your unconscious goals, you are going to have trouble reaching any goals at all, or you will be dissatisfied with the ones you do reach. Finding out about blocks on this level is fundamental to clearing away what is keeping you from your good life.

9. The Vase

The vase represents our perception of love. What we love and how we love is basic to all human life, and love perhaps more than any other human characteristic comes from the deepest level of our beings. We can no more rationally choose a love partner than we can choose what we will dream tonight. We *can* marry for rational reasons—he's a good provider, she will be a good hostess, we make good business partners, my mother is crazy about him or her, and so on. But love is another matter. Love springs from within, from that deepest level of the unconscious, which, remember, knows what is best for us. The image of your vase will tell you about love and your perception of it in your life.

Whatever your image of the vase, trust it to reveal to you your deepest feelings about love. If you fear or distrust love, or think it is difficult to find, or if your vase is cracked or broken, remember that you can change that image by releasing what is blocking your love.

In a dramatic rejection of what she found, one woman said vehemently, "I don't want *that* vase. It's chipped and ugly and I inherited it from my mother." We returned to the meditation and she smashed the old vase of her mother's interpretation of love and replaced it with a lovely new one of her own choosing. Trying to love by her mother's standards was keeping her from finding a rewarding relationship.

Another woman found a beautiful crystal vase, but she was distressed because it was empty. She went into the garden of the house and picked a bouquet of flowers to put in it. Upon contemplating both the image and her response to it, she discovered that she was a very loving person who had not allowed herself to fulfill her affectionate nature.

10. The Fence

The fence represents our perception of death. Many people fear death or consider it an unfair intrusion into life. We all know that death comes, that nobody lives forever, yet most of us consider death to be the enemy—something to be conquered, coerced into going away, or, failing that, totally ignored. Yet death is as much a part of life as is birth. Whether there is "life after death," in the sense of a continuance of *this* life, I cannot say. I rather doubt it. But this does not mean that death is the end of everything. It is the end of a chapter, not the end of the book. Or, it is a sequel. Whatever you believe about death, it will come one day and your perception of death, embedded as it is in your psyche, colors how you live your life. Fear of death is a great inhibitor of living your life fully. If you have unresolved feelings about your death (and most of us do), this image will reveal to you your own reality. Facing it means looking at it from within.

Having stared death in the face more than once, prior to experiencing this meditation I thought I was completely reconciled to my own demise. I was not bothered by the desire for an afterlife. However, my first view of the fence was of a high brick wall just behind the house, not off in the distance, and I was furious that my view was blocked. This experience sent me in search of deeper levels of my own being. Eventually my fence became a low stone wall far off in the distance, with grasses and flowers growing through the cracks in the masonry. Beyond it I could glimpse the sea gently rolling in upon the shore.

An old man I knew experienced a weathered picket fence, already lying flat on the ground. He saw himself walking over it into a broad meadow filled with light and flowers. His life was almost over, and he was at peace.

Whatever your feelings about death, it remains for all of us a mystery. It's not death itself that's important—for it will come and others will go on—but how we live that matters. Fear, anxiety, anger, and depression about death are only *thoughts*. They can be changed like any other thoughts. A positive relationship with the end of life makes the living of it more pleasurable and productive. Fear of death is a roadblock on the path of life. If you experience fear or anger at the fence, you can go back into the meditation and allow yourself to confront the feelings safely.

One man, raised with visions of hellfire, saw a frightening vision of flames leaping beyond a high concrete wall, like that of a prison. He returned to the meditation with a fire hose and in drenching the flames realized he had nothing to fear. Hell is a construction of the mind, not a real place. He had believed that he no longer was influenced by his parents' old-fashioned religion, but his unconscious showed him that the fear implanted in him as a child was still active inside him. Armed with that knowledge, he was able to free himself from the rigid and crippling notions of his past.

There are many images for the fence. What is important is your reaction to the image your unconscious gives you. Examine this reaction and see if you want to change it.

This meditation should enable you to get a glimpse of the hidden powers you already have inside you. By now you should be able to experience the power of your imagination, begin to understand your own intuitive process. Eliminating blocks is just one of the things your psychic self can do for you. As you continue to work with the material in this book, and begin to evolve positive consciousness, you will be amazed at what you can do.

Change Your World by Changing Yourself

Part IV

The Practical Psychic

Relationships

If I had my life to live over, I should devote myself to psychic research rather than psychoanalysis.
—SIGMUND FREUD

As you continue to practice your psychic skills, you will develop a higher state of consciousness not only in regard to your own needs and aims but in relation to others in your life. You will engender in yourself a sense of *knowingness* about those for whom you care. As you more and more connect with this faculty within, you will realize that there are invisible threads along which information is carried. We are all traveling on the same psychic "information superhighway," no matter where we are in time and in space. As you recognize and accept this truth, you allow yourself to connect with the universal intelligence that is in you and in everyone else. When this happens, you experience a state of oneness that does not require a physical presence. You can tune in to what another person is doing or thinking even when you are physically separated.

You already know everything you need to know to make your relationships work. The trouble is that you don't know you know, or you aren't willing to admit that you know. You are constantly receiving and storing information about your spouse, a parent or a child, a friend or a boss— and about yourself in relationship to that person.

Relationships are a prime area where intuition can be of help, where it is probably the best tool available. If you have relationship problems of any kind, turn to your intuition to find out the truth of the situation. You can learn to use your psychic abilities to find out what to do about relationships that are in need of repair, or nourishment, or understanding. Love is a component of your psychic landscape. You can consult your psychic self about love and ask it questions. It will tell you what you want to know.

Suggestions for Improving Relationships

FIRST, *make it a priority.* Use your practice sessions to focus on any relationship that bothers you. Concentrate all of your energy and effort on the single issue, for as long as it takes. In opening yourself up to the truth about the relationship, maintain a neutral, nonjudging state of mind. If you are judgmental about the situation, you will weaken the line between your conscious mind and your state of inner knowing. Stay open to the truth.

❤ Using the relaxation and meditation exercises given, ask a carefully worded question. Simply asking to know the truth about a relationship works best. The key is being willing to accept the truth and act on it. So many people want to turn from the truth because it is unpleasant or doesn't suit their illusions. Remember, "The truth shall make you free."

SECOND, *practice loving and releasing.* Whatever the problem, generating love about it will work wonders. It is even possible to love what hurt you in order to heal yourself. Loving does not mean putting up with bad behavior on the part of another, nor does it mean condoning what is wrong. Love comes from the deepest part of the Self and has a power all its own. However, do not mistake emotional need for love. Love is free and unfettered. Your love belongs only to you and you are free to use it as you choose.

❦ Releasing is a potent tool for getting at the truth of a situation. Once you have asked your question and given love, it is time to let go. You can use a simple affirmation for this, such as, "I now let go of this situation and trust my psychic intuition to reveal its truth." Or, make up your own release statement. If release is difficult, and it often is, persist but don't be harsh with yourself. All of these techniques should be applied gently.

Practice centering, knowing that happiness is the product of a quiet mind. Concentrate your thoughts on serenity, poise, peace, security, and inner guidance. Know you will prevail.

THIRD, *generate love to yourself and others.* Love is energy. Use the energy meditation to generate love. This type of generating of love is very powerful, for it saturates the atmosphere around you with loving vibrations. When you send out positive, loving vibrations, you attract positive, loving vibrations from others. Be careful not to give yourself double messages. The deep mind takes your thoughts literally, and if you are harboring resentments, anger, or judgmental thoughts, you will hamper your ability to see clearly. Negative thoughts poison the system and rob your psychic intuition of vitality, weakening its ability to give you strength and guidance. Create images of how you want the situation to be and let those images sink into your non–conscious, which has the power to bring them into being.

FOURTH, *don't use relationship problems to avoid your own life issues.* This is probably the most frequent situation I encounter in my therapy practice. All sorts of relationship problems fit into this category, and often they act as a distraction to keep the person from concentrating on the real issues of his or her own life. If this is the case with you, review the twelve steps in chapter 10 and apply them to the situation.

FIFTH, *let your intuition help you to develop positive relationships.* If you have avoided satisfying relationships because of guilt, neurotic patterns, other people's expectations, or any other of a host of reasons, turn inward and consult your inner Self. Using the program outlined, focus your attention on what fulfilling relationships would mean to you, how they would feel, how they would change your life. Only honest inquiry will produce the desired result.

SIXTH, *jettison relationships that aren't working.* Negative relationships can poison you, and you owe it to yourself to become and remain emotionally healthy. Bad energies can even make you physically sick. Relationships can wear out and need to be replaced with new ones. There is no one to blame for this situation, and only an honest appraisal will do. Often we stay in relationships long past their natural life because we don't want to hurt someone's feelings, or because it is a habit. Consult your intuition, which knows the truth, and listen carefully. You will also be doing the other person a service by not hanging on to something that is ready to end.

As you weed your garden of relationships, you will find you are lighter, freer. Affirm that intuitive intelligence guides you in all your decisions, and remember that the only person on earth you can change is *yourself.*

SEVENTH, *Remember that you do not control of others environments.* It is always possible to tune in to a clogged or unclear channel. Information is not always precise, especially when it concerns other people. If you are "sending," you need to clear your own channel so that the message is not garbled. If you are "receiving," you equally want to have your inner set attuned so that its functioning isn't impaired.

Channel-Clearing Exercise

To do this exercise, first use any of the breathing and/or relaxation exercises already given. When you have reached your deep level, you will create your "meeting" with the person with whom you wish to contact or converse. Imagine any setting you like—it should be comfortable and well furnished, conducive to a meeting place. Take several minutes to do this, arranging furniture, flowers, music—whatever makes the place seem especially hospitable. Once you have created your meeting room, invite the person you wish to contact to come in and sit down. This may happen immediately or it may take longer. Be patient. If he or she does not appear, the channel is not open at present and you can try later.

When the person does appear, act like a polite host, offering a chair and refreshments. Then, say what you have to say (sending), or ask what you want to know (receiving). Wait for a reply. If no reply comes immediately, the channel is not clear at present and you can try later.

If you experience difficulties making contact, repeat the exercise at a later time and say, "My channel is clear. I can now successfully send and receive messages." Keep using this technique until you get results. It is important to be calm and relaxed when doing this in order to keep a clear channel clear.

As you practice channel clearing, you will find that you have a connection with the other person. This is "thought transference," and happens when you both learn to know what the other is thinking or wanting. For example, when you telephone someone with whom you have developed this connection, that person will know you are calling before answering the telephone, and vice versa. More and more you will find yourselves having such seemingly uncanny encounters, but this intuitive touching is a product of your own inner Self.

When you concentrate on another person's welfare, not what you want from that person, you will find that you receive guidance about the relationship, that you "know" what is needed at any given time. If strife or hurt feelings occur, your intuition will tell you how to proceed to correct the situation. Soon you will accept this process as normal because you will be making a connection on a higher level of consciousness.

Strong emotion is often the catalyst for psychic experience. Once, when I was living in Italy, I was overcome with an overwhelming sense of sadness. Feeling uncontrollable tears rising in me, I rushed home in a state of confusion. I had nothing to be unhappy about. I was on a beautiful Mediterranean island filled with gaiety and sunshine. Puzzled and unable to shake the mood, I went into a meditative state and realized that the sadness did not belong to me. I received a strong sensation that a dear friend in New York was crying. I had not seen her for some time, so I promptly wrote a letter asking if anything was wrong, or any way I could help. When I received a reply, I learned that at the time I had received her tears, she was about to undergo a serious and life-threatening surgical procedure. In her anxiety, without family or close friends nearby, she had concentrated on me as the person she would have liked to be by her side. As she was being wheeled into the operating room, she felt my presence expressing concern and love. The feeling that I was there with her buoyed her up during her ordeal.

Neither she nor I found anything odd in the communication, but many of us find it extremely difficult to credit our own experience, even when it is most powerful. We've been told since childhood that such things are "impossible," or else figments of our imaginations. By affirming your ability to communicate with others on your psychic wavelength, you open up to more experiences. By recognizing that we are indeed all connected, you transcend the idea of separateness. Albert Einstein says,

> "[We experience ourselves] as something separated from the rest, a kind of optical delusion of consciousness....Our task must be to free ourselves from this prison."

What Not to Expect from Psychic Work on Relationships

Relationships exist on many levels over different spans of time. The central core of any relationship is always yourself and your thoughts and feelings. The other person in the relationship is also his or her own central core. The most important thing to realize in applying psychic work to relationships is that *you can control no one but yourself*. Those for whom the attempt to control others is central to relationships are doomed to failure; those who wish to relinquish control over their own lives will never be successful in relationships. Psychic information will not make a bad relationship good. One of the most frequent questions asked psychic counselors, especially those who work on telephone services, is, "Is my spouse or lover cheating on me?" Assuming that we have the ability to answer that question accurately, what difference does it make? Knowing that another is cheating will not create faithfulness.

The purpose of using psychic ability in relationships is not to confirm or deny errant behavior. In such cases, "to ask the question is to answer it" is usually the rule. Nor is psychic ability capable of making one person love another. Despite our universal yearning to believe otherwise, there are no magic potions. Remember this: *what you have to struggle to get, you have to struggle to keep*. This dictum is especially true of romantic relationships. Many feel that if a psychic tells them that the desired person loves them, that will make it so. It won't.

However, psychic work *can* allow us to connect with our own true selves. Only at the level of deep inner truth can *love*, not fantasy or need fulfillment, occur. The only way relationships can be made to work is by contacting that which is inside *us*, where relationships actually are located.

Effective Use of Psychic Work in Relationships

Though psychic work is useful for a wide variety of specific situations, including relationships, it is not a quick fix for what is wrong. To engage in psychic development is to embark on a life-long process, one that is ultimately life-changing. And, whenever we change ourselves we change our relationships to others. We blame many factors for holding us back from achieving satisfying relationships, but we seldom look inside ourselves, which is where the solution to the problem lies.

With these thoughts in mind, jettison any worrying thoughts about the specifics of any relationship and move instead to the central core of yourself, where the truth resides. Here are some guidelines.

Believe in your ability to be in right relationships

Just as you have the capacity to contact your deep inner mind through psychic practice, you have the ability to use your inner truth to create happy and fulfilling relationships of all kinds. If nagging doubt creeps in, send it away with the releasing meditation. Go often to your sanctuary or other special place where you stay in touch with your intuition, which will always guide you.

Trust your intuition to tell you the truth

Intuition is there to help you, not to hinder you, but in order to use it properly you must accept the truths you encounter. Knowing things are one way and wanting them to be another leads only to confusion and lost direction. When you get a message from your inner Self, do not attempt to ignore, change, or deny it just because it does not suit your conscious purposes or emotional needs of the moment.

So often people run from the truth. A client asks, "Does he love me?" She does not want to hear the truth if it is "no." She wants reassurance. Another says, "Is she faithful?" and the question answers itself. It does not matter whether she is in fact faithful or not—his mistrust is enough to poison the atmosphere.

Recognize that your psychic Self is unlimited

You are not stuck with what you already have. The universe is in a state of flux at all times; changes are constantly taking place. As a limitless being, you can create whatever you want in the privacy of your mind and bring it into manifestation if it is your truth. Belief in limitations stunts relationships, but it is just another mental construct you can reshape. Do not accept others' evaluation of you as limited. Following the twelve-step program regularly will allow you to stay in contact with your higher Self, which recognizes no limitations.

Understand that all relationships, even difficult ones, serve a purpose in your life

So often a bad relationship sours us on other relationships, but all relationships—good and bad—are there for a purpose. There are no accidents in the Intelligent Universe. Often we are guided to our good by forces that at the time seem negative. Sometimes someone comes along who serves a hidden purpose, perhaps sending our lives in a different direction. Even if the experience is painful, when put in perspective its purpose can be discerned. If you want information about such a relationship, go inside and ask, "What is the lesson for me in this experience?" The sanctuary meditation is useful for this purpose.

Form the habit of listening to your intuition about relationships

What is important is to *listen* to the inner mind, which will always give you the information you need about your relationships. However, if you have negative experiences, don't blame your intuition or yourself. Don't do the "shoulda, woulda, coulda" blame trip. Realize that everything in your life serves a purpose.

Learn the lessons the universe sends you about relationships and examine yourself to see if you ignored intuitive direction. If you did, it was because you did not value it properly. When you value it, you listen and are guided.

How many times I've heard a person unhappy in a relationship say, "I knew I shouldn't have married him but I went ahead with it anyway." Or, "I knew I couldn't work with that woman and I never should have accepted the job." Or, "Something told me she would never settle down to one man."

Examples are endless. So many people are in relationships for wrong reasons because they failed to listen to their inner selves. Perhaps the relationship has failed to live up to their expectations, or has taken a turn for the worse, but the inner voice, which always knows what's best, is shut off, stifled, muffled, ignored.

Understand that relationships are psychic structures

From our thoughts, feelings, needs, desires, hopes, wishes, and reactions, we create psychic structures of each of our relationships that are every bit as real as buildings made from steel and concrete. They may bear little actual resemblance to the real person, but they are an accurate portrait of our inner *perception*. Many of us carry these psychic structures—some created in childhood—to the grave. All relationships exist secretly within the psychic structures we have created. And like other mental constructs, these psychic structures can be dismantled and/or rebuilt *mentally*.

The psychic structure you have created of another person needs energy to sustain it, just as you need food. When you withdraw energy from it, it will cease to have power. Although you cannot change another person, you can change what you are projecting inward to yourself about that person. You can take responsibility for what you experience. For example, many individuals are in relationships with an addictive partner. This causes worry, aggravation, exasperation, anger, hopelessness, abuse. By withdrawing psychic energy—by not participating mentally in maintaining the psychic structure you have erected about that person—you will automatically change the relationship by changing what you are carrying around inside yourself. Your partner's reaction to this inner shift in you will be a change in behavior.

If you wish to demolish the negative or self-defeating psychic structures of any relationship, use the releasing and/or mind-clearing technique. Think of a plant which grows from a seed, puts out roots, shoots, leaves, buds, flowers—it is in a constant state of being energized. In the return to the seed stage, the energy is dormant. Affirm often, "I now let go of outworn structures, outworn thoughts, outworn feelings, outworn ideas about this relationship." Then release and let go. A feeling of peace and cleansing will follow.

Learn to resolve conflict by nonparticipation

You are always in charge of your own state of mind, and it is your state of mind that determines the quality of your relationships. If conflict is a problem, it is often the result of negative psychic projections. It has been said, "Two cannot quarrel when one will not," and by taking the route of nonparticipation at the psychic level you can circumvent conflict.

The withdrawal of psychic projections is a powerful tool to influence the behavior of others. It does not require anything more than your *determination* to neutralize your own inner energy, to stop projecting it outward. The decision to be a nonparticipant in conflict can be an illuminating experience, giving you a sense of wonderful power. This, however, does not mean mere silence or a stiff-upper-lip approach with angry feelings simmering below the surface. It requires a genuine inner transformation.

To do this, you mentally withdraw all psychic energy into yourself that you have been projecting onto another person and recharge it with positive energy. Then, you radiate out this positive energy to the other person. It acts like a mirror, returning positive energy to you.

Monitoring is an especially effective means of keeping watch on what you are projecting outward. Use breathing and relaxation exercises to neutralize negative projections and affirm inwardly, "I choose only good to go forth from me and I allow only good to return to me."

Use visualization to benefit relationships

Visualization is a powerful tool for use in maintaining and nurturing relationships. Right now, you can visualize all your relationships just the way you want them to be. Over time, you can manifest what you visualize. Believe in the power of your psychic Self to create the reality you want and deserve in all your relationships.

A son was estranged from his father and in pain from the separation, but so much hurt had occurred between them that he saw no opening for repair. I asked him to remember some happy time between them and to hold that image in his mind, replaying it over and over. Slowly, his anger and hurt began to dissolve and the real love he felt for his father reemerged into his consciousness—it was an emotionally liberating experience.

"I can forgive him," he told me in an exultant voice. "I see how it can be with us again." It took time, but he kept visualizing himself and his dad in the loving relationship they had had before the rift. From deep within, he sent his love out to his father, and when "chance" threw them unexpectedly together, instead of being cold and aloof he spontaneously rushed to his father and threw his arms about him in an effusive greeting of love. Astonished and pleased, the older man returned his hug and all animosity between them vanished. It was like a miracle—but the son had created it all through visualization.

Use your personal psychic journal for relationships

Writing in your journal is a good way to keep track of your progress in working with the above guidelines. Make notes of what you want to achieve, what techniques you used, and the results. This will also help you to determine which techniques and exercises work best for you and for specific situations.

Also, the act of writing is itself a powerful stimulus to the psychic process. Words are probably the most important ingredient in our list of power tools within the psyche. Nonverbal images are potent and play an important part in how we communicate with ourselves and others, but words for most of us are the primary form in which we process mental activity. The Bible tells us that the *logos*, or word, generated God. "In the beginning there was the Word, and the Word became God."

Fueling our psychic process with the written word adds to its effectiveness. Though it is at present unclear precisely how this works, writing as an adjunct to the psychic process connects left-brain with right-brain functions, promoting wholeness. Currently, writing-as-therapy is a technique that is being investigated and there is much still to be learned on this subject. My experience, however, has taught me that writing activates deep non-conscious psychic centers and promotes the healing-into-wholeness process.

Magnetically Attract the Right Partner

It has been said that the best time to prevent divorce is before marriage. Finding the right partner and forming a long-term, committed relationship is probably the single most important factor in the lives of human beings. Yet the vast majority of people put more time and energy into choosing a new car than into choosing a life partner. This major component of our lives is usually left to chance and circumstance, with the predictable result that the divorce rate is over fifty percent.

As a psychic consultant, the most common question I hear is, "When am I going to find a man (or woman) and get married?" The answer is, "When you are ready."

A woman in her mid-thirties came to me for a Tarot card reading. By her account, she was "desperate to get married and have children before it was too late." She was trim, outgoing, attractive. I said that I could not understand why, if marriage was truly her most important goal, it had eluded her. She insisted that she had made a consistent effort for years, but she always seemed to "find the wrong man," or she herself ended the relationship. She complained bitterly about her unmarried state, saying that without a husband her life wasn't worth living.

After the usual preliminaries, I laid out the cards and to my surprise found her mother dominating the layout. My experience with the Tarot is that the true issue of a situation will present itself, no matter what the client claims to be her concern. If marriage is the issue, cards pertaining to marriage will show up. I told her what I was seeing in the cards, and asked what her mother might have to do with her wishes to marry. Her reply astonished me.

"My mother calls me every week and asks me when I'm getting married," she said agitatedly. "She keeps telling me I'm ruining her life because I'm not married and giving her grandchildren. She's already got twenty-eight grandchildren. That's why I left home. There was so much pressure on me to get married and I wanted to be free."

This was an independent, feisty woman with absolutely no desire to be in a conventional marriage. She wasn't married for the very simple reason that deep down she didn't want to be married. She kept picking the "wrong" man in order to have an excuse to break up the relationship.

It is a fact that we attract what we give energy to, including romantic partners. If we are spinning negative energy, we will get negative results. We are magnets to other people, and we can attract or repel them as we wish. Anyone truly seeking the right life partner need only put magnetism to work and, in time, that person will achieve the desired results.

Life is energy, love is energy, thoughts are energy, feelings are energy. We constantly send out our energy into the psychic ether where it picks up information and returns that information to us. Our energies carry information that can be read by other energies. This is a constant process, but it is usually undirected and therefore brings in spasmodic or uneven results. Or, we don't trust ourselves and shut off that power source.

Learning to magnetize is easy, but it takes time. When you first work with psychic energy, the results are bound to be inconsistent, but if you stick with your program you will eventually get the results you desire.

Word Portrait Technique

You must first construct an accurate portrait of yourself in detail. Pretend that you are writing an advertisement for a personals column and that you are going to describe yourself to a total stranger whom you want to attract. You don't need to limit the number of words, as you would in a real ad. Take as much space as you like in this imaginary newspaper, even a whole page. Describe yourself *honestly*.

Next, describe the person you want to attract in the same detail. Be specific. Create a picture of this person in your mind. If you want a specific hair color, or eye color, or height, or weight, include those characteristics. (This isn't going to be easy. Even the simplest person is amazingly complex.) Make a mental portrait of this person down to the smallest detail. Fill in the background—what kind of education, family, and so forth. Do you think the person you have described would be attracted to the first person you described—yourself?

Now ask yourself some questions. Must you find someone with the exact same lifestyle as your own? How like-minded must your preferred partner be? Are you willing to open yourself to new experiences? Is your self-portrait the real you or an idealized version? Have you imagined a real other person or just a cardboard cutout, like a picture in a magazine or on TV?

The purpose of this portrait-painting exercise is to get you to look at both the real you and at the reality of the person you want to attract. If your inner Self's reality does not match what you are consciously projecting, results will be spotty at best. And if the person you describe is not reality based but only an idealized concept of a real person, you will be disappointed. Here again, as in using your psychic journal, the act of writing acts as a stimulus to clarify your intentions.

Make magnetizing your right partner a part of your daily practice, using the following specialized techniques. Constructing a treasure map is also a good idea.

Visualization for Magnetizing

In a calm and relaxed state, spend some time imaginatively experiencing what it would be like to be with the person you want to magnetize. Imagine yourself in a relationship with this person in as much detail as you can. Experience how your life is with this person. The more you bring yourself into harmony with the situation as you wish it to be, the more successful your magnetizing will be.

Invite the person you wish to magnetize into your meeting room, using the channel-clearing technique, and have a conversation, getting to know him or her. You can ask questions and receive answers. Remember, extrasensory or psychic abilities are *channels of information.* As you work with the magnetizing process, you will be getting information. It is important to act on this information.

One client of mine had resolved her inner conflicts about having a relationship and she was ready. She began to magnetize, envisioning her perfect partner in glowing Technicolor detail. For a few months, nothing happened, but she kept at it. Then, one day while she was meditating, she got a very strong impression that she should visit her aunt in another state.

When she arrived at her aunt's home, she discovered that there was a boarder. Her recently widowed relative had decided to rent the upstairs section of the house to a gentleman whose company had transferred him from out of state. That evening when she met the man she knew at once why she had been compelled to visit her aunt. She recognized the man she had envisioned and apparently he saw the connection just as quickly. Today, they are happily married and Jenny credits her psychic magnetizing with giving her the right road map to happiness.

The Magnetizing Technique

Using your preferred relaxation/deep relaxation method, reserve a half-hour for your first magnetizing session. You can do it as often as you like, subsequently using as much time as you see fit. Remember that frequency and consistency will produce better results than sporadic effort. If at first you have feelings of doubt, simply set them aside. If they persist, use the mind-clearing technique before continuing. As you work with magnetizing, you will become more relaxed and confident. Fully believing that you have the power to attract the person you want will bring quicker results. If you are skeptical or don't really believe you can get or deserve to get that person, you will have less success.

First, in a relaxed and calm state of mind, create a symbol for your magnetizing—some people like the image of a rose-colored heart, or of two hearts intertwined. Your symbol can be abstract, such as the astrological glyph for the planet Venus. The symbol should represent something meaningful to you.

Using the energy technique, begin to energize your symbol while visualizing it. See yourself filling it with pure love energy.

Imagine within you, at the heart center, a power source that will attract the right partner to you. This power source generates energy, and you send the energy out into the psychic ethers at the level where all is connected to all. As you do this, you are activating the magnetic field around yourself that will spread out the energy like ripples in a pond. You are generating energy into this magnetic field, which, like a physical magnet draws iron, draws like energy back to it.

Imagine your symbol sending out waves of this magnetic energy toward the person you desire. Place the symbol among the waves of magnetic energy you are sending out. Continue until you can feel the sensation of *sending*. Some people experience this as a pulsating in the forehead; others as being pumped outward with each beat of their heart; for me, it is a whole-body sensation that feels as if I were a powerful beam of magnetic energy radiating out into the universe.

Continue to feel your magnetic energy build. Imagine a golden cord being drawn out of your heart, going out and linking you to the person you want. Mentally hold out your arms to receive that person. Try to feel the magnetic field of the other person as you do this. Feel the connection you are making.

Continue this energizing of your magnetic field until you feel a natural cutoff, a sort of "click," which will tell you that you have generated sufficient energy. When you feel this ebbing of the energy flow, allow yourself to rest in the certainty that the process is working. Do not strain to energize. Just do what feels comfortable.

When you have finished the exercise, rest with your eyes closed for a few minutes and feel the sense of being at peace, relaxed, full of confidence.

Gently breathe yourself back to your normal world. Repeat this exercise as part of your regular practice program. Ask your inner self to tell you how often to magnetize.

As you go about your daily business, be open to receiving guidance and acting on it, and be open to answers you might not have expected. Be accepting if the person isn't exactly how you physically pictured him or her. It is the spiritual qualities of two people that bring them together and keep them together. A diamond ring in a brown paper bag is still more valuable than a zircon in a velvet jeweler's box. Have faith that you will know what is good and appropriate for you. And be patient.

Crystallize Desire into Action

13

The Material World

Our science is totally incomplete and will remain so until we include the study of consciousness as a causal element in the universe.
—WILLIS HARMON

The idea that using our psychic potential can affect our material reality is still a startling one for most people. We have been taught that the material world is outside ourselves, that we are subject to economic forces that have nothing to do with us personally but operate in some impersonal vacuum we are powerless to affect. However, this is not the reality of the universe in which we live. Throughout this book we have demonstrated that mind and matter interact, that proper use of our psychic and mental faculties can affect our lives in powerful ways. The material plane of money and goods is no exception.

Chester Carlson, the inventor and founder of Xerox Corporation. He knew intuition and ESP were important *because he used them*, and he funded research into these fascinating subjects at the New Jersey Institute of Technology, the fourth-largest engineering school in the country. Carlson was interested in practical results for the simple reason that his personal experience supported the concept.

At the institute, two researchers posed the question, "What is the X-factor?" What single component in the success of individuals stands out when all the usual components—education, intelligence, experience—have been factored out? They performed an experiment involving numbers and a computer and on one test found that of twenty-one company presidents who had more than doubled their firm's profits during the preceding five years, nineteen scored high precognition while only two scored at chance.

Dr. John Mihalasky, who helped conduct the tests, says,

> Intuition, it seems, is part of the whole person. We are endowed with it for a reason—to help us create more successful lives for ourselves and others no matter where we are. In any of life's decisions, from rearing kids to buying a house, it makes sense to use all of our abilities to make better choices.

Priming Intuition to Achieve Practical Results

The mind is capable of producing energy, and it is capable of connecting us to the entire world around us. When we turn the great energy of our intuitive thinking upon ideas of abundance, we draw to us what we need. You are an irresistible magnet with the power to attract to yourself everything that you truly desire. This is done through the power of the thoughts, feelings, and mental pictures that you constantly feed into your subconscious, where intuition can act upon them. Remember that you are the center of your own universe and that you magnetize whatever you visualize.

Just as you can change your state of mind by changing your breath, you can alter your material world by changing how you think about it. As you used the guided meditation in Chapter 11 to develop positive consciousness about yourself, you can use the images your mind makes to revise your ideas about money and material goods. Check yourself now: do you believe that the only way to increase your prosperity is to work ever harder? Do you believe that there is a general scarcity of goods and that it is hard to get your share? Do you believe that others are to blame for your current financial status? If so, you have created a a consciousness of scarcity in yourself. You can, however, enter your intuitive mind and there create a consciousness of abundance.

How to Create Abundance Consciousness

✗ **Realize that you already have everything you need to create abundance in your life—in your mind**

If money, material goods, or a career are your goals, you can turn the power of your intuitive mind upon those goals and bring them into reality.

Do: Our first key to psychic awareness was *attention.* Begin now by focusing your attention upon your material world. To do this, take half an hour of quiet time, and put yourself into a calm and relaxed state of mind. Then, using either your personal psychic journal or a separate piece of paper, list all of your desires in the realm of the material world, whether money or goods. Do not stop to think whether these desires are possible in your present state.

As you make your list, *do not wonder or doubt where the money or goods will come from.* Following Key #2, *accept that* your deep mind has the power to produce what you desire.

Once you have made your list, spend fifteen minutes a day going over it to implant it firmly into your subconscious. Revise and expand your list on a daily basis, and be definite about what you want to achieve. If, for example, you need a specific amount of money, list that amount. Do not be vague.

Trust your intuitive power to bring you what you want and then be open to receive it in whatever form it comes. Keep your expectations high and give thanks on a regular basis. In their book, *Executive ESP*, Sheila Ostrander and Lynn Schroeder report interviewing not only top executives but "teachers, consumer advocates, newspeople, salespeople, weather forecasters. Those at the top almost always said, 'Sure, I use it.'" "It" was of course psychic ability—called by many names, such as "hunches, gut feelings, intuition, or, sometimes, outright ESP."

The third key to psychic awareness is concentration. What we concentrate on is what we get. If you continually focus your thoughts on what is lacking in your life, you will perpetuate lack. If you want prosperity but tell yourself it is beyond your powers, you will confuse your psychic mind with double messages. Be positive. Be definite.

Review the list you made of what you wanted to bring into your life. How does it compare with the list you made just now of your desires for money and material goods? Is there a conflict? It's vital to know what you truly want, for your psychic Self already knows. Many people complain about not having enough money, but when they face what they actually want they discover it is not money after all.

For example, an artist I know is always short of money. Talented and competent, she is a hard worker. Yet, she is often in arrears and frequently borrows. What emerges from a study of her inner attitudes is a desire for the appearance of penury. Her prosperous father financed her art schooling in Europe, and there, in rebellion against her family's solid middle-class values, she adopted a schoolgirl's attitude toward being an artist. True artists, in this romanticized view, lived in tiny, unheated garrets and suffered for their art. Only after they died were their talents recognized and rewarded. Though she is shielded from the harsh reality of actually living this way by a stipend from her family, what she really wants is the *image* of herself as being a poor but talented artist, always struggling, never succeeding, an idea modeled on the real travail of artists whose work she admires.

Prosperity is something we create in the mind first. There is not a building on earth, no matter how complex or ornate that was not first just an *idea* in the mind of someone. The Empire State Building in New York City was built in the middle of the Depression because someone believed it could be done and constructed that tower mentally without asking where the capital to build it would come from. The set of inner invisible beliefs you carry around inside you is what makes you prosperous.

Know what you can conceive, you can achieve

The fourth key to psychic awareness is *imagination*, and it is one of your most powerful assets on the road to your prosperity. You cannot manifest in your life that which you cannot imagine. It's that simple. Yet, your imagination can create whole universes, just as a novelist creates a fictional world. The difference between you and the novelist is that you can create in the real world. By understanding that you have no limits, and by letting your imagination soar, you contact the part of you that knows you lack absolutely *nothing*, that all things are possible to you. It is when you bombard yourself with negative thoughts, such as "I'll never have enough money," or "I don't have the right education, training, connections," or "Others have all the luck," that you shut off your imagination and shut down your prosperity consciousness.

To overcome ingrained beliefs, which may be so subtle you don't even know you have them, such as the artist who had no conscious awareness of what kept her poor, review the fifth key, *optimism*. It is our expectations of good that bring good. Heed these words of the German poet-philosopher Goethe: "What you can do or dream you can, begin it; boldness has genius, power, and magic in it."

Conversely, expectations of lack bring lack, as in the case of a woman who has a home-based typing service. Although she works hard, she never has enough money. She firmly believes that jobs are scarce, hard to get, and low paying. To the suggestion she charge more for her fine work, she says, "They'll never pay more." And so she continues to earn less than she is worth. To the suggestion that she advertise her services, she replies, "No one will ever come." And so no one knows what she has to offer. To the suggestion that she ask her customers to recommend her to their friends, she responds, "They won't do it." And so it goes. Unfortunately, this story does not have a happy ending. Some people refuse to change their mind-set.

At one time when I needed money, I made a treasure map, using money symbols and play money. Then I boldly wrote a check out to myself for the amount I wished to manifest and signed it "Universal Prosperity." Several weeks later I was informed by my agent that a previously published book had been sold in paperback. I had not even known the negotiations were going on. My share was exactly the amount I put on the check!

Believe psychic ability is entirely human

When you use your psychic abilities correctly you strengthen yourself as a whole human being, and it is this integrity that is at the core of your ability to bring prosperity into your life. By implanting ideas of abundance into your deep mind, you replace the idea that the material world is "out there" somewhere with the truth that it is "in here," waiting to be brought forth.

A real estate tycoon who came from poor surroundings and now flies his own plane on his deal-making trips commented that "You are thinking all the time, so you might as well dwell on prosperity." What this means is that as you think, so you reap. Prosperity is not an event; it is a chain reaction produced by your inner Self. When you fully grasp this concept, your actions begin to reflect your inner reality and produce manifestation in your outer reality.

Be willing to accept the unexpected or unusual

The sixth key to psychic awareness is *curiosity*. Unfortunately, curiosity is often dead in us by the time we start first grade. The wonder and joy of being curious in this fascinating world are stifled by enforced competition—for grades when we are in school, for power and position when we are adults. John Holt, in *How Children Fail*, says,

> We destroy the…love of learning in children, which is so strong when they are small, by encouraging and compelling them to work for petty and contemptible rewards—gold stars, or papers marked 100…or A's on report cards, or honor rolls, or dean's lists, or Phi Beta Kappa keys….

Our stifled curiosity prevents us from exploring our inner selves, which in turn keeps us within boundaries in the material world. Remember, these are self-imposed boundaries. In reality there are no boundaries. By stimulating your curiosity about yourself and your world, you activate your psychic abilities to generate the energy you need to take appropriate action in the material world. Today, find something that you want to know more about.

A therapist went to a conference outside her field, just to experience something new. There she met a college administrator who invited her to teach a course in her own specialty. It was a wonderful opportunity, not only to make extra money but to expand her repertoire of marketable skills. Had she not been motivated by curiosity, nothing would have happened.

Always choose the higher value over the lower one

This may sound unnecessarily lofty, but it is important. The seventh key to psychic awareness is *purpose*. Without purpose, we are forever adrift in the material world on a raft of confusion. It is purpose that takes us from wishful thinking into action. Purpose fuels our thought processes into positive consciousness. Purpose puts us into the flow of the universal prosperity process.

The experience of *flow* is the sense of being at one with the universe and one's Self. It is a state I experience when writing well, reading an astrological chart, or giving a Tarot reading. I am "hooked in" to the higher power and no effort is required. Artists call this inspiration. Flow is the result of purpose, for when we are purposefully engaged at anything, whether in the material world or in the invisible world of the mind, all things fuse into the state of oneness that produces flow.

We impede flow in our lives when we clutter them up with the trivial or superfluous. On the mental plane, we entertain unimportant thoughts while on the material plane we accumulate unnecessary possessions. One of the best ways to induce flow into your life is to get rid of what you don't need or want. Go back to the list you made earlier stating what you want to eliminate from your life. Add to that list any material possessions that belong there. By eliminating what we do not need or want from our lives, by cleaning out and clearing up, we open to flow. In effect, we create a vacuum for prosperity to fill.

Creating a Vacuum

To create a vacuum, get rid of what you do not want. This will make room for what you do want. Earlier we noted that working on one area of your life through psychic methods would affect all other areas. Mind-clearing opens the way for prosperity while uncluttering your material world opens the psychic door wider. Not only that, but working in tandem as they do, these two aspects of you—the material and the mental—together bring in new prosperity. The rule here is to let go of the lesser in everything and all your affairs.

Go through your closets, your house, your garage, your car, your jewelry box, your cupboards, your office, your desk, and either throw out or give away whatever is unnecessary or superfluous. This is an amazingly simple technique that really works to bring new good into your material world. It also opens you up to more advanced psychic development. When we reduce clutter in our material sphere we automatically produce clarity in our mental sphere, which opens channels for us to receive new prosperity.

Recently I responded to a letter in a networking publication from someone requesting donations of clothes. As I read the notice, I realized I had clothing in my closet that I no longer needed, for my life had changed. Some items were new and unworn. With no thought of reward or even of doing a good deed, I packed and shipped four large boxes of clothing and then stood back to admire the empty hangers in my now unstuffed closet. Three days later I received confirmation of a new book contract.

On another occasion, I decided to empty out my kitchen of everything I did not use, including some gifts of expensive glass-ware I didn't like. I called a thrift shop that benefits the home-less to ask if they could use the sort of things I had, which included a service of expensive bone china with 24-K gold rims—pretty but not my style. The thrift shop was delighted with my donation. A week later I received in the mail a check for $500 from a relative who had been thinking kindly of me.

Flow is another word for circulation. Money is a form of ener-gy. Spending represents energy flowing out from you, income rep-resents energy flowing in. Both are necessary to proper balance. If you are in a situation where both ends of the cycle are flat, you may be experiencing a blockage of energy. If that's the case, go to your intuition and ask it where your energy needs to flow more freely. Remember always that you are a whole person, and block-ages in one area, seemingly unconnected, like emotional or phys-ical problems, can affect other areas of your life. If one part of you gets shut down, the rest will suffer accordingly.

Once you have created a vacuum and engendered flow, give thanks. Gratitude is the eighth key.

Attracting Money and Material Goods

Make attracting money and material goods your top priority until you achieve your present goal. Do not dilute your effort by switching back and forth among other topics.

Ask yourself what are the reasons you want more money, or why you need a specific material object—say, a new car. Perhaps what you need is not a *new* car, but a dependable one requiring little maintenance. Your intuition may direct you to a used car that will suit your purposes at a price you can afford.

➤ Using the techniques given, make a mind movie of what it ~~Do~~: is you want, and impress that image on your unconscious while you are in a relaxed state. *Exer.*

Go often to your sanctuary and use your imaginative powers to sharpen your images of prosperity. Be specific and enrich your images with details. Imagine checks being written to you for a specific amount. Imagine such a check showing a current date. Visualize yourself receiving the check, feel what it would be like emotionally. Mentally receive the money, deposit it in your bank, take out cash, pay your bills, or buy goods with it. You don't have to win the lottery or a horse race to bring this picture into reality. Keep your images of prosperity clear and sink them deep into your psychic Self with confidence in your ability to manifest them in the real world. Claude Bristol in *The Magic of Believing*, says:

> And this brings us to the law of suggestion, through which all forces operating within its limits are capable of producing phenomenal results. That is, it is the power of your own suggestion—that starts the machinery into operation or causes the subconscious mind to begin its creative work…that leads to belief, and once this belief becomes a deep conviction, things begin to happen.

What happens with this process is that after you program your psychic Self with the proper images and questions during a relaxed period, and write down on paper precisely what you would like to manifest in the material world, a technique that serves to firmly implant the idea, you begin to *act* upon the images in a natural way—in the flow—and this brings in what you want to receive.

Choosing and Energizing Your Symbol

Creating a symbol for prosperity is a powerful tool. This is because symbols act at a deep level, bypassing the ingrained attitudes of your old belief system and reaching into your deep psychic Self.

You can use one of your regular practice sessions for this exercise, or devote special time to it. First, pick a time and place where you can be quiet and uninterrupted for at least fifteen minutes. Use your favorite relaxation method to reach a state of calm. Eyes closed, rest quietly and concentrate on what prosperity means to you. Then ask your psychic Self to give you a symbol. Take whatever image comes, since that will be the correct one for the present time.

Once you have received your symbol, send it energy. Imagine that you are holding it in your hands, that it is becoming a part of you. Energize it as you did your hands in the energy technique. Picture energy flowing from your center into your symbol until it glows with light. Now, take your symbol and send it out into the world where it will attract to you the money and material goods you want.

Impress your chosen symbol into your unconscious during your daily relaxations and meditations, and as often during the day as you like. Use any spare few moments—walking to the bus stop, waiting to make a purchase—as an opportunity to prime your psychic pump. Know the essence of what you want and allow your intuition to connect you to it. Tell yourself often that you are linked with the unlimited abundance of the universe.

Recognize that there is a natural ebb and flow to cycles of money. Money, like air, must circulate. Often a scarcity consciousness makes us hold on tightly to what we have, which suffocates the energy in our psychic Self. The wonderful astrologer Isabel Hickey once said, "If you have only five dollars and the rent is due, go out and buy hyacinths."

While I am not suggesting that you spend the rent money on frivolities, it is important to recognize that a refusal to participate in the energy-circulating process that is the flow of money in and out of your life can block the incoming channels. I confess that it can sometimes be scary to spend when you don't know where the next money is coming from, but my experience has proved that loosening up opens the flow. When I am uptight and watching every penny anxiously, I never seem to have enough, but when I release the energy and spend I never seem to run out.

A freelancer I know—afraid to spend a dime because of the uncertainty of work coming in—had a birthday. An aunt, wise in these matters, gave her $150 with the stipulation that she spend it on something that would give her pleasure. This woman enjoyed spending a day at Atlantic City, not for gambling purposes especially but because she liked the elegant atmosphere of the casino. The trip, with a modest sum for game playing, cost $150, so she decided this was how she would spend her windfall. She wasn't focused on winning money, only on having a nice day. Her habit had been to play the slot machines, quitting when she had lost a small fixed amount. But on this day her intuition directed her to the gaming tables. She thought it was because she wanted to sit quietly with a drink and observe people. Sitting down at an empty blackjack table, she struck up a conversation with the dealer who persuaded her to stay and play cards. She ended up winning $1,000.

I told her about circulation, and she spent her winnings on some equipment she had been wanting for a long time. Almost immediately, her business increased and the incoming flow came in her direction.

As physicist John Wheeler has observed, "We are inescapably involved in bringing about that which appears to be happening."

Your Money Attitude

Attitudes we carry unconsciously affect how we encounter experience in our lives. Many of those who experience financial lack do so because they have been programmed to believe in financial lack. Some people think that money is "evil," or that they are somehow "unlucky." Others have a victim mentality, believing that their suffering is someone else's doing. Refusing to take responsibility for your own attitudes and beliefs will not be cured by developing psychic abilities. There are those who deep down feel they are undeserving of prosperity. You must examine your beliefs to find out if negative ones are preventing you from having the money and material goods you want. Or *think* you want.

Sometimes we think we want something just because someone else has it. Or we think we want something because our parents have trained us to believe we should want it. Or we think we want it because we are supposed to want it, or everyone else has it, or it is the societal norm. If you only think you want a certain level of material success, but your heart isn't in it, then you will not get it through psychic intuition. When the conscious attitude is in conflict with the unconscious reality, which is always the true picture, the unconscious will always win out. That's why affirmations alone will not work to change your life.

For example, a client was working as a college instructor, but nothing went right for her. Courses she applied to teach were canceled, or if they were not she found the work boring or unsatisfying. She was working with positive affirmations, declaring better for herself, with no results. She meditated to find out what her true inner reality was and discovered that she was at heart a free spirit who wanted to roam the world with a backpack. As hard as she had tried to satisfy the demands of an academic career, she had always failed. This was because it did not represent her true Self but was a result of her education and society's expectations. When she admitted to herself that what she wanted was to travel and see the world, she became excited and happy. The next week she presented herself to a tour company as a lecturer and went off on a cruise ship to her true destination in life.

If at *your* most basic level you crave to be a free spirit who is not tied down by material possessions, you must acknowledge that reality and not blame yourself for how you choose to live. Find out what you truly believe, and if necessary change your beliefs. Limited thinking can be expanded. You can release that which has been holding you back by consciously choosing the images and concepts that will benefit you.

How to Change Your Money Attitude

• Using any of the relaxation exercises, go within to discover what is keeping you from getting what you want. Examine yourself honestly and acknowledge your present attitudes toward the material world. Perhaps your goals are unclear or limiting. Or perhaps you secretly feel you don't deserve prosperity. You can change that.

• Using the sanctuary meditation on page 118, go into your private space and ask intuition what is the best way to achieve your financial goals. Notice your emotions and feelings as you do these exercises, especially negative ones. Cleanse yourself of negative emotions by releasing them. One method is to mentally write them down on a blackboard and then erase the letters. You can imagine them enclosed in a balloon that you let float off into the air until you can see it no more.

• Use your practice time to concentrate your intuitive mind on the subject of material abundance. See yourself sending out your desires through the psychic ethers, where they will connect with the best means of fulfilling them. If you are in an ebb, a flow will soon follow.

• Realize that prosperity, like everything else in your life, is experienced first on the mental plane. It has been said that being broke is a temporary experience while being poor is a state of mind. If, no matter your circumstances, you can believe that you are a prosperous person, knowing that no one outside yourself can take that belief away from you, then you will manifest prosperity. There are millionaires who feel poor. One entertainer who made millions in his life died bankrupt and several million dollars in debt. Material possessions do not equal prosperity, which is first and foremost a mental attribute.

No matter how much money you have or do not have, you can feel the riches that are present inside you right now. Go back to your list of what you have to be thankful for. If you are unemployed, you still have energy, desire, and the ability to change that situation. If you need training, you have a brain with which to acquire it. Whatever you need in the material world to make your life better already exists in your mental world. You have only to make use of the power that resides there to feel rich every day of your life. Your experiences are gold just waiting to be mined. Be grateful for every blessing you have already brought into your life, however small, knowing that more are on the way.

The other side of this coin is represented by someone whose scarcity consciousness rules her life. Her parents grew up poor during the Great Depression, and although her father later became a wealthy businessman, her mother continued to believe in scarcity. For example, she never bought more food than the family would eat in one day—a practice left over from Depression days. Despite her husband's success, she could not believe there was enough to go around, and she passed this deep-seated fearfulness on to her daughter. Although my friend owns her own house and earns a respectable income, she continually "talks poor" and complains about the high cost of everything. When she inherited a substantial sum of money, I thought that at last she would feel secure and be happy, but I was wrong. She complained about the cost of administrating the will, the lawyer's fees, and the taxes eating into her inheritance. I have another friend who quips, "That's a high class problem." But it is indeed a problem. Do not allow yourself to become trapped in the consciousness of scarcity or you will never be able to hold onto the *feeling* of prosperity, no matter how much money you acquire.

• Do not complain constantly about what you have, emphasize what you don't have, and dwell on how difficult it is to get ahead. Otherwise you are creating internal images of lack, scarcity, hardship, loss, difficulty of all kinds. If you find yourself discussing these topics frequently, STOP. The words you speak sink into your unconscious, which acts like a mirror to bring forth what you think. Using the monitoring technique, watch yourself carefully and mind what you say. Each time you catch a thought reinforcing scarcity consciousness, gently turn it away and replace it with its opposite. If you think, "There's not enough," say "Abundance is for all." If you worry about how to pay the bills, instead of complaining about high prices, tell yourself that you have riches within. In time, you will begin to act on these new thoughts and images and you will create bountiful circumstances in your life.

What Not to Expect from Psychic Work in the Material World

Almost everyone these days is looking to improve their financial condition. As a psychic counselor, I find that questions about money are prominent on anyone's list, and most people are confused about how psychic abilities can help them to improve financial conditions.

Wishful thinking is *not* psychic ability. When we speak of "psychic work," we mean making both the *mental* effort necessary to contact intuition and to program the subconscious mind *and* taking appropriate action based upon information received.

To become prosperity-conscious is a necessary first step, and to translate your new thinking into actual belief is vital. However, you must also follow the leads given to you by your psychic Self, even if that involves taking risks. If you feel an inner motivation, you must have the courage to act on it. This is your intuition giving you guidance, telling you to strike out boldly. Unless you learn to heed the information you are receiving, you will get nowhere. People others call "lucky" are simply those who, like Conrad Hilton, followed up on their intuitive promptings.

Many people prefer the fantasy of winning the lottery to the reality of doing psychic work. They ask foolish or unrealistic questions, such as "Will I win the lottery?" Even if the answer is "yes," it may only be a small amount. Others ask open-ended questions, such as, "When will I get a lot of money?" To such questions, I answer, "Where are you accustomed to money coming from?" The person on welfare daydreaming about getting rich is not using the power of intuition. Though these techniques work, they must be applied regularly and consistently in order to achieve results. Using psychic ability is a way of life, not a one-shot quick fix for what ails you. In other words, you have to start from where you are. If you are in Chicago and want to go to Dallas, you can't fly on an airline ticket from Los Angeles to New York. If you are unemployed, you need a job.

Although you can attract money and material goods, it is important to realize that these do not materialize out of thin air. True, a few people win big money in the lottery or at the horse races, and they may have used intuition to pick their numbers or their horses, but unless you are content to be poor while you take long shots, you need to inject some realism into your use of psychic abilities. For example, if there are no jobs in your area, you might have to move to another town or city. Intuition can guide you, but it can't pack your bags.

Trying to use your psychic abilities for frivolous or unserious purposes will bring unsatisfactory results. Your intuition is there to help you live a better and more rewarding life, but it is not there to enable you to avoid the work of living your life. Don't expect your psychic Self to produce rabbits out of hats. You can't find a job if you don't look for one, but the action of looking coupled with a mental attitude of expecting the best may lead to greater results than you anticipate. One man looking for part-time lawn-care work found a job as a full-time gardener on a large estate. Money does not fall from the sky but comes as the result of doing something positive. Using psychic ability is like planting a garden. You put the seeds in the ground, but then you must water and weed, prune and propagate. The true gardener loves his work and loves his garden for itself, for the marvelous process that is life, and for the gift of being a participant.

Find a Job, Develop a Career

Whether you are looking for your first job or have been a victim of "downsizing," your intuition can be a valuable asset. It is an undeniable fact that work and love are interconnected. If you love your work, you will do better at it. Some of us are required to take work we do not love as an interim measure, but never, never abandon your inner Self's desires. Work is not only a means of earning money, it is a potent form of self-expression, and the more of your Self you express, the stronger your Self will become.

You are a special person, with a unique contribution to make to the world. Since you did not pop out of the womb with a user's manual in your tiny fist, you must make your own way among the job and career thickets. The best compass you have is your intuition, but it cannot operate at its maximum capability without purpose. And it is you who must decide what your purpose in life is. Whether you know it or not, you do have one.

Discovering your life's work is an exciting adventure, one that will take you on many paths during your lifetime For some of us, our life's work is aligned with how we earn money. For others, it is a separate activity. A woman client of mine considers her life's work to be growing beautiful roses. For a long time, she worked at a secretarial job and grew her roses in her spare time, eventually adding a small greenhouse to her house. Although she felt her job was a dead-end, she had no training for anything else.

I asked her to meditate on work and love in her life for a week and tell me what images her unconscious produced. At the time, I did not know about her passion for roses, so when she began dreaming of heaps of rose petals I was puzzled. As we delved into the subject, I suggested that she might use her love for roses as the starting point for a business. She really liked the smell of different rose varieties. We looked at the recurring image of rose petals—and came up with *potpourri*. The idea of creating wonderfully scented packages of rose petals excited her, and she began doing it, selling her concoctions at a local shop specializing in fine soaps and perfumes. In time, she was able to quit her job and now has a thriving at-home business. It not only supports her but gives her joy and love.

Finding your life's work not only allows you to bring money into your life, it lets you grow emotionally and spiritually. What you do with the bulk of your time has a definite effect on the rest of your life, and if you are unhappy or frustrated in your work it will spill over into everything else.

Especially in today's changing world economy, we are called upon to invent new ways of working and making money. Your intuition can serve as a guide to your life's work by showing you where your deepest desires lie. During your relaxed time, you can summon up images about your life's work by allowing images to flow. You can try on a variety of careers in your imagination before settling on a specific course of action. The more you open yourself up to intuitive guidance, the clearer your purpose will become.

Wherever you are at present in your life, it need not limit your imagination of where you want to be in the future. Even if your life's work doesn't exist as a job today, that does not mean it cannot do so tomorrow. As we reach the twenty-first century, old ways of working are being dropped and new ones are coming into being. Depending on where you are in your career, you may create your work out of past experience, or invent something wholly new.

Discovering Your Life's Work

What are you doing right now? Whatever it is, it has the germ of what you will do in the future. It doesn't matter if you have had one job or a hundred. Each new job or pleasurable activity engenders new skills. You already possess skills you probably don't know you have. You can assess your skills easily by writing down everything that you *like* to do and everything you already do well. Notice what you do naturally, what comes easily and gives you pleasure. These are clues to your life's work, which will involve using those skills.

Begin by asking yourself questions to break down what you do into its parts. What routines of your job do you like or dislike? Using the list-making technique on page 126, break down the component parts of your job into things you would keep, things you would get rid of, and things you would bring in. Do the same with any hobbies and cultural or leisure activities.

Once you have identified your skills, you can decide whether you want to add to them or concentrate on what you already do well. Whatever you do, whether it is an income-producing job or a nonpaying activity such as a sport, a hobby, or community work, it can become a part of your life's work. Nancy Kerrigan, for example, said during a television interview that she originally took up skating for recreation.

One of the best ways to draw your life's work toward you is to create a symbol for it and then energize that symbol, knowing that it has the power to scan the psychic ethers and connect you to what will bring your desires about. Your symbol might be anything—it must be of personal significance to you. A symbol I have found effective with my clients is the one of the Path. You experienced a path in the mediation on page 154. Did you like that path? Were you happy with it or did you want to make changes? Using the same meditation, but focusing on the path, enter the space again to find the symbol for your life's work. Then energize your symbol as you did the one for prosperity above.

Keep energizing your symbol by thinking of it often, especially on waking and before sleeping. Notice if it appears in your dreams. As you work with your symbol for your life's work—or even for a temporary job if that is what you want now—you release energy into the cosmos where it can connect with those who can help you. And, as you meditate on your symbol, you create the right conditions in your intuition from which will arise the specific ideas and plans to bring your ideal job or career into being. Don't rush this process. Keep at it until you get results. *Intentionality* is major here, as is persistence. Miracles do happen, but don't expect to make a major life change overnight. Make a list of all possible vocations you might explore, or skills you already have or might acquire, of combinations: for example, you might be skilled at office work but not want to work in an office. Where else might you apply those skills? And do you enjoy the skills themselves? Suppose you also like to cook. What combination might come from administrative skills and cooking skills? Catering is one that comes to my mind, or writing cookbooks or articles, or teaching cooking, or organizing other people's kitchens. Be creative. Listen to your inner guidance and take action appropriately.

Although it is a good place to start, you don't have to limit yourself to skills you already possess. You may not now have any skills. Ask yourself what you truly enjoy doing. How do you spend time not allocated to work or school? What interests you passionately? What comes naturally? What makes you happiest? No matter what you are currently doing, you are planting seeds for future growth.

One woman loved hairdressing work, but she hated working in a salon. She also liked to nurture older people. Now she works independently, traveling to residences for the elderly, combining her love of hairdressing with her nurturing abilities. Not only are her services much in demand, but the ladies give her much love and affection in appreciation for making them look and feel better.

Discovering your life's work requires listening to your inner Self. You are already the world's authority on yourself and what is good for you. Creating your life's work is a process of discovery, and everytime you go within the mansion of the Self and explore its rooms, you will be putting yourself on your true Path.

Follow Your Inner Wisdom

14

Personal Growth

*Human beings possess capabilities of mind
that are literally beyond genius.*
—DR. BARBARA BROWN,
Supermind

Your psychic potential can not only enrich your relationships and draw money and material goods to you, it can enhance your personal growth in many areas. You can learn faster, decrease stress, improve performance, be more creative, increase your self-confidence, and be the person you always wanted to be.

As you harmonize the forces of your mind/body/spirit, and use your practice to move out in one direction, you create a momentum that carries you into a more boundless life overall, giving a sense of being enlivened and enriched in every area of life. Connecting the urge for outward performance to the process of inner expansion results in a melding of awareness and sensitivity with practical results in the here and now.

Are these shimmering promises too good to be true? Or are we treating ourselves as limited beings when in fact we are limitless? Albert Einstein said, "Imagination is more important than knowledge," and Leonardo da Vinci's work confirms this. Leonardo wrote, "Man shall have wings. He shall be as the gods. If it be not for us, then it shall be for those who follow us."

Leonardo knew that humans would one day have the power of flight, even though he knew nothing of today's principles of aerodynamics. The Wright brothers also used their imaginations, but their true motivating force was the belief that flight was possible. From the sixteenth century to the twenty-first century, a mere second of geological time, we have gone from being earthbound to soaring above our planet into outer space. Why? Because a few dared to believe the impossible, and others dared to act on that belief. Who can say what the future holds for humanity? The possibilities of what it would mean to be fully human are inspiring indeed.

However, we have been sold a bill of goods, and we have bought into the mistaken notion of our limitations. Our history is of humans believing themselves less than they potentially are. The powers of the non–conscious mind have been denigrated by church and state and establishment science alike, institutions whose power results from confining the minds of the populace into narrow and straitened modes.

Dr. Brown says that "Human potentials have gone largely unrecognized because science has not spent its energies exploring what it means to be human." And writer Colin Wilson comments that "While men will devote their whole lives to problems like squaring the circle or trisecting an angle, they seem to experience no similar compulsion to solve problems connected with the 'occult.' "

It would seem that scientists live in fear of not being able to "prove" their theories; of ridicule by their colleagues; of being thought far-out; of not getting government grants for research; of seeming irrelevant. This fear prevents the majority from pursuing investigations into the real nature and vast capabilities of the non-conscious realm, which by its very nature is ephemeral and cannot be pinned down absolutely. To scientists, what cannot be quantified, measured, and proved in laboratory tests has a distinct bad odor—the odor of superstition.

Even the great psychologist Dr. Carl Jung was careful to couch his writings on the unconscious in the most punctilious of scientific language out of fear of the accusation of being thought "unscientific."

We have been badly short-changed by those who are in charge—from parents to politicians. We are wearing self-images many sizes too small, and like too-small shoes they are cramping our growth and deforming our spirits. It is time to wake up and—not only smell the roses and the coffee—but declare for ourselves the liberty that is mandated in our Constitution. Who is to say what we can achieve if we only put our minds to it?

There is today right now inside you a wonderful and able human being just waiting to be released from the bounds of self-imposed restrictions. You can begin immediately to develop yourself as a person who is inner–directed and not dependent upon the whims of the outside world. You do this by choosing to honor and rely upon your psychic Self. Right now a frontier is open to us all.

Shiela Ostrander and Lynn Schroeder in their book *Superlearning* say:

> Delving into untapped reserves, businesspeople found that another sort of apparent limitation—inflation, hard times, uncertainty about the future—could be eased using intuition and making the most of the metaphorical mind....Right-brain potentials, so long shunned by science, are rapidly coming into their own. Suddenly, to people in a great many different disciplines, this is where the really human action is. This is where the most revolutionary and even evolutionary discoveries await.

Psychic development is not a pill you can take, nor is it a magic potion to cure all your ills. What it is—available to you now and forever—is a powerful way to nurture your own Self, to grow into that unlimited being that you were meant to be.

Guidelines for Improving Self-Image and Self-Confidence

Cancellation of doubt

We hear proposals for "debt cancellation" to help poor nations. I propose that we all adopt a policy of *doubt cancellation* in our personal lives. A shortfall in your inner Self is much more serious than one in your bank account. Money is replaceable—time is not. Do not waste your precious time and energy on doubts. Issue them a cancellation notice *now.* Remind yourself often that you create yourself minute-by-minute by your thoughts. You are today the result of a lifetime of thinking and feeling. These thoughts and feelings are the seeds that bear fruit in the real world. For every thought there is a physical reality. By changing your thoughts, you change your reality.

Self-confidence, self-esteem, and self-image are all inextricably linked. Those who lack self-confidence generally lack self-esteem and have poor self-image. You can improve all three by using your psychic/intuitive abilities, by following a regular program of relaxation and visualization techniques. It is all a matter of focusing your attention upon the desired result. The next time you are beset by doubts about yourself, use the following guided meditation.

How to Increase Self-Confidence

This exercise has been especially designed to give you a self-confidence boost by improving your self-image and self-esteem.

Take whatever image you received of the cup during the meditation in chapter 11 and examine it honestly. It's important for you to take a thoroughly honest look at who and what you are—or think you are—in order for you to be able to create an improved self-image, which will increase your self-confidence. In addition, increasing your self-confidence will give you greater access to your psychic potential. Each, working in tandem, will enhance the other. Also, as you work with your psychic development and experience success in accessing your deep knowing mind, your confidence in your ability to use this part of yourself will increase.

Allow about thirty minutes for this exercise. You can make it a part of your regular practice program or you can add it as an extra. Depending on your need and on the results you get, do this exercise regularly, from once a day to three times a week.

First, get into a comfortable position wearing loose clothing. Some people like to take a warm bath or shower first, as an aid to relaxation. Make sure you will not be disturbed. Now, close your eyes and look upward to the center of the forehead, the "third eye." Breathe slowly and deeply several times, feeling the tension leaving your body. Next, take a deep breath and while exhaling feel the warmth of total relaxation flow through your entire body. Stay with this feeling for a few moments and enjoy it before going on.

Next, use whichever relaxation/deep relaxation method you prefer, letting yourself go into utter relaxation.

When you feel totally relaxed, begin to visualize yourself in a beautiful outdoor surrounding—it could be a beach, a woodland, a flower-filled meadow, a park. Choose a time of year you enjoy—spring, summer, autumn, winter—and begin taking a walk. As you stroll, feel the sun on your face. If you have chosen the beach, you might want to take off your shoes and feel the warm sand between your toes. Create as many details for this scene as you can, making it thoroughly pleasurable. Fill in the sensual details—hear the birds singing, smell the fresh, flower-scented air, hear a bee buzzing by, watch small animals at play, notice the play of sunlight on the water.

As you continue on your walk, you will find a large ball, like a beach ball. It is bright yellow, full of cheer. Take the ball and throw it into the air. Watch it rise up and fall down, catching it. Do this several times, and each time throw the ball higher and higher. As you throw, inhale deeply on the throw and exhale on the catch. Over and over, higher and higher, inhale, exhale. You are relaxing into your deep inner Self. As you relax fully, your body feels lighter and lighter, as light as the ball floating in the air. Visualize yourself as able to rise into the air like the ball and float out to where the clouds are.

Now, imagine a rainbow appearing in the sky overhead, a lovely multicolored band arching from one side of the sky to the other. Follow the colors of the rainbow one by one—red, orange, yellow, green, blue, violet, purple. You are sitting under the protective arch of this beautifully colored natural phenomenon. You are in a place where you can accomplish anything you want with little or no effort. Here, under the rainbow, you are fully confident of your abilities. Your mind soars to new heights of what is possible. Sit beneath your magic rainbow and begin to think about yourself. Ask questions. Ask yourself what you like about yourself and what you dislike. Look at your attitudes toward yourself—are they negative and critical? Attach any negative or critical feelings to the yellow ball and throw them up into the rainbow where they will dissolve never to trouble you again.

Now, begin to construct an image of who you want to be, of who you really are when you are free of negative programming. Think about the effect you have on others. See yourself through the eyes of someone else. What do you see? How do you want to change that picture? Imagine that you have a TV screen with your self-image on it in front of you. The set has a whole row of knobs you can use to adjust the picture. Begin making adjustments until you have the picture you want. Now, imagine you have a split-screen on your TV. Put the old, negative picture next to the new positive picture and compare them. Now choose which one you want and erase the other picture. Did you choose the new you, the one you actually are when all the old negative programming is erased? I'll bet you did. Good.

Now spend a few minutes with that new image, even if it seems a bit strange to you. Feel how it feels to have a good self-image, to feel good about yourself, to be brimming with "can do" self-confidence. Congratulate yourself on being able to accept this image. Praise yourself for being courageous enough to shed that old, erroneous image.

Slowly breathe yourself back to normal consciousness and when you are ready to return to the everyday world, get up and go and take a long look at yourself in the mirror. You should be able to see a difference, even if it is subtle. As you gaze into your reflection in the mirror, see and feel yourself actually becoming the person you saw on the TV set under the rainbow. Know that you already possess all you need to do whatever you want. You are not telling yourself a lie. Your deep mind *can* accomplish whatever you want. Say out loud, "I now claim my power. I am supremely self-confident. I succeed in all that I do."

Now, take the image from the TV screen and superimpose it on your image in the mirror. Believe that you are now the person you found under the rainbow. Feel yourself and the image you created becoming *one and the same thing.*

Repetition of this meditation will allow you to implant into your deep mind the image of who you truly are. Don't lie to yourself, but do de-emphasize the negative. If you need to make changes, set about making them in a consistent manner. Each time you return to your special rainbow place, you will be reinforced by the good image of yourself you have created and can now bring into being.

Remember to thank your intuition and to praise yourself for being willing to take a chance on the real you.

Watch the words you use when you speak to yourself and others

We have already mentioned the power of words. They are particularly significant to your self-esteem. If I say to you, "You're getting fat," and if you have a sensitivity to that issue, my words will have a serious impact on your psyche. They might even throw you into a paroxysm of self-doubt leading to depression. It will make no difference if I immediately retract the words, saying, "I was only kidding. Don't take it so seriously." The damage will already have been done.

On the other hand, if I say to you, "That's a *stunning* outfit—it really makes you look *super*," my words will act as an instant uplift, especially if you've been feeling a bit down about yourself. They will buoy you the whole day. The same holds true for words about yourself to yourself or to others.

If you consistently use denigrating terms when referring to yourself, silently or out loud, you will impress those ideas into your subconscious, which, being the mirror-mimic it is, will return those images to you in the form of concrete experience. If you call yourself *stupid*, or *clumsy*, or *lazy*, or *weak*, or *afraid*, you will be issuing a self-fulfilling prophecy. Do you use such words about yourself, even in supposed jest? If you do—**STOP RIGHT NOW.** Bombarding yourself with the negative images contained in the words you use will clog your psychic channels. You can unblock them by the simple method of being aware of what you say and think.

If, for example, you make a mistake, *do not call yourself stupid.* Say instead, "I made a mistake." Everyone makes mistakes, and most mistakes can be corrected. Making a mistake does not make you stupid, it makes you human.

Many people confuse being self-effacing with politeness. When complimented, instead of saying a simple thank you, they disparage the compliment. Someone says, "That's a nice dress you're wearing," and the reply often is, "Oh, this old thing? I don't know why I put it on." This is because they have been taught that accepting compliments is somehow akin to an overweening and sinful pride for which God will strike you down.

Realize that you can *at this very moment* make major changes in your life merely by changing your vocabulary. You do not have to spend years in therapy or invest inexpensive self-improvement seminars to do this. You can spend a few dollars on a dictionary of synonyms and antonyms and look up all the related words to those you regularly employ. If you use "stupid" about yourself, look up *stupid* and find all the antonyms for it and start applying them to yourself.

Begin to speak with confidence of yourself and your abilities. This is not boastful, it is just common sense. Remember that what you give your attention to is what you manifest, and if you are stressing the negative you will be manifesting it. Use the monitoring technique to review what you are saying during the course of a day and make corrections to your course. Steering true means speaking true. Suppose you really do feel inadequate about something. Instead of saying, "I can't..." or "I'm afraid..." say "I am learning a new skill" or "I am now about to undertake something that is entirely new to me." Find the *truth* and speak it.

Think of all the times when you were a child that you heard words that wounded you, even if said casually. Look at the emotional damage they left behind. When I was a girl just blossoming into puberty, my thighs raced ahead of my upper body in development. I was blissfully unaware of this bodily imbalance until my older brother's 20-year-old girlfriend said to him in a loud voice, "I didn't know your sister had such BIG LEGS." I spent the next ten years in long skirts hiding my defect. And I have *never* forgotten the remark, which contributed to a bad and incorrect body image.

If words can wound, they can also heal. Every negative word you have ever heard about you can be changed into a positive. And if you take nothing else from this book but the knowledge that words have great power, you will have achieved much. Whatever words you choose to tell yourself is accepted by your subconscious mind as truth. Do not let negative lies become your truth. If you suffer from a poor self-image, get up right now and go to the mirror and look yourself in the eye and say, "You are a *wonderful* person!" Say this with utmost sincerity, for it is the truth. Repeat this affirmation every morning and every evening religiously for one month and you will be amazed at what a difference you will see. If at first the idea of praising and complimenting yourself seems silly or ridiculous, do it anyway. Very soon you will make such a positive connection to your real self that it will feel right.

Unlocking your creative energies

Intuition and creativity are intimately connected. Art is an intuitive function, but many kinds of creativity are not artistic in nature. Creativity enters into the thinking of those in many different fields. Imagination also comes into play during creativity, and the use of imagination fuels intuition.

There is a free-flowingness in the intuitive/creative/imaginative sphere where these characteristics blend into one another. Who is to say the scientist developing a new theory is less creative than the artist creating a painting? The end result is different, but the process is similar. No two painters receive their inspiration in the exact same way, and no two people perceive their deep inmost intuitive/creative urges precisely the same. I make this point to emphasize the individual nature of the psychic process. Our brains function in similar ways, but the deep inner reaches of each human differ from all others, just as every snowflake—made alike from the simple process of cold air and water forming the tiny crystals—is unique. Of millions, no two are ever alike.

Suspend rational thought

Although rational thought is important at the verification stage of the intuitive process, those seeking to enhance their creativity through intuition must be willing to shut off the left-brain, rational/analytical mode.

Suspension of rational thought for the purposes of enhancing creativity is a *temporary* condition, but the idea of letting go of this control for even a short time seems to frighten many people, especially those who consider anything *non*rational to be *ir*rational. The more control-oriented you are, the more difficult it will be to suspend rational thinking.

You may be one of the many people who were brought up to believe that nonrational meant crazy. Women, especially, are denigrated by being called "irrational." And men short-change themselves by relegating their intuitive "flashes," or insights, to the dustbin of the irrational.

Creativity is inherent in all human beings and can be nurtured by paying attention to the intuitive process. To enhance your own creativity, you must open up your awareness to your inner processes, even when they seem to contradict your rational mind. You do not need to know in analytical detail how or why your intuition works. Accepting that it does work is all that is needed.

Get the "go with the flow" mental habit

Following the images your mind makes without having any specific goal in mind is called "free-form thinking," and it is useful for tapping into your unconscious resources. Daydreaming is another form of this, and both function at the alpha-theta level of brain wave. But free-form thinking is not without purpose. It may seem silly to your rational mind, but like Freud's free association there is method in its apparent madness. It allows you to connect with the right-brain, image-making part of your brain, where creativity is spawned.

Practice purposeful repose

One writer on creativity has called this "masterful idleness," and asserts that it is the "hardest part of the creative discipline." Note that word *discipline*. This is *purposeful repose*. Doing routine work is easy, but releasing the creative flow is difficult. This doing of nothing is the proper activity for priming the creative pump through intuition, which allows our inner minds to arrive at creative solutions to problems, to come up with original ideas, to release us from the restrictions of the rational-only mode of thinking.

Using Intuition to Aid Learning

Your intuition can be a valuable learning aid. As Dr. Karl Pribram has pointed out, the brain's structure is holographic. Information is distributed throughout, and each memory is encoded to contain the whole. Intuition lets us tap into that resource to enhance learning abilities. Students who practice getting in touch with their intuitive selves will find that more of the mind's capacities light up and the totality of the learning experience shifts into clearer focus. One of the main benefits of tapping into deeper resources is the overthrowing of limiting ideas about learning abilities.

Overcoming these psychological blocks is critical. The first of these is the belief that learning can only be accomplished in the rational mode. This cuts off a large part of the learning capacity. Another facet of this block is the idea that there is a "norm." Everyone is supposed to learn the same material at the same rate. With ninety percent of our mental ability lying unused and fallow, there is a lot of room for opening up and expanding not only what we learn, but how we learn it.

"We are hoarding potentials so great that they are just about unimaginable," says psychic Jack Schwarz.

The second block to learning is the sense of "I can't do it," either as a result of past failures or the idea that one has a low level of learning ability. This notion is generally imposed from outside sources, such as critical parents and teachers. Many people have accepted an other-imposed evaluation of their learning capacities and simply lost heart. Years of denigrating remarks such as, "You're hopeless at math," or "You'll never make college," become, to the uncritical child, the only truth. A variety of experiences then usually ensues to reinforce the person's feelings of insecurity about learning abilities. Anxiety and emotional overloading beset the student, and failure follows. But it need not be so. Whether you are a student or an older person wanting to return to learning, you can use your intuitive abilities to help.

The following steps will allow you to use intuition to enhance learning capabilities.

- Use the relaxation exercises to combat the tension and worry which accompany fear of failure
- Use the visualization exercises to "program" your deep mind with images of success.
- Implant affirmative statements to dissolve blocks and build self-confidence.

Here are some statements you can use in conjuction with your relaxation/visualization program to enhance learning.

I learn quickly and easily through my intuition.
Learning is easy and fun.
I remember everything with ease.
Remembering is pleasant and fun.
My mind shows me what I need to know when I need it.
My mind stores information for me.
My mind releases information when I need it.
I am a good learner; I enjoy learning.
• I am calm and confident.

Make up your own affirmations to use while you are in a state of relaxation. Words that are meaningful to you are best. Some people like to make up rhymes or use alliteration. Repeat your affirmations slowly to yourself a few times and imbue the words with meaning and emotion. You can use your affirmations at any time to reinforce the image.

The visualization for mind-calming below is especially good prior to an exam or if you are feeling tension about new material, but you can use it any time you are feeling anxious or want to release the tensions of the day. Precede it with breathing and/or relaxation exercises.

Mind-Calming Visualization

Begin by following the instructions for preparing for a relaxation exercise. After relaxing, let your mind take you to a beautiful natural setting. It can be a place you love to visit, or a place you have only seen in a magazine picture or on a TV travel show.

It might be a walk through snowy woods, a hike up a mountain pass, a leisurely sit-down by the side of a cool lake, a beach scene at whatever time of year you like best. The idea is to pick something that you find calming and soothing. Try imagining sitting by a lake in spring when the wildflowers are just beginning to bloom.

Visualize yourself walking to the shore of the lake, enjoying the cool-yet-warm spring air, breathing in its freshness, feeling invigorated yet relaxed.

Feel the warmth of the sun on your shoulders. Maybe you take off your jacket and turn up your face to the gentle warmth.

Take off your shoes and dabble your feet in the lake, feeling its refreshing coolness. Watch a pair of mating ducks land on the lake and see the birds soaring overhead in the blue sky. Feel at one with the scene. Notice how the water catches the sun's light. See the reflection of a passing cloud on the water's surface.

Take your time to enjoy this place, letting all your worries and tensions slip away until you feel utterly calm.

Once you have done this meditation, you can return here whenever you like. With practice and the use of a symbol to represent this calm place, you can evoke it in only a few minutes anywhere, even on a crowded commuter train. You can change or vary the scene at will. For example, I have a special place I go, which is perched on a mountainside. It is the retreat of a Buddhist monk I call Genji. I have been going there for about five years now, at all seasons, in all weathers, at all times of the day and night. The place changes with the hour, the month. One day a female cat appeared and presented Genji with five kittens, who have now all grown up. In summer, Genji grows herbs and in autumn harvests and dries them. I never tire of this place, which serves as a refuge whenever I need one.

Using Intuition to Solve Personal Problems

Everyone experiences problems at some time in their lives. Problems are not only a part of life, but they are a growth potential. How we react to our problems has a great deal to do with how we solve, or do not solve, them. Our attitudes toward our problems programs our unconscious, which takes our conscious thoughts literally, to reflect back to us what we think and expect.

We can all choose how to respond to our life problems, even the most severe. And, our psychic abilities can help us to reach appropriate resolution. Sometimes, we have only to ask. This takes practice—one of the twelve Steps—but the answers are always available to us if we but learn to listen to the "still, small voice within."

Napoleon Hill, the author of *Think and Grow Rich*, was commissioned by the philanthropist Andrew Carnegie to research a practical method for living a successful life. He tells of his experience with Dr. Elmer Gates, a well-known teacher/scientist/inventor of the day.

When Hill called upon Dr. Gates, his secretary said that he was busy. Offering to wait, Hill asked how long he might be and received the reply that it might be a few minutes or a few hours or a few days. Amazed at this rather odd answer, for surely one could approximate how long a business meeting or a specific task would require, Hill asked what in the world the good doctor was doing. The puzzling reply was, "He is sitting for an answer."

Upon further questioning, Hill learned that when he was beset by a problem, Dr. Gates locked himself away in a special room, soundproofed and darkened. There, he cleared his mind and asked a question, focusing intently on the one idea. And he waited until the answer came no matter if it took a minute or a week. He didn't fidget, get nervous, become impatient. He waited. When the answer appeared on the screen of his mind, he arose and wrote it down and emerged into the regular world.

Finally, Hill got to see Dr. Gates and asked him where the answers to his questions came from. He was told by Dr. Gates they came from three sources:

1. Accumulated evidence, knowledge, experience
2. Telepathic contact with the minds of others
3. The great repository of Infinite Intelligence—"which may be contacted through the subconscious section of the mind,"

Often when we are facing personal problems, we are not clear about what the problem is. It may be necessary to probe deeper to reach clarification. As stated earlier, forming the right question is the key to getting the right answer. I call this looking for "the question underneath the question."

Let me give you an example. A woman came to see me for a Tarot card reading. As I always do, I asked what problem or area of life she wanted me to concentrate on. She replied that she was thinking of going into business for herself, which would mean quitting a good job and taking some risks. She wanted to know if the timing was right, if it was a good idea.

That seemed straightforward enough, and I laid out the cards after the usual preliminaries. To my surprise, there was nothing I could read that had anything at all to do with the issue she had presented. Occasionally, I do draw a blank—find a person for whom I cannot read—in which case I cancel the reading and charge nothing. But this woman had been recommended by a regular client and I wanted to help her. As I gazed at the cards, I saw her husband and another man. I also saw a crossroads in her marriage and illness. What could these things have to do with her going into business for herself?

When I told her what was coming through, she at once responded, "I'm thinking of getting a divorce." This was the question underneath the question. Her husband had recently had a serious operation, which left him partially disabled, and she felt guilty about wanting to leave a sick man. Going into business for herself would give her an excuse to spend long hours away from home, and the tensions of so doing would drain off her energies and attention, effectively divorcing her from him physically and emotionally. The other man was the business partner she had selected, who was also her married lover.

A complex situation, but not unsolvable. Her affair was an emotional buffer zone, not a case of true love. The business idea was an escape route. It was only when she acknowledged the problem and set out to solve it that she began to get answers that worked.

No one can lay out an exact laboratory-style plan for solving personal problems through applied intuition, and although there are methods, there are no hard-and-fast, guaranteed procedures. However, general rules do apply.

FIRST: Be specific about the problem; look for the question underneath the question

SECOND: Gather all the information you can about the issue at hand. If you want to buy a house, research real estate and mortgages.

THIRD: After you have collected data, study it and fill your mind with pertinent data. If you have a health problem, learn all you can about symptoms and treatments. Saturate yourself with information.

FOURTH: Put the entire issue aside for at least 24 hours, unless it is an emergency.

FIFTH: (5) When you are ready to "sit for an answer," go to your usual meditation spot or to some other quiet and peaceful place and spend fifteen minutes doing your favorite relaxation exercise.

SIXTH: (6) Drop the question into your intuitive mind and visualize it sinking to the bottom.

SEVENTH: (7) Continuing to remain relaxed, let the answer float up from your intuitive depths. You might visualize the answer on your screen, or hear a voice in your head. It may be a bodily feeling you recognize as your psychic response.

EIGHTH: (8) Be prepared to wait, if necessary. Do not attempt to rush your process.

The purpose of this technique is to circumvent your rational mind, which has a tendency to worry a problem like a dog with a bone. When you program your unconscious with the right question and then switch your focus to something unrelated, the answer pops up, sometimes unexpectedly.

For Every Question There Is an Answer

Part V

The Invisible World

Dreams: Your Hidden Resource

We are such stuff
As dreams are made of, and our little life
Is rounded with a sleep.
—WILLIAM SHAKESPEARE,
The Tempest

Dreams have fascinated the human race for all time. They seem magical—in our dreams, we can fly, stop roaring locomotives with our bare hands, meet and converse with interesting people, receive intricate teachings, solve problems, be creative, converse with the dead, become aware of psychological changes, receive intuitive promptings.

Dr. Carl Jung wrote,

The dream is a little hidden door in the innermost and most secret recesses of the soul, opening into that cosmic night which was psyche long before there was any ego-consciousness, and which will remain psyche no matter how far our ego-consciousness may extend. For all ego-consciousness is isolated: it separates and discriminates, knows only particulars and sees only what can be related to the ego. Its essence is limitation, though it reaches to the farthest nebulae among the stars. All consciousness separates; but in dreams we put on the likeness of that more universal, truer, more eternal

man dwelling in the darkness of the primordial night. There
he is still the whole, and the whole is in him, indistinguish-
able from nature and bare of all egohood.

It is from these all-uniting depths that the dream arises, be
it never so childish, grotesque and immoral. So flowerlike is it
in its candor and veracity that it makes us blush for the
deceitfulness of our lives.

The world of dream is many-layered, infinitely rich and varied,
capable of astonishing metamorphoses. Dreams weave the
events of the day into a new pattern; they combine with previously dreamed—a sort of recombinant dream chemistry; we
dream of those we know and love or hate; dreams of people we
have never met; dreams of the living and the dead; dreams of
fantastic adventures; dreams of magical beings; dreams within
dreams. This list does not cover the entire territory—which is
unfathomable—but it will give you an overview of what is possible in this mysterious land that we all visit every night of our
lives. Joseph Campbell says in *The Mythic Image*.

For in dreams, things are not as single, simple, and separate
as they seem, the logic of Aristotle fails, and what is not-A
may indeed be A. The goddess and the lotus are equivalent
representations of this one life-enclosing sphere of space-
time, wherein all things are brought to manifestation,
multiplied, and in the end return to the universal womb that
is night.

It has been estimated that the average person spends four or
five years of a lifetime dreaming, but it is my opinion that this
figure is low. According to sleep lab studies, we dream on average one and a half hours during a normal eight-hour night's
sleep. I dream much more than that, even three times that
amount. However, it does not matter how much time you spend
dreaming; I suspect that the amount varies with the individual
and with interest in the dream process and level of interaction
with the dream world. I always find it sad when people aren't
interested in their dreams—it's like not being interested in your
emotions, or your love life. It's like not being interested in poetry, or music, or art. Those who find dreams a waste of time are
truly wasting their time. What is more, they are throwing away
a precious resource.

For your dream world is a hidden resource, one that you can access freely, one that you can control and command, one that will enrich your life immeasurably.

The richness of the hidden vale of dreams is exemplified in the fairy tale about the twelve princesses, whose slippers were each morning discovered to be in shreds. With so many daughters to feed, clothe, and provide dowries for, the king of this otherwise happy land was not a rich man. The expense of having daily to cobble the princesses each with a new pair of shoes was quite bothersome to him. Questioning the daughters had proved to be of no avail. None would tell what they did during the night, when they were always locked in their chambers behind guarded doors.

Finally, the king proclaimed an offer to give half of his kingdom and his choice of the daughters in marriage to any knight who could uncover the princesses' secret. Many knights showed up at the castle to strike the bargain; all, however, failed. Each was locked in at night with the princesses, to keep watch, and each morning the knight was found asleep and the princesses' slippers in tatters. Then a new knight—in shining white armor— rode up and threw down his gauntlet to the challenge. That night, he was locked into the bed chamber of the princesses, who cordially offered him wine—drugged, as it had been with the others. But he only pretending to drink the wine and then feigned sleep.

When the entire castle was fast asleep, the princesses arose from their couches, one by one, donned fine ball gowns and their new shoes, and slipped away down a secret passage that led underground. Wrapping himself in a magic cloak his mother had woven of her dreams, which made him invisible, the knight followed the princesses down, down—into a fabulous underground world, filled with jewels and treasures of every kind. At the bottom there was a lake, and twelve little boats waited at the shore. Each princess got into a boat and each boat sailed of itself across the glasslike surface of the underground lake.

On the opposite shore, the princesses disembarked and were met by twelve handsome troubadours. The princesses and their escorts danced their way through a series of bejeweled gardens.

The first was paved with pink marble—the trees and bushes grew rubies; the second, floored with amber, was filled with flowers made of emeralds; in the third they walked on shining silver and every tree held dazzling blossoms of sapphire; the fourth glittered gold underfoot and danced with the light from thousands of blossoms of diamonds. The knight had never seen such splendor, and he could hardly believe his eyes.

All night the princesses and their troubadours whirled and spun in the jewel-encrusted underground garden to the strains of celestial music which seemed to come from everywhere and nowhere. At break of dawn, the eldest princess summoned the sisters together for the return trip across the mirror-still lake.

"Hurry," she said, "it is almost light and we must return before the knight awakens."

Knowing his marvelous tale would not be believed without evidence, as they returned the knight surreptitiously plucked a bejeweled twig from each of the gem-flower gardens. As the twelve princesses each stepped into her little boat, he noticed that the thin-soled slippers had been reduced to satin rags.

When the boats reached the other shore, the knight—concealed in his cloak of invisibility—raced up the long stairway to the sleeping chambers ahead of the princesses. When they returned and tossed their ruined shoes into a heap, they found him asleep as they had left him.

The next morning, the knight was summoned to the throne room, where the king demanded to know if he had discovered the princesses' secret. The knight told all, to the amazement of his host and the astonishment of the princesses, who proclaimed him a liar. But when he opened his cloak and presented the king with the jeweled twigs of ruby, emerald, sapphire, and diamonds, the eldest princess confessed all to her pleased father, who decreed that henceforth the princesses should have all the new slippers they desired, so long as they would share with him the experiences of their wondrous nocturnal world.

And the knight—whom did he choose to be his bride? The *eldest* sister.

I find this little tale a perfect paradigm for the dream experience. The princesses are our nonlinear, nonrational faculties that, at the onset of night, slip away to a private realm of inexhaustible treasures. That there are twelve princesses suggests the twelve hours of the night. The knights who failed are those who don't remember their dreams—they are the rational-minded who think there is nothing else in this world except what one can measure with the five gross senses. The knight who succeeds is the one whose mother wove him a cloak of her dreams—in other words, someone who is not afraid of the feminine, nonrational side of life, who can walk its ways in protection. My explanation of the choice of the eldest princess as bride is that she, being the oldest, represents wisdom. The king is the masculine counterpart, or the waking consciousness, which is incomplete without knowledge of our nocturnal wanderings in the jeweled lands hidden beneath the castle of ordinary everyday reality.

What Dreams Can Do for Us

Dreams are fascinating. They can also be baffling. They can entertain, mystify, uplift, frighten—but what, the practical-minded want to know, can they do for us? Dream researcher Patricia Garfield, Ph.D., writes in *Creative Dreaming,*

> We can deal with our problems at their origin in our own minds. We can learn about ourselves and grow. We can unify our personalities. We can transform our fear-producing dream enemies into dream friends. It is true. We can build into our dream world friendly images that will help us not only in our dreams but in our waking life as well. We can make dream friends who will provide us with solutions to our problems and with marvelous creative products. Dream friends can show us how to solve a knotty problem at work, provide a theme for an advertising campaign, create an original dress design, compose an epic poem, or sing a new song. Whatever our problems are, dreams can provide novel ideas and sometimes magnificent resolutions.

I believe that in the various dream states we have the ability to connect up with other dreamers, to share a vast and fluid world, just as all the marine creatures share the ocean. We, in our usual state, are like little boats bobbing on the surface of this immeasurably huge ocean of dream. We need to become divers and submariners, going deeply into this fascinating medium where we can swim freely, without restrictions.

True, we sometimes encounter frightening experiences or images—nightmares—but these also can teach us about ourselves and allow us to develop new strengths. Once I dreamed I was attacked by demons—the kind you see in medieval paintings— which were truly fearsome. I fought long and hard with them, in what seemed a very physical sense, and conquered them. They left with their forked tails between their hairy legs. I was, of course, fighting my own fears, which had become demonized, as if they existed outside of me rather than inside. These fears I had not acknowledged appeared as adversarial creatures. You can fight your own demons of fear and negativity and overcome them.

The world of dream is multilayered. It is the medium for many psychic experiences, which live in it like fish swim in the sea. Get to know your own private dream aquarium, explore the images there, find out what you like and what you don't like. You'll be amazed at how much control you have over your nighttime productions—for you are the writer, director, produc- er, and leading actor. Dreams may seem to come from out of nowhere, but they are all a part of you and your world.

Interpretation of Dreams

Most dreams are not to be taken literally—just because you dream of someone dying does not mean that the person will die. In fact, the literal interpretation of dreams is a cause of fear and anxiety and a source of numerous old wives' tales. From my expe- rience, dream books that give meanings for various symbols are not to be trusted. Your inner symbol producing mechanism is yours alone, unique. What cats, or a particular cat, mean to me, an avid cat-lover who has had special relationships with several cats, would be quite different from what that symbol would mean to someone who was not interested in or who was terrified of cats.

Whereas it is true that some symbols have universal signifi- cance—the sea is a universal symbol for the unconscious—it is important for you to learn to interpret your own *personal* symbol system. Dream interpretation is an art, not a science, and no scientific sleep lab can read the content or measure the mean- ing of dreams. Isis, the Egyptian goddess queen, says, "No man has lifted my veil," and this can well apply to the scientific efforts to penetrate the mysteries of dream in sleep labs.

If you are just beginning to pay attention to your dreams, begin the process of interpretation by recording the symbols that appear most frequently. Ask yourself the significance of these motifs. In my case, I know that when my cat Fuzz, who has been dead for ten years, appears in a dream that my heart center is being activated. Another frequent symbol in my personal dream system is that of a house, or an apartment. This symbol stands for the Self, and the dream's content is a clue to my self-development.

Dreams are a part of your psychic/intuitive self. They can be used in the same way as any other facet of your intuition—to enhance creativity, to solve personal problems, to gain information, to peer into the future.

Here is an example of a precognitive dream, which presaged my becoming a professional astrologer. At the time, I was studying astrology as part of my work on symbolism, with no thought of ever reading charts for other people or of in any way "going public" with what I knew.

The Dream: I am on a train and engage in conversation with a man about astrology. He is very knowledgeable and to my surprise I tell him that I am an "astrologist." He questions me and I give answers. Next, we come to the place of a famous astrologer—a sort of palace in the woods. There, I look at a pile of charts and see an error in one of them, which I point out. He thanks me and sets me to checking a pile of charts for him. I feel I don't really know enough, but I manage nonetheless. Later on, I find myself lecturing on astrology. The subject is Cancer rising. I answer questions from the audience, and one man says that he has Cancer rising but that he cannot identify with what I have said. I explain to him eloquently that each sign contains within itself its opposite. At one point, still in the dream, I realize that in real life I will one day lecture on astrology.

The world of the psyche and intuition is not divorced from our everyday reality, not a thing apart. We are all of us multifaceted beings with complexities of which often we are little aware. All of these facets are in operation all of the time, just like our body chemistry goes on about its business when we are totally unaware of its functioning. Dreams reflect our many facets, and they can be put to use to benefit us if we but pay attention.

While the symbolism in dreams may require interpretation and understanding, it is not there merely to mystify us. As Carl Jung says in his autobiography, *Memories, Dreams, Reflections,*

I was never able to agree with Freud that the dream is a 'façade' behind which its meaning lies hidden—a meaning already known but maliciously, so to speak, withheld from consciousness. To me dreams are a part of nature, which harbors no intentions to deceive but expresses something as best it can just as a plant grows or an animal seeks its food as best it can.

In addition to working with your own personal dream symbols and motifs, you can use the mind-mapping technique to connect you with the meaning of your dreams. To do this, take a large sheet of paper and some colored markers. Starting with a central theme (a word or a picture), draw the characters, actions, and objects in the dream, using the cluster method discussed on p. 000. Note which colors you choose, and pay attention to the feeling tones the dream evokes, selecting a color to express them. This technique is especially useful for those who function less well in the strictly verbal mode.

Dreams and Creativity

Writers, artists, and other creative people have recorded their dream experiences, depending upon them for inspiration. Psychologist Eliot D. Hutchinson reports cases of numerous scientists who have received information through dreams and says of dreams that "by them we can see more clearly the specific mechanism of intuitive thought." He goes on to say that "a large number of thinkers with whom I have had direct contact admit that they dream more or less constantly about their work, especially if it is exceptionally baffling...they often extract useful conceptions."

Dream researcher Patricia Garfield, tells of an "astounding dream discovery" made by Hermann V. Hilprecht, professor of Assyrian at the University of Pennsylvania: Working late one evening in 1893 Hilprecht was trying to decipher the cuneiform characters on drawings of two small fragments of agate. He thought them to be Babylonian finger rings and he tentatively assigned one fragment to the Cassite period, c. 1700 B.C., but he was unable to classify the other. About midnight, feeling uncertain about his classification, he went to bed and had a dream.

Garfield relates the anthropologist's dream, which was of a priest of pre-Christian Nippur who led the doctor to the treasure chamber of the temple and then told him in exact detail what the fragments were and how to fit them together. It was a long, involved sequence, but Hilprecht remembered it all and upon waking told it to his wife. He says, "Next morning...I examined the fragments once more in the light of these disclosures, and to my astonishment found all the details of the dream precisely verified in so far as the means of verification were in my hands."

Hilprecht, who had been working with drawings, went to the museum in Constantinople where the actual fragments were kept and found that they fit together perfectly. Garfield says, "In all respects they confirmed the information in his dream. Clairvoyance? Prescience? Magic?...Whatever the essential verity, the combination that unlocked the 3,000-year-old secret occurred in the dream state."

From time immemorial, people have used dreams in ways that benefited their waking lives. The more you learn to interact with your dream world, the more you integrate your total personality. Truly, this is a realm of magic and mystery, but one well worth exploring. Those who go fearlessly into the caverns of the night can return with untold treasure—and, intrepid explorers all, discover new territory in the vast, as-yet-unexplored continent of the human mind.

The ability to devise creative products and solutions to problems advances as you draw upon your dream life and develop skills in both dreaming and the interpretation of your dreams. As you consciously pay attention to your dreams, and use your dream symbols in the waking state, you will be integrating yourself, creating the greatest artwork of your life—your whole and unique self.

Guidelines for using dreams for specific purposes

- Learn to eliminate fear-producing dream images by being willing to overcome them in the dream state.
- Activate your creative dream faculty by filling yourself with images of the variation that exists in the real world. Read, travel, look at art, listen to music, study what interests you, absorb yourself in the external world and feel the

internal. Remember, your unconscious records everything you experience and feel.

- Solve problems by filling yourself with information. The more deeply involved you are with a subject or an intense emotional involvement, the more you will get out of the dream experience.
- Program yourself to produce creative solutions to problems. Accept that all the elements necessary are within you, in your existing body of knowledge.
- Give yourself specific dream assignments. Ask for a dream to resolve a particular issue and then work with what comes. Produce first; evaluate later.
- Be patient with your process. Persist in dreaming and working with the symbols from your dreams. Develop positive symbols for yourself and invite helpful dream figures.
- Give special attention to recurrent dreams. They are message carriers of what is ongoing in your psyche and are wonderful clues to your future.

Dream Recall

Not all dreams are remembered, even by the most careful and dedicated dreamers. Some people swear they never dream, but they only have no recall. Others recall only the most vivid of their dreams, forgetting the rest immediately upon waking. Some of us have trained ourselves to remember dreams regularly, almost every day/night cycle. But even to those of us who work steadily with the dream fabric of our lives, total recall is not possible.

Remember that attention is the first key to psychic awareness. Paying attention to dreams increases both the volume and the vividness we experience. The same is true of dream recall. The more you attend to recalling dreams, the easier it is to recall them.

✳ One popular method, which seems to work, is to tell yourself before you fall asleep, "I will remember my dreams in detail," and then to drink half a glass of water. The other half is drunk upon waking up.

The best time to remember dreams is when you awaken spontaneously, not by an alarm clock or an outside noise. When you wake naturally, it is always at the end of an REM (dream period). Also, the last dream is the longest and most vivid, thereby giving you more to hold on to when you wake up.

If you must use an alarm clock, and if you habitually begin thinking about the coming day's activities before you even open your eyes, you will have great difficulty catching dreams. An antidote to this is to reserve a time when you can "sleep in" and wake naturally. Vacation time or a weekend of quiet can be a fruitful start. I find that clients who begin the process of remembering their dreams are so fascinated and rewarded that they find ways to awaken naturally amid busy lives. One of these is to set your internal alarm clock so that you are not ratcheted out of sleep by a loud mechanical sound.

Once you have waked naturally, lie still with your eyes closed and review your dreams. If nothing comes at first, continue to relax until you recover either a feeling about a dream or actual images. Usually there is a story, and sometimes the plot will follow later. Jot down whatever you remember, no matter how fragmentary. You will get better at this in time. Fragments collected over time can function like pieces of a puzzle. Here is a fragment, a mere scrap of a dream that had great meaning for me and seemed to presage my psychic work.

The Dream: A blond man speaks to me at a hotel of some sort. He breaks into French as his English fails him, and though I don't know French well I understand what he is saying. He gives me a key, which looks like the key to the security lock on my front door in real life. I ask what it is for and he replies that I will find out. When I go back to my room I find that the key fits a TV-like set, tuning it to a higher octave or channel, like UHF but much higher than that. I watch something on this "TV," but I don't understand how it works.

My impression of this dream is that I am being given the "key" to a higher channel of myself. I don't yet how to use this channel. Therefore, I am receiving communications in a language I don't fully understand.

Watch for anything that seems to have particular meaning or significance—such as a particular word, place, object, number, color—especially as symbols tend to be repeated frequently. As you become accustomed to this process, you may find yourself recalling portions of the night's dreams during the day. When this happens, write them down.

Here is an excerpt that is an example of a particular word having great significance.

The Dream: I am taken to a place where seminars are being held. A tall man is teaching a group, but I am not part of it. Someone tells me that this is the same place that B. (a psychic healer) studied. I peek around the corner and hear the man say, "Abadie is doing rocks."

I woke up feeling there was significance for me in "rocks," but at the time I could discern no particular relevance. It was a year later that I began working with crystals and healing.

Keeping a Dream Diary

You can record your dreams in your personal psychic journal, or you can keep a separate dream diary. I do both, depending on the circumstances of the moment. The more psychic you become, the more you will dream and be able to remember. In time, you can develop an amazing ability to recall in great detail. Sometimes I get four or five dreams per night or as many as eight or ten, and these often *each* take one or as many as three or four pages of single-spaced typing to record. In the beginning, however, be content with notes you can expand later in your diary.

Always keep a pad of paper and a pen beside your bed, along with a soft light you can reach easily. A penlight is good. The more often you wake in the night, the better chance you have of remembering your dreams. This is because the average REM dream period lasts for an hour and a half. Write down your dreams in as much detail as you remember as soon as you wake. Don't wait until you have become fully conscious, as after a shower and breakfast.

Patricia Garfield suggests not opening your eyes at all, and gives a detailed method of writing with eyes closed in her book *Creative Dreaming*, but I think this is an individual matter. Personally, I have no trouble getting up and going to the word processor and typing out my dreams, but this may be the result of years of dream work. At first, it is no doubt best to write while remaining in bed.

Attitude is everything. Valuing your dream product is the first step to remembering it. Always title your dream and date it. This is important. Giving a title to a dream makes it special. Here is a dream I titled *Dream of the Blue Light:*

The Dream: I am with a small group of people and suddenly I feel this force. Astounded, I say, "The energy is here," and I see a blue light—like very intense DayGlo™ neon—in the shape of a right angle. It is in me and not coming from the outside. I know I am being used as a medium by this force, and I say to the group, "Ask me questions!" They do, and I give answers.

Though I remembered only this fragment, it was a powerful sensation. I felt that "the energy" was a real force which had contacted me in the dream state was using me as a channel for its expression.

Use the keys to psychic awareness in your dream work. *First,* pay attention; *second,* accept what you produce; *third,* concentrate on the subject about which you want dream help; *fourth,* use your imagination to interpret the symbols; *fifth,* expect positive results and experiences; *sixth,* be curious about your dream world and eager to explore its vast reaches; *seventh,* have a definite purpose when you want a dream to serve a specific purpose, whether it is the solution to a problem, creative input, or just a wonderful experience; *eighth,* be filled with gratitude that you have this wonderful nightly opportunity to explore your inner world, which, like an Aladdin's cave, is filled with treasure.

Be a Dream Explorer

16

The Other Side: Guides, Teachers, and Angels

> *Hermes is constantly under way...and one*
> *encounters him on every path.*
> —KARL KERÉNYI,
> *Hermes: Guide of Souls*

Guides and teachers come in many forms and contact with them is equally varied. Angels appear both as personages and as events, such as the "miraculous" saving of a life. It is asserted in esoteric tradition that we have certain guides with us from birth until death, and many people believe we also have a guardian angel assigned to keep watch over us at all times. In my experience guides and teachers can come and go, changing according to our needs and level of progress.

The mysterious figure of Hermes, the Greek god who was the guide of souls and messenger of the gods, is the perfect paradigm for the guides and teachers we encounter on "the other side" during our journeys into the mysterious unconscious realm of our selves.

Hermes, whom the Romans renamed Mercury, is first known to us through the Greek epics of Homer, the *Iliad* and the *Odyssey*. He is most powerful, the mediator between the worlds of being and nonbeing, of reality and unreality, of conscious and unconscious. He is also known as the Lord of the Roads, and he accompanies humans on their journeys, especially to the places in between waking consciousness and the realm of the non-conscious.

According to classical scholar Walter F. Otto, the world of Hermes/Mercury is a complete one, "…a world in the full sense which Hermes animates and rules, a complete world, and not some fragment of the sum total of existence."

Here is how this magical, mystical, mysterious figure injected himself into my life.

For some time I had been thinking about a book on the mental processes, but it hadn't quite jelled. I needed a concept on which to premise the book. In addition, I was attempting to decide among a number of projects on which to concentrate my energies, and I was in quite a quandary.

The first hint that I had somehow entered another sort of reality came on a trip I made to upstate New York to visit a crystal collector, accompanied by my friend and fellow astrologer Mary Orser. I had already made two trips to the collector, an elderly man who was selling off a huge collection he had gathered over a lifetime, and we had become friends. Though he was most protective of his treasures, he allowed me to prowl at will through his back room where he kept crystals not on display in the main room, many of them his personal treasures. Usually, however, he allowed me to buy what I found out there, and I had found some wonderful specimens. This day, I was going through an upright filing cabinet originally made for library cards, which was neatly labeled from A to Z. Each drawer contained crystals beginning with the letter marked on the front panel. I already had spent about an hour thus engaged when I opened the drawer marked M. There were a dozen or so crystals inside—and something else. It was a small, dark, opaque vial and when I lifted it out of the drawer I realized it was extremely heavy for such a small object. Holding it up in my hand, I called out to Dr. F., "What's this?" He looked over at me from where he was conversing with Mary and replied, "Mercury."

What was a vial of mercury doing in a chest full of crystal specimens? There was nothing else but crystals in all the other drawers. I felt a jolt of recognition, as if the god himself had actually spoken to me. Being an astrologer, I knew that Mercury, the planet, is representative of our mental processes. However, I put the odd incident out of my mind, I concentrated on what I was there for: to buy crystals.

Elated over our crystal purchases, we drove back to Mary's house in Woodstock, where I was to spend the night. There the subject of Mercury came up once again. Another guest commented that Mary and I seemed to "finish each other's sentences," and Mary laughingly said it was because of our conjunct Mercuries in 26 degrees of Sagittarius, the astronomical center of the galaxy. As we had often discussed this conjunction between our charts, which gives us extraordinary mental rapport, I didn't consciously connect the conversation with the vial of Mercury in Dr. F.'s crystal drawer.

The next clue came the first night upon my return home from the trip. I had a dream in which an attractive young man was romancing me, boldly enticing me into his bed. The overture was extremely vivid and lifelike, and I obligingly crawled into bed with him, frankly amused at how quickly things were moving. But before any action could take place, I stopped him with a question.

"I'm an astrologer," I said laughingly to my dream-man, "and I'd like to know your birth date."

"Mercury," he replied.

As Mercury rules the sign of Gemini, I said, "Oh, you're a Gemini!" He was pretty typical of the breed, tall and slender, talkative, charming.

"No," he said, gazing deep into my eyes. "I'm *Mercury.*"

At this point I woke up realizing that Mercury was clearly presenting himself to me in a manner I couldn't refuse. The rogue was seducing me! After that, it was like falling down the rabbit hole! Amazing things began to happen. Books I needed came to my hands unbidden, or I would be reading and suddenly a thought would occur to me to look something up in another book on my shelf. I found myself deeply immersed in Jung's alchemical researches, which I hadn't reread in years. And much of what was merely arcane material suddenly began to make a lot of sense. For days I was so absorbed in my own process that I was hardly aware of it—and then realized that what I was doing was just that: *processing.*

Suddenly everything clicked into place. That insight told me the book I was to concentrate on was the one about the mental processes and Mercury's role in them. And then, just when I thought I was home free, he threw me a curve ball: I hit a block and couldn't do *anything!* I just couldn't figure it out. Mercury is also known as the Trickster God. Had he been leading me astray?

Then a fellow astrologer called and happened to mention an astrological technique known as midpoints. Talking with her, I realized that I had a Mercury-Pluto midpoint in operation at the moment. It seemed Mercury wanted to hook up with Pluto through me. As I pondered the meaning of Pluto, the answer came: *power.* I then thought about the mental processes and power and almost instantly came the phrase, *power thinking.* I had been given the perfect concept!

The realm of the gods is within us—it is a world–view we can make use of by getting in touch with our own unfolding intuitive powers and the guides and teachers that visit and help us through them.

"Life is individual: it actualizes itself according to the inherent laws which govern the particular [individual] in question," Kerényi notes in *Hermes,* and he goes on to say:

> The journeyer is at home while under way, at home on the road itself, the road being understood not as a connection between two definite points on the earth's surface, but as a particular world. It is the ancient world of the path, also of the "wet paths"…of the sea, which are above all the genuine roads of the earth. For, unlike the Roman highways which cut unmercifully straight through the countryside, they run snakelike, shaped like irrationally waved lines, conforming to the contours of the land, winding, yet leading everywhere. Being open to everywhere is part of their nature. Nevertheless, they form a world in its own right, a middle-domain, where a person in that volatized condition has access to everything. He who moves about familiarly in this world-of-the-road has Hermes for his god…he is also called *angelos*…the messenger of the Gods.

The deeper expression of Mercury's role as messenger of the gods is that he mediates, or delivers messages between the conscious mind and the unconscious realm, or altered states of consciousness. This is a more subtle meaning than is usually encountered, but it is one of the most important factors in understanding how your guides and teachers operate.

In answer to the question, "What appeared to the Greeks as Hermes?" Kerényi states,

> ...he is the supra-individual source of a particular world-experience and world configuration. Certainly there is also an experience of the world that rests on the basic assumption that a man stands in the world alone, endowed only with a consciousness that is exclusively restricted to the ability of receiving scientifically evaluated sense impressions. No such assumption exists, however, when it comes to that other experience of the world which the antique statements correlate with Hermes. The experience of the world in this manner is open to the possibility of a transcendent guide and leader who is also able to provide impressions of consciousness, but of a different kind: impressions that are palpable and manifest, that in no way contradict the observations and conclusions of natural science, and yet extend beyond the attitude described above, which is the common one today.
>
> This Hermetic aspect is thoroughly empirical, and it remains within the realm of a natural experience of the world. The sum total of pathways as Hermes' playground; the accidental "falling into your lap" as the Hermetic material; its transformation through finding...the Hermetic event...into an Hermetic work of art, which is also always something of a tricky optical illusion, into wealth, love, poetry, and every sort of evasion from the restrictions and confinement imposed by laws, circumstances, destinies— how could these be *merely* psychic realities? They are the world and they are *one* world, namely, *that* world which Hermes opens to us.

Kerényi speaks also of the "activity of Hermes" as referring to "alternatives of life, to the dissolution of fatal opposites, to clandestine violations of boundaries and laws." In other words, the overturning of the rational-mind-dictated world and the discovery of the magical powers of the inner world.

About fifteen years ago, I encountered a group of guides. They first appeared to me in an exceptionally vivid dream, which I titled The Dream of Green Fire:

The Dream: I am in a large house in a wooded area with a young woman friend and I hear my name being called. Outside, it is dark and stormy, snowing heavily, and very cold. I cannot imagine who would be calling my name or how I could hear it over the blast of the storm, but I know I must go and find out if someone in trouble needs my help.

Bundling up, I forge out into the storm, following the sound of a voice calling my name. Soon I come to a clearing in the woods, surrounded by a ring of green fire. Inside the ring of green fire there is no storm. It is quiet, placid, peaceful, and warm. Nine men robed and hooded like monks, in long woolen olive-brown gowns, tied at the waist with knotted golden ropes, are sitting in a circle inside the ring of green fire, and in the center of the circle formed by their bodies there is small green bonfire. They seem to glow with the same soft light.

By gesture, they invite me into the circle. I step out of the raging storm into the this center of absolute calm and safety and I can see their faces beneath the hoods. All are very old and appear to be very wise, with deep, dark eyes. I feel a sense of protection coming from them.

Then I see that one of them is holding my cat Fuzz, cradling him in his arms. I realize that the voice I heard calling me was that of Fuzz, who was lost in the terrible storm and needed rescuing. They give him to me like a gift, telling me that he is all right. I feel a sense of complete and utter peace and safety.

When I woke, I pondered the symbolism—and the answer came immediately: Fuzz was my heart. They had told me something very important, that my *heart*—most fearfully broken more than once—was safe and whole. And though I feared it beyond rescue, they had returned it to me intact and healed.

The nine men appeared to me several different times over the next several years, during the most active time of my psychic development. Always, they were accompanied by ice and snow, to which they were immune and within which they created a warm center. Symbolically, snow has to do with the powers of imagination (water) and of manifestation (crystallization).

Astrologically speaking, this corresponds to the planet Neptune (the sea), which rules imagination and the psychic realm, and the planet Saturn (the earth plane), which rules manifestation in the material world. I concluded that somehow I was to bring my many years of internal psychic experience into external reality. But I didn't have any idea how this was to come about at the time. Then, in 1988 during a year I spent in Arizona, I had this dream, which I called *Dream of the Magic Book:*

The Dream: I am summoned at night to a mountain top covered with snow. The road itself is clear, but I am afraid to leave the car and go upward into the snowy dark woods. I hang back, reluctant to take the risk, until I hear the plaintive meow of a cat. Recognizing the unmistakable sound of my cat Fuzz, and thinking him lost, I plunge ahead, now without fear or anxiety. Again, I encounter the nine old men inside the ring of green fire. This time they give me a large book made of parchment sheaves, ancient and yellowed but not fragile. The pages are covered with a mysterious writing I cannot decipher, but I understand that this book holds important esoteric knowledge and that the nine men are great magicians from the timeless world.

I interpreted this to be a message saying that when I follow my heart—the meow of Fuzz—I am able to go forward into unknown, and possibly dangerous, situations without fear or trepidation, and by so doing I receive the reward of greater knowledge.

This was the last time I saw the Council of Nine, as I came to call them. There is no doubt in my mind that these "men" guided me through a crucial period of my life, and I remain grateful to them.

When I read Betty Eadie's book *Embraced by the Light,* I was astonished to find that one chapter was entitled "The Council of Men." In her vision (if that is what it was), she met twelve men seated around a kidney-shaped table who radiated "absolute love" to her. She also learned from this council of men many fascinating things about herself and her life. In addition, she describes three men who meet her at the beginning of her near-death experience. The description she gives is eerily like that of my own Council of Nine:

They wore beautiful, light brown robes…a hood on the back.…Each wore a gold-braided belt that was tied about the waist with the ends hanging down. A kind of glow emanated from them, but not unusually bright. [They] appeared to be about seventy or eighty years old, but I knew somehow that they were on a time scale different than the earth's. The impression came to me that they were much older than seventy or eighty years old—that they were ancient. I sensed in them great spirituality, knowledge, and wisdom.…I began to think of them as monks—mostly because of the robes—and I knew I could trust them.

I am not suggesting that Betty Eadie's council and mine are the same group of guides. What I do think, however, is that we are all capable of experiencing contact with our own deeper dimensions symbolically. It is through the use of symbols that we can connect with what cannot be seen, heard, touched, tasted, or smelled. Whatever symbolic form your guides and teachers will take will depend on what forms are palatable to you, to which forms you are most open and able to respond. In my case, these often have to do with art and books. For example, during a sabbatical year in Arizona, I had many interesting and exciting psychic experiences, including this *Dream of Initiation:*

The Dream: I am taken to a large private library of the type one might find in an English country estate. I am told that I am here for an initiation. I lie down on a Persian rug on the floor on my back, and I am injected through the Third Eye (sixth chakra) with a long needle. Next, another injection is made into my throat (fifth chakra). I am afraid it will hurt, but it does not. These two injections are all that there is to the initiation process. Afterward, I fall asleep (in the dream), and later on I wake up and go through exactly the same procedure a second time.

Again I sleep, and when I wake I am shown a painting-in-process; it is in the first stage, a charcoal sketch. My sense is that the painter is one of the French Impressionists, whose work I admire. Someone says, "Use the green filter," and instantly the painting changes dramatically and I am able to see color where there was before only shades of gray.

This process continues and I realize that I am seeing the painting *as it develops in the artist's mind.* I am able to see straight into the mind of the artist as he works and see each step of the painting as it forms and comes into being in his mind *before it is put on the canvas.* This seems to me quite remarkable, and I wonder what substances were injected into my forehead and throat.

Then, I suddenly remember that I know all about this initiation, that I read about it in a comprehensive article by the writer Lawrence Durrell, a writer I admire greatly who has, in real life, written about esoteric matters.

This dream coincided with a major turning point in my life, which involved a deepened understanding of the inner mental and creative processes, and of the extent to which thought and imagination affect how we live our everyday lives. A New Age tenet had been, *Thoughts are things,* but it was through this dream experience that I understood fully that this is literally true. I noted in my diary that,

> It [the dream] somehow seems to answer a question
> that I have been vainly seeking an answer to for a long
> time. It is the first time 'initiation' has been clearly stated.

The term *initiation* refers to being inducted into the mysteries, of being given understanding of the higher order of things. The initiate is one who now *knows internally* what cannot be communicated by mere words but what must take place at a deep inner level that connects the individual to the universal. The closest word we have for this is *telepathy.*

Another dream occurred during this time period in which I met a teacher is titled, *Dream of the Great Library.*

The Dream: I am at the house of a man who goes by the nickname "Winnie" (which may be a pun on the word win). He tells me that if I will forego getting my Ph.D., he will teach me everything in his library. He shows me a magnificent library full of ancient texts on papyrus, handwritten tomes, illuminated manuscripts, medieval books on herbalist lore, esoteric teachings of all kinds and from all ages. The books seem to glow with magical power. I ask him, "What will I accomplish if I learn all this?" and he replies, "Nothing."

The message is that I must relinquish my conventional thinking—that is, getting a Ph.D.—and take in its place this powerful ancient tradition, which is far superior. But learning this will not "accomplish" anything in the usual sense, as that is not the purpose of esoteric learning.

Later, just before leaving Arizona while in a deep meditative state I was "given" this diagrammatic concept.

PURE ENERGY
[The Universal Source—God or Consciousness]
Becomes/is transformed into

THOUGHT
[Mind Stuff without Form]
Which inherently contains

STRUCTURE
[Corresponding to Matter]*
To activate physical manifestation
DESIRE
[To Manifest]
Uses thought structure to mold

SUBSTANCE
[Prana]
Which then becomes manifest in

MATTER
[Physical Reality]

This experience signaled the start of my writing about astrology and psychic matters, and led to my first astrology book, *Love Planets*.

The teachings that we receive from the "other side" may not be remembered after the particular altered state of consciousness in which we experience them is gone. There was a lot you learned at school that you "forgot," but that somehow sunk in as part of an overall pattern of learning a subject.

Some people, however, are able to regularly receive lessons while in an altered or dream state, and remember everything

---

*Structure refers to the *archetypal patterns* already existent in Universal Mind prior to becoming manifest. For example, there is a crystalline structure in *unformed thought* that corresponds exactly to the physical structure of a crystal.

and record it. Viola Petitt Neal, who wrote *Through the Curtain*, reports how she attended "night classes," which she dictated to Ms. Shafica Karagulla while in the altered state. In this book, the authors speak of the "Council of Seven." So it would seem that the symbol of a council is a common one.

It's even possible for one person to receive guidance from another person's guide. I had such an experience when I first began to practice astrology professionally. My friend, Josephine Corado, a blind psychic, had invited me to spend the weekend at her home on Long Island and had arranged for me to read the charts of several of her clients. I arrived on a Friday afternoon carrying some astrology books. At that time, I was accustomed to spending three or four hours of preparation time on a chart, and although I had prepared most of the charts I was to read over the weekend, one remained undone.

That evening as we sat chatting in Jo's living room—she in the recliner from which she did her readings, me on the couch—she suddenly burst out laughing.

"What's funny?" I asked in puzzlement.

"Akenaton," she replied. "He's standing right in front of you."

I knew Akenaton was what she called her guide, but there was nothing in front of me but the coffee table.

"Where?" I asked, looking around.

"Right *there*," she pointed a finger to the spot where my tummy was.

"What does he want?" I asked.

"I haven't any idea," was her unhelpful reply.

Shortly after this conversation, she announced that she was going to bed early. I reminded her that I had a chart to prepare the next morning for a reading at noon and she promised to get me up by nine. It was about ten P.M., and I'm a late-night person, so I was at loose ends to occupy myself. Since Jo was blind, there were no books and no TV. We'd had wine with dinner, and I wasn't in the mood to study astrology, the only books I had, so I lay on the couch to meditate.

As I lay there, wide awake but very relaxed, a curious thing happened. My entire body began to vibrate as if someone had plugged me into an electric socket. It was very intense, though not actually uncomfortable. The source of the sensation seemed to be the center of my forehead. I didn't understand at all what was happening to me, but as I was in what I knew to be a psychically saturated atmosphere, I made no effort to get up. The room was not dark; there was a streetlight just outside the uncurtained window. I looked about myself, but saw nothing out of the ordinary.

The sensation finally stopped—*three hours later.* As unexpectedly and inexplicably as it started, it stopped. I felt none the worse for the experience, and I got up and went to bed. In the morning, Jo woke me as promised and I sat at her dining room table to prepare the chart for my noon reading. I worked away, consulting my books only occasionally, and when I had finished, I asked Jo, who had a talking watch, for the time. "It's nine forty-five," she told me.

I knew that could not be right, for I had finished with three hours' worth of work and I had started at nine. "That's impossible," I said. "Please check your watch again." She came over to me and I heard the little voice say, "Nine forty-six." How could that be? I had not felt any sense of time speeded up, had worked at my usual slow and thorough pace, checking everything twice. To make sure, I telephoned the time service. Then I remembered the previous evening's strange experience and Jo's telling me her guide had been standing in front of me. Could there be a connection?

It became evident to me that I had far more astrological knowledge and understanding than I deserved, based upon the length of time I had been studying the subject. I understood that I had received a powerful teaching that night. And, ever afterward it has taken me only a short time to prepare an astrological chart. Since that time, my readings have risen to a level of comprehension that amazes me, for I know that I didn't earn the knowledge I have—it was given to me.

Guides and teachers are a very personal experience. There is no way any of us can pass on information about them except by relating our own experiences. Here is one more of mine, perhaps the most dramatic of all.

In 1986 I had reached a point in my practice of psychotherapy where I was working intensively with clients rather than doing the usual fifty-minute hour once a week. Several of my clients responded especially well to this intensive method of working several hours a day for one or more days in a row. I decided to rent a house in the country to facilitate this way of working. The client could live on the premises and we could work with her dreams in the mornings when they were fresh. Also, it gave me space to hold seminars in a quiet surrounding.

I took possession of the house over the Labor Day weekend, a friend having come along to help with the transport of gear. He stayed a couple of days and then I was left alone in the house for the first time around midnight on Sunday. I was sitting on the porch having a stargaze when I distinctly heard the crunch of underbrush. The house was in a copse of pine trees and cut off on all sides by bushy growth. Who could be out walking in the woods at this time of night? Suddenly, I *knew*.

A dark figure appeared out of the woods about ten yards from where I was sitting. I could "see" him clearly. A native American, about forty years old, tall, lean, muscular, who wore unadorned buckskins the color of blueberries. His dusky-looking skin had a bluish undertone. He wore no headdress and his long straight hair was blue-black, like ink. He simply stood there and stared at me. I thought, "If I stay out here one more minute, he is going to walk up to me and speak and I can't handle that." Getting up, I went into the darkened house and turned on all the lights. Recently I read that blue is the color of wisdom, but at the time I was unaware of this.

The next week at the house, a young woman arrived for an intensive session of several days. A sensitive person who had suffered abuse as a child, she was a "natural" psychic. She had come to me for help in kicking a drug habit.

During the first afternoon, I was taking her through a guided meditation when to my consternation I saw her slip away into trance. When she returned, I asked her what had happened and she reported matter-of-factly that she had been "with the Indians." She described the same man I had seen coming out of the woods exactly as I had perceived him. I did not know what to make of this. Upon further probing, I elicited from her that the man had given her some herbal concoction and that the entire tribe had said prayers over her.

The following afternoon, she was outside having a cigarette and I was preparing lunch. Suddenly she burst into the kitchen and said excitedly, "He's out there!" To my question of "Who?"—although I knew the answer—she replied, "That Indian I saw last night." It seemed we were very close to something powerful and mysterious.

During the week she spent with me we both experienced his presence daily. She was "taken" several times for healing treatments, given herbal drinks, and met the women of the tribe, who treated her as a daughter. I have no explanation for these occurrences—I only am a witness to their happening. When she left, she told me she felt strong and whole for the first time in her life and that she would never use drugs again.

Later that fall, during a weekend mask-making seminar I was conducting, the Woodstock shaman, as I came to call him, once again manifested. One participant, Jean Ready, a gifted medium who required a cane, was seated at the end of the big work table. She asked me to pass her the vial of blue glitter for her mask work. I reached out for it and as I did something told me to put the lid on first, or it would get spilled and make a mess. But she was impatient and I couldn't locate the top, so I handed the vial to her open. As predicted, she dropped it and it spilled all over the black rug under her chair. She wanted to help clean it up, but I told her to stay put, that I'd vacuum later.

After the seminar, when I lifted Jean's chair, to our amazement, we saw that the spilled blue glitter had, in clear outline against the black rug, created the face of the Woodstock shaman. Bits of different colored glitter had fallen in such a way as to furnish the details of the portrait. Oddly, Jean had brought not only a camera but had gone out of her way to purchase film on a Sunday because she had a strong feeling she was going to want to take a picture of something. Thus, we were able to photograph the manifestation for posterity.

On New Year's Eve, a friend came to spend the holiday with me, but she caught a terrible cold and had to go to bed. It was extremely cold and the guest room heater was not working properly, so I tucked her into my bed early and she went off to sleep. After welcoming the New Year alone in utter and peaceful silence, I joined her. She woke up saying she had to go to the bathroom, which was across the large studio that formed the main part of the house. Scooting out into the now cooling room, she returned a few minutes later, hugging herself. As she jumped back into the warm bed, she said,

"Who are all those Indians out there? That big guy—he's really good-looking!"

Before I could respond to this extraordinary remark, she was asleep again. The next day I asked her if she remembered what she saw, and she described a "bunch of Indians" sitting in a ring in the studio, silent and motionless. The "big guy" was the Woodstock shaman as I had first seen him and as my client had described him.

During the months that I lived and worked in that house, I experienced the shaman many times and others also felt his presence. Always, my experiences were at night. Once I woke from sleep as if a hand had touched me, and I was instantly alert in the thick dark of a winter's night. I felt all my senses were sharpened and into my mind came the following passage, which I wrote down verbatim immediately afterward:

> *Magic is constructed on the mental plane. [Learn to] create such structures on the mental plane in order to work magic power. Magic is SYSTEM. Not hocus-pocus. ORDER. Not mental (intellectual) order as in logic or an orderly thought process but on the mental plane. Not in the mind but OF MIND. Understand difference between MIND and mental or thinking.*

I understood MIND (called manas by the ancient Egyptians) to mean Universal Intelligence. This teaching is supported by the one, shown on p.244 as a diagrammatical concept, which I experienced at a later date.

The shaman told me the story of his life and work, which I found fascinating. How did he "tell" me? Obviously not in ordinary conversation—I suppose it was a kind of telepathy where the thoughts simply arrived in my mind. As I could not have originated these thoughts, I can only conclude that they came from another source. This is what he told me:

He was an advanced practitioner for his time, interested in "spiritual technology," or the art of bringing forth into manifestation what could be created in the mind. One might say he was a Native American alchemist. His tribe was somewhat suspicious of his research, even though he was an official "medicine man," or doctor. Like people everywhere, I suppose, they were leery of new ideas that were contrary to the prevailing religion or cultural norm.

Because of this suspicion, he conducted his work in secret, going to an old burial ground (which I later discovered was the site on which my house sat). One of his interests was to contact directly nature spirits—what I have called "elementals." As a shaman, he knew how to put himself into a trance, knew how to use psychotropic plants (like psychedelic mushrooms or peyote) as an adjunct to out-of-body travels into other dimensions of reality. As a Native American shaman, he would have believed that he could absorb animal and vegetal powers into himself, and as a shaman he would have had training for this. But he wanted to know more, to experience more, and so he took risks. With each success, his confidence grew, and he became careless, taking greater risks than were prudent. As he always worked alone, there was no one to back him up, hold on to him, so to speak. Finally, one night when he felt he was on the verge of his great discovery, he went too far out of his body and was unable to return. He died. Now, his spirit had been activated and he wanted someone to carry on his work. He said he would groom me for this task. I was flattered, eager to learn, but circumstances intervened and I was forced to give up the house a few months later.

On my last night in the house, feeling sad about having to go, I was packed and ready to leave the empty-feeling house when my friend who was driving me back to the city telephoned to say he would be a couple of hours late. There was nothing to do, nothing to read. I lay down on the bed to meditate and pass the time and I must have dozed off. I saw bright light, like that of the full moon, and I roused to go and look at the moon shining on the snow, a scene I love. But when I got up I discovered the moon wasn't full or even visible. The room was in darkness. I lay back down, puzzled. Then, I felt the shaman's presence. He touched me gently, told me he was going to give me a healing treatment. For more than an hour, I felt a gentle pulsing going through my body, felt it connecting to parts of myself that had been outside of my awareness for a long time. My legs, which had been damaged by polio, felt alive for the first time I could remember. I felt myself open like a flower under the beneficence of this healing vibration. It was a parting gift.

You might wonder why the Woodstock shaman didn't come along with me to the city, since time and space are of no importance in the psychic world. I don't know the answer to that, but it has been my experience that there are locational factors— that particular experiences are common to certain spots, just as UFO sightings seem to cluster around certain areas. It could also be that there are psychic energy fields. And, just as the right tone sounded by a singer can shatter a crystal glass, it may also be a matter of resonance, of vibrating in tune.

It is not necessary to perceive an actual *figure* as a guide, though this seems to me the most usual form in which guides appear to us. However, one can simply sense or feel guidance, or the presence of a guide. In my own life, I have known many guides of different qualities. During one period, when I was intensively studying the Tarot cards, I received information and guidance from guides who manifested to me as sounds. I identified three of these "energies," one of which was a thin, high-pitched tone, barely audible. The second tone was lower, but still in the high range, and seemed to cover a slightly wider band of the sound spectrum. The third sound was much lower, almost a bass, and broader. Each of these sounds conveyed information differently. For example, when I heard the highest tone, I knew it was time to sit quietly and meditate, that a "message" was coming in through this energy vibration. These sounds occurred at all times of the day and night, but always when I was wide awake. You may receive guidance and teaching in any of a number of different guises.

Here is a meditation you can do to get in contact with a guide/teacher. Remember that you can do this anytime you feel the need. You may meet a guide who will stay with you for a long or a short time. You may meet many guides. There is no right or wrong way to contact a guide. Some appear spontaneously, without your asking, like the Woodstock shaman. Others respond to your call.

Meeting Your Guide

You are going to meet a teacher/guide whom you trust and rely on; there is great love and respect between you. To prepare yourself do the following:

1. Articulate a question that you wish to ask your teacher. This question should be stated as succinctly as possible. The clearer the question, the clearer the answer. Write your question on a piece of paper.

2. Do not ask questions requiring a simple yes or no answer. The purpose of the exercise is to give you an opportunity to

communicate with a teacher/guide and to get to know this energy, to become familiar with how your own deep level of knowledge and awareness operates.

3. Refrain from asking a question about some large and complex issue in your life covering a broad generality, such as "When is my life going to get better?" Be as specific as you can. For example, if you are considering a job change, you might ask, "What are the advantages/disadvantages of making a job change at this time?" Avoid emotionally loaded questions. Don't ask, "Does So-and-So really love me?" Instead, ask, "What is the truth of my relationship to So-and-So at this time?"

4. Do not ask a question requiring a prediction, such as "When will I find the right man and get married?" When you ask such questions, you put pressure on your intuition to come up with the "right" answer—the one you want, not the true one. Ask instead along these lines, "What will concentrating on getting married accomplish for me at this time?" The aim is to keep the process as simple as possible in order to tune in to a clear channel. Asking for the truth about any issue is always a good question.

5. Do not ask a trivial or silly question. By doing so, you dishonor your deeper self. Ask a question that is of some importance to you, to which you honestly want an answer. An example of this is, "How do I serve my best interests in the matter of _____ ?" Also, do not ask a question to which you already know the answer. Do not try to test your inner Self nor demand "proof."

6. Tell yourself that you can trust your teacher/guide and open yourself to receiving the answer to your question. Take whatever answer comes, even if at first it seems not to make sense or be relevant. Your deeper Self is talking to you. If you draw a complete blank, be patient and try the exercise until you get an answer.

7. When you do meet your guide, pay attention to the form in which he or she appears. Some people will "see" a human

figure, some a light or other appearance. Do not have pre-conceived notions of what a guide is or looks like.

8. Be prepared to write down the experience in your personal psychic journal.

After you have completed the above steps, do the following meditation. It helps to have someone do it with you, but you can do it alone as well by memorizing the steps before beginning your relaxation.

Meditation for Contacting Your Teacher

Get comfortable in a position you can hold for about twenty minutes. Breathe in and out deeply several times until you feel yourself totally relaxed. If you like, play some soft, soothing music to aid the relaxation process.

Now, find a setting somewhere in nature—a forest, the seashore, a flower-filled meadow, a lakeside, or whatever suits your personality. Once you are in this place, look around you and notice all the details—sights, sounds, colors, smells, flora and fauna.

As you relax yourself completely, enjoying your perfect surroundings, you are going to talk a walk and during that stroll you are going to find the place where you can meet your teacher/guide. It can be any place you choose. Some people like to envision a schoolhouse, perhaps a one-room little red schoolhouse. Others might find a grander site, like a Greek temple. Still others might want a familiar place, even a place where they actually attended school.

In these guided meditations, the specifics are not important; there are no right or wrong situations. Whatever springs into your mind is the right place, because you are using a process to contact your own deep inner self. Your guides and teachers are within the realm of the non-conscious part of your being, which is connected to all reality everywhere and at all times and places. Some people call this the "superconscious." Use whatever term appeals to you; terminology is irrelevant; the experience counts.

When you locate the place where you will meet your teacher, pause a moment to notice the details. The more details you notice, the more complete the experience. Do not rush yourself. After noticing the details of the building, walk slowly and confidently to the door and enter the place. Once inside, notice the details and pay attention to how you feel. If you have any negative feelings, acknowledge them and put them aside for the moment. Nothing can hurt or harm you here. Know that your teacher/guide loves and respects you and wants only your good.

Take a comfortable position inside the school room and if you do not immediately see your guide, wait until he or she arrives. Again, you may not see a human figure. You may see a white light, a cloud, a puff of blue smoke, or hear a sound or tone.

Accept whatever occurs to you as the representation of your guide. When you see your guide, image a beam of light passing between you, from the center of the forehead. You are connected by this beam, which transmits information.

Ask your question and wait patiently for the answer, which may come immediately or take a while. Don't analyze the answer, just accept it verbatim.

If you do not get an answer, or if the answer seems to make no sense, accept that also. Remember that you are practicing, learning a new skill.

Ask your guide for a sign by which you can recognize him or her in the future. Express your gratitude for the communication.

When you have completed these steps, take a few deep breaths and bring yourself back to normal waking consciousness. You may want to yawn or stretch.

Then immediately write down what you experienced and how you felt about it. Describe your guide to yourself in as much detail as you can. Write down the answer to your question, even if it seems nonsensical. The non-conscious speaks in symbols and metaphors. Record any significant sensations you experienced, such as the smell of perfume, or a colored light. Your teacher/guide may have offered you a gift. Remember something specific about your teacher/guide as a sign of future recognition.

After you have written down your inner experience, ask yourself these questions:

1. Did I enjoy going to meet my teacher/guide or was I anxious, nervous, or apprehensive?
2. Did I get the answer I expected or something entirely different?
3. Did the answer make sense to me?
4. Was I comfortable with the entire experience?
5. Did I feel a rapport with my teacher/guide?

As you continue to use this process, your experience of guides and teachers will both change and expand. It is an exciting experience, one you will want to repeat often. Once you have created and are familiar with your "schoolroom," it will take you only a few minutes to reach the deep level of inner guidance.

Angelic Encounters

When I was a child, I held conversations with angels on a regular basis, finding the experience neither odd nor disturbing. Angels were my friends. In examining this from a psychological perspective, it is tempting to conclude that, as a motherless and lonely child growing up in a Catholic convent, I was merely imagining converse with celestial beings, that talking with angels was a childish projection resulting from being immersed in a religion-soaked atmosphere. Not so. The nuns did not encourage such independent spiritual activity, and I became quite secretive about my angels. According to my much older brother, I was "extremely reluctant" to disclose what they said to me.

Although today I have no exact memories of these early conversations with angels, angels have kept me company in one form or another for most of my life. Interestingly, today the subject of angels is a popular topic. In pondering this fact, I can only surmise that the angels have decided to come out of the closet, as it were. My feeling is that they are doing so in response to many heartfelt prayers, not always directed to the conventional "God" of the Christian church, who has failed so many.

What are angels? No one knows for sure, but I believe that they are celestial intelligences—some say beings of pure light—

who vibrate at a very high rate, which makes them invisible to us. However, unlike ourselves they have the ability to change their vibrations at will and assume different forms. When they lower their vibrations to the approximate rate of humans, they become visible. Also, they can assume form and appear as other people or even as thoughts and experiences. My own first clear memory of angelic interfacing with my life came at the age of nineteen, when I was in college.

At the time I was sharing a house with two other girls. One fall afternoon when I was alone I lay down on the living room rug in front of the piano for no particular reason. I was not accustomed to lying on the floor, and I wasn't sleepy. What happened is what I would now describe as an out-of-body experience. First, I heard music and thought the piano was playing itself, which my logical mind knew was impossible. Next, I had the sensation of being lifted up—up, up, and away I flew out into the stratosphere, carried by an angel who held me upside down by the feet. I knew nothing of symbolism then, but the feet are related to Pisces, which is ruled by Neptune, which in turn rules the psychic realm.

The angel told me that I was about to see my future. We soared on until we reached outer space. I could see all the stars and planets, and—believe it or not—I saw Earth exactly as it was later photographed by the astronauts. I distinctly remember the shock of recognition when years later I first saw the actual pictures of our planet photographed from space. *I had already seen it.* This experience would be called déjà vu, or a sense that one has been somewhere one could not logically have been before.

On three separate occasions, angels have saved my life, twice through the agency of other human beings.

The first time, also at age nineteen, was an attempted suicide. My despair was deep, but I did not communicate my bleak feelings to anyone. That night I had been out with two friends, a man and a woman, who accompanied me to my apartment. The hour was late and as they were leaving he offered to escort her to her home, a forty-five minute drive across town, by following her car with his. After I had seen them off, my mood descended into utter blackness. I turned on the gas jets and prepared to die. The next thing I knew, I was in the front yard and the man was bending over me, forcing air into my lungs. He had returned to encounter the telltale smell of gas and had pulled me unconscious out of my apartment into the air where he administered timely resuscitation.

He later told me that he and my girlfriend had decided to stop at a bar near her house for a nightcap, but when the drinks were served he began to feel extremely uncomfortable about me, not knowing why. The logical action would have been to telephone, but a rising sense of urgency sent him outside for some fresh air. Near his car he saw a hovering light and the words came to him, "Get back to M.J. now." Leaving my girl-friend at the bar, he speeded back and rescued me.

The second time occurred on my twenty-first birthday. I was living in Houston, and my housemate had arranged a birthday party for me aboard a Holland-America Lines ship, which was docked in the Houston ship channel. I had never been to the dock area, which is complex, and we were met and guided by the shipping line's local manager. The evening was a festive one, replete with Scandinavian cheer in the form of aquavit chased with beer and numerous wines with each of several courses at dinner, which was followed by champagne and cognac. Nancy I were both more than a little tipsy when we left the ship and began the long, unfamiliar drive home along dark and deserted roads.

Our car had an unreliable starter. Usually, when the car stalled it took fifteen or twenty minutes of coaxing to get it started again. This time Nancy drove, and I passed out in the passenger seat. Suddenly I woke—absolutely cold sober—to discover that Nancy was slumped over the wheel of the car, which was straddling a rail-road track on an embankment. Behind and in front were inclines. As I took in the situation, I saw the glaring headlight of an oncom-ing train. I assessed the situation with lightning speed, as if some directing force had taken over my brain. Nancy was a tall girl, heavier than I, and I knew I could not move her body. I also knew there was no time for me to get out of the car, run around it, open the door, and try to shove her aside. I also knew that there was not enough time for me to drag her out of the car to safety. The only possible solution was to get the car started *immediately.*

With the train bearing down, I shoved back the seat, climbed into Nancy's lap, turned the ignition key—*and the car started.* As it rolled down the embankment the speeding train raced by. I could feel the wind in its shuddering wake. At the bottom of the incline, the engine immediately died. As I looked back at what might have been the disaster scene to see a glowing light hovering about the track. Writing this now gives me chills as I remember that predawn reprieve.

Safe at the bottom of the hill, I managed to get the still unconscious Nancy into the passenger seat. It then took another twenty minutes for me to coax the car to restarting. During this time I was my "normal" self with no extraordinary abilities. However, when I finally got us under way—in that bleak, deserted, and utterly unfamiliar industrial dock district—it was as if I became a homing pigeon. I drove unerringly through a maze of unknown territory for more than an hour before I reached familiar ground. Not once did I get lost and have to retrack. Somehow I just *knew* the correct route. As I have always been known for my lack of a sense of direction—friends used to say I could get lost in a phone booth—this finding of the way was remarkable.

The third angelic occurrence was during a sailing excursion when I was twenty-two. I couldn't swim, but I liked being in the water, and the sailboat's owner indulged me by tying a twenty-foot line around my wrist so that I could be pulled through the sea by the boat. On this day I was playing porpoise when the rope slipped off my wrist and I was suddenly untethered in the open ocean. Relieved of my weight drag, the boat shot off toward the horizon and I watched her almost disappear. I remember little else, except that I was extremely happy under the water. I saw visions of light and could communicate with the fish and other marine animals. Everything was beautiful and serene. The next thing I knew I was flat on the deck being given artificial respiration by strong arms. I vomited up a lot of sea water.

The man at the tiller knew immediately that I was no longer tethered to the boat, but under full sail it had traveled a considerable distance before the crew could tack and come around to return. In open ocean, with no markers, how had they managed to find me?

Unusual for our group, that day we had two extra men who were excellent swimmers aboard, one of whom I had never met before. When we returned to the dock, the stranger took me aside. He was older—mid-thirties or so—and he looked at me intently. I can still remember the clear green color of his eyes flecked with little spots of amber. Taking my hand, he said gravely,

"You lead a charmed life. Did you know that?"

I shook my head in the negative. Once again, I had not found the experience to be out of the ordinary. Being close to death had not made much of an impression on me. He continued to look at me oddly, penetratingly.

"I was the one who found you," he said. "And I wasn't supposed to be on this boat today. I only came because my flight was canceled. I'm supposed to be in San Francisco today. I don't even know Harry [the boat owner]. My roommate asked me to take his place because he wasn't feeling well. But I came because of you."

Without understanding this, I accepted it as fact. I never saw the man again, and he never again sailed with Harry. I later learned he was a professional diver.

Although he did not actually say so, I understood uncanny guidance had led him to find me. Considering the time-lag and the open sea, he knew the odds were against it. Clearly, the experience had impressed him deeply.

The question also arises, why didn't I drown? I can only say that while I was under water I felt buoyed up by a force of light. That I did not sink was a major factor in the rescue. Did an angel really hold me up until they got back? You decide.

Aside from lifesaving, angels carry messages. In this respect, they may be related to the function of Mercury. Early in the beginning of my excursion into the psychic realm, I was visited by a soft pink light, very diffuse but compellingly powerful. It filled my entire apartment and produced in me such a holy feeling that I spontaneously fell to my knees beside the bed, as a child in prayer.

This light communicated to me that it had traveled far, from the stars, and it was there to give me approbation for the course I was about to embark on, which included the study of astrology. There is no way for me to describe the sense of peace and happiness I received from this pink glow. I think it might be the way a baby feels when, bathed and powdered, dry and cuddled, it drinks its mother's milk.

Why speak of angels in a book about psychic potential? Simply because they are *there,* and when you begin to have contact with your own deep inner Self you are likely also to come into contact with higher beings and infinite energies.

The more alert and open you are to these extraordinary experiences, the more likely it is you will find them in your life at some time or other.

Expect A Miracle

The Lunar Connection

*Geophysical evidence reveals the power of the stars and the planets in
relation to the terrestrial...astrology is like a life
giving elixir for mankind.*
—ALBERT EINSTEIN

There is a charming Yiddish folktale about the relative
value of the light of the sun and the light of the moon to
earthly life.

Learned rabbis of the Orthodox faith in small villages spend
their time pondering questions of vast and cosmic importance.
Theirs is a theoretical rather than practical approach. In this
revealing story, the rabbis of a Russian village had for many
years daily debated the all-important issue of whether the light
of the sun or the light of the moon benefited humanity more.

Finally, the head rabbi announced that a decision had been
reached. The excited villagers gathered in the square to receive
this long-awaited revelation. A hush of reverential expectation
quieted the clamoring crowd as the chief rabbi, ceremoniously
robed as befitted such a momentous occasion, appeared.

Solemnly, he proclaimed that the light of the moon is of
greater importance to the human race than is the light of the
sun. As the villagers strove to assimilate this news in stunned
silence, a child cried out, "Why?"

Though not accustomed to the impertinence of having his wisdom questioned, the rabbi smiled benignly and replied, "Because, my son, it is dark at night. So we need the light of the moon more."

This tale, though it appears simple-minded, hides an important truth, as do most folktales, legends, and fairy tales. The rabbi's assertion that we need the light of the moon more—because it illumines what is naturally dark, the night—metaphorically refers to the realm of the non-conscious, from whence our psychic powers stem. Though scientifically absurd, the rabbi's conclusion reveals a deep psychological truth about the human psyche, one which, in our busy, almost exclusively sun-oriented (logical, rational) lives, we often are not in touch. Symbolically, the moon serves to illuminate the non-conscious side of human life, and in that diffuse light we can often see more clearly than in the glare of the noonday sun.

The light of the sun enables us to see the world around us—what is *outside ourselves*. But the moon allows us to shine light into our inner, psychic world, to illuminate what springs naturally from *inside ourselves*. In moonlight we perceive the reality of our inner psychic abilities more clearly, we are more aware of the shadings and nuances of feelings and inner perceptions, we tune in more accurately to the vibrations of others, and our psychic Self is more in tune with the information universe.

This is because during the hours of night our subtle senses are more open and receptive to the information flowing along the psychic network. In mythological terms, when the sun sets the god embarks on the "night sea journey" to the secret realm where the moon mysteries are enacted.

The moon has been called the "soul of life." Without it, we would have only the mechanical, an endless solar efficiency, which, in the end, is soul-less. Without the moon we would have no poetry, literature, art, music, dance, or dreams. Artists are notorious for being "dreamy," and it is at night when the moon reigns that we dream.

That other half of life, the one that is unseen in the bright light of day, comes alive in us at night, when the moon sheds her gentle light. Then, doors open to magical realms of the imagination and human creativity. Then, the wonderful world of the psyche is wide open to us.

Try this experiment to prove this to yourself:

Choose an hour of the day—say, from three to four—and sit quietly in a room by yourself with no distractions. See what comes to your mind, how you feel, what you think, where your awareness goes. Afterward, take that same hour in the night and repeat the procedure. Notice the differences. If you let yourself be in tune with the cosmos, you will *feel* the Moon's energies, not only "out there," but in you.

Symbolically speaking, the moon gives birth to herself every month. She goes from new moon (black, invisible) to the full, and then slowly "dies" in the waning period only to be "reborn" again as it reappears as a slender, shining crescent. How thrilling is that first sight of the newly waxing moon!

The moon's cyclical and ever-changing nature is analogous to the great flux and flow of life itself, regular and rhythmical as the ocean tides she rules, and of our inner, psychic lives. Surely, no one has not at some time or other been impressed by the magical power of the moon—perhaps newly risen, full, and still red in the Mediterranean sky, or hanging huge and golden as the Harvest Moon, or silvering the snow of a winter's night. In contrast to the sun's powerful gaze, even the brightest light of the fullest moon only serves to gleam and soften what it touches. That's how the moon works in you as well.

Astrologically speaking, the moon symbolizes all that is receptive in human nature—the unconscious, the emotions, the instincts, the psychic realm. It speaks to us of the deepest, darkest, most interior place where all is gestated before birth, be it a child, a work of art, or a psychic perception. The moon resonates with the psychic. It reveals our inner contours to us.

Unfortunately, for those of us living in cities, the moon is often not visible and her energy loses its power. It can be difficult to get an unrestricted view of the moon, to find an uncluttered patch of sky in which to view her, and contemplation of the moon's luminous glory can be hard to attain. However, that does not mean we cannot access our inner moon's influence on our lives and our psychic ability.

There are two ways to do this:

One is by knowing your natal Moon. This refers to the sign the moon occupied at the moment of your birth. (If you do not already know your natal Moon sign, see the Appendix for how to order a computer astrology chart.) Each Moon sign has specific characteristics, which, like your psychic profile, will help you to understand your psychic Self. Each Moon sign relates to the inner psychic nature differently.

The second way is to keep track of the *transiting* moon. Each month, the Moon passes through all twelve signs of the zodiac, and as she occupies one or another of the signs, her influence varies. In addition, there are *lunations*—new and full moons and eclipses—that bear substantial psychic weight. Also, each month you get a "lunar return," which is when the moon returns to the Zodiacal sign it occupied at your birth.

To do Moon work, you will need a lunar calendar. This is a calendar or a diary showing the phases of the moon, times of rising and setting, and the astrological signs through which she moves.

Your Natal Moon

Moon in ARIES
With your natal Moon in the active sign of Aries, your psychic nature is active and adventurous. You will get the best results by stimulating your psychic Self regularly. Your approach to psychic development is enthusiastic, and you will obtain success by challenging yourself.

Moon in TAURUS
With your natal Moon in the receptive sign of Taurus, your psychic nature is rooted in Earth magic. It is stable and will thrive in a relaxed, sensuous, comfortable atmosphere. Your approach to psychic development is basic and conservative and you want practical results.

Moon in GEMINI
With your natal Moon in the communicative sign of Gemini, your psychic nature naturally tends to both sending and receiving information. You may need to set aside your intellect in order to tune in to your deeper levels, and you must learn to avoid distractions and being scattered.

Moon in CANCER

With your natal Moon in the water sign of Cancer, you are a "natural" psychic type, but you tend to be fearful of receiving negative information. It is important for you to do your psychic work in an atmosphere where you feel safe. Do not go beyond your comfort limits and practice releasing.

Moon in LEO

With your natal Moon in the robust sign of Leo, you use your psychic ability for self-expression. You need to be creative and playful with your psychic work, and you will succeed by making a game of it, finding pleasure in it. You will want to share your psychic insights with others.

Moon in VIRGO

With your natal Moon in the mental sign of Virgo, you need to set aside your analytical tendencies to achieve results. When embarking on your psychic practice, be sure that you have given yourself an orderly atmosphere. You will want psychic information to serve a useful end.

Moon in LIBRA

With your natal Moon in the harmonious sign of Libra, you approach psychic development in a balanced manner. You need to cultivate an atmosphere of calm around your psychic work and to practice in a setting of harmony and beauty. You will want to receive information about relationships.

Moon in SCORPIO

With your natal Moon in the intense sign of Scorpio, you are psychically gifted. As you approach your psychic work intensively, it is important not to overdo until you are familiar with your psychic landscape. Do not push yourself beyond your level of current ability.

Moon in SAGITTARIUS

With your natal Moon in the philosophical sign of Sagittarius, you are naturally gifted with optimism, one of the hallmarks of a strong psychic nature. You are unafraid of exploration and love to learn, especially about yourself. Your psychic nature is freedom-loving and can bring wisdom.

Moon in CAPRICORN

With your natal Moon in the disciplined sign of Capricorn, you approach psychic work in a controlled and specific manner, seeking practical results. You can use your psychic ability to enhance your career, to succeed at business, and to increase your productivity.

Moon in AQUARIUS

With your natal Moon in the detached sign of Aquarius, you approach psychic work with an open mind. Whatever you discover in the psychic realm will interest you because you like what is unusual. With your unconventional attitude, you will roam far and wide on the psychic landscape easily.

Moon in PISCES

With your natal Moon in the sensitive sign of Pisces, you are already a "sensitive" with a strong intuitive nature. You may have difficulty sorting out the information coming in to you and you need to be especially careful in the verification stage. Results will often seem inspired.

The Transiting Moon

No matter what sign is occupied by your natal Moon, you can moon-tune yourself to the sign of the transiting Moon. Using your lunar calendar, determine the exact time that the Moon enters the new sign, and the exact time that it exits that Sign. The last few degrees of the Moon's leaving a sign are known as "void of course," and this is *not* a good time for psychic work. As you look at your Moon calendar, determine what work you want to do under which influences of the Moon, according to the listing below.

Transiting Moon in ARIES

These two days are a good time to begin any psychic projects you have in mind. This is a time for you to be adventurous and daring. A seeding time, results will come later. Avoid rushing through your practice at this time.

Transiting Moon in TAURUS

These two days are a good time to work for practical results, especially money and finances. Concentrate your energies during this time for best results. This is an excellent time to practice relaxation techniques.

Transiting Moon in GEMINI

These two days are a good time to practice telepathy and channel-clearing techniques. Information flows freely under the Gemini Moon, and both sending and receiving are enhanced. You may have to weed out trivial information.

Transiting Moon in CANCER

These two days are a good time to work on family and related matters. The Moon rules Cancer and is especially psychic in this sign. It's also a good time to concentrate on bringing more security into your life.

Transiting Moon in LEO

These two days are a good time to work on career and creative issues. Paying attention to the psychic at this time will engender increased feedback from the information network. Child-related questions will be answered now.

Transiting Moon in VIRGO

These two days are especially good for job-related questions. Psychic work now will bring practical results. Under the Virgo Moon, verification is enhanced. Routines should be followed precisely for best results.

Transiting Moon in LIBRA

These two days are the best all month for working psychically on relationships and marriage issues. An excellent time to do magnetizing for the right partner. Also superb for harmonizing mind, body, and spirit.

Transiting Moon in SCORPIO

These two days are a time for going into your psychic depths with utmost seriousness. Under the Scorpio Moon, the psychic door is open wide and profound insights can be gained. An excellent time to practice channeling.

Transiting Moon in SAGITTARIUS
These two days are excellent for practicing remote viewing. They are also a good time for learning about your psychic Self and being exploratory. No need to concentrate on one issue— feel free to roam the psychic landscape

Transiting Moon in CAPRICORN
These two days are an excellent time to concentrate on your career and to achieve practical results in the real world. Business decisions are especially open to psychic guidance, and questions about money matters are in order.

Transiting Moon in AQUARIUS
These two days are "hot" psychically and generally give rise to unusual experiences (especially if the Moon is full). Be prepared to meet guides during an Aquarius Moon, and ask questions of serious significance to your life.

Transiting Moon in PISCES
These two days are most propitious for psychic work. Under a Pisces Moon, the psychic door is open widest all month and sensitivity to the psychic realm is heightened. A good time for delving into emotional issues.

The Lunar Return

When the transiting Moon returns to the sign in which it was placed at your birth, you are said to have a lunar return. This is an important moon progress to you personally. Use your lunar return for anything that is especially important to you at the time, depending on the sign in which it is placed. During these two days, you have the opportunity to renew your lunar energies and to reorient yourself to the natural energies of your natal Moon. It is a powe]rful time. Use it well.

The Phases of the Moon

From the nights in which we observe the newborn Moon's slim shining crescent to those when her full and glorious face illuminates all, and back again to the opposite-facing sliver, she is passing through what are known as "lunar phases."

The *waxing* Moon brings an energy of *expansion*. This is a positive influence promoting growth. It is the best time to concentrate on issues of relationship or romance, of a new beginning in your love life, or to effect a reconciliation. It is also a good time to focus on begining new projects at work, or a new job. Whatever you start during this phase will grow into fruition.

When the Moon is at the *full* the energy is toward completion. The lunar energy is at its strongest and most powerful. This is a time to promote *enlightenment,* and to look for results of what you have seeded in the past. It is an especially good time to work on clairvoyance and clairsentience as the light of the full Moon eliminates shadows. Also, issues related to blocks can be cleared up.

During the period of the *waning* Moon, the energy moves toward *decreasing* and finally, eliminating. Emotional problems can be put into perspective at this time, and this phase is ideal for dealing with negative issues you want to eliminate from your life. Now is the time to practice releasing and letting go, especially of outworn relationships or bad love affairs. Use the waning phase of the Moon to help you discharge all negativity.

The night of the *dark* Moon, when she is invisible, is a time when it is advisable not to do any Moon work, unless you wish to totally eliminate something, to have it "die" forever. In this lightless phase, the energy for *banishment* is very strong and it is a time to symbolically kill off whatever is contaminating your psyche. Fix the feeling or issue firmly in your mind and then say, "I banish you from my life forever and always. Amen."

Remember that the energies of the Moon change slowly during the phases, seguing from one into the next. After the dark moon, for example, the energy of the new Moon slowly increases into the expansive growth phase. The full Moon's energy begins to culminate two days before the total fullness is achieved, and it continues in effect for another two days afterward. The energy of the waning Moon heightens toward decrease as the visible area shrinks.

The New Moon

The period of the new, or dark, Moon is a mysterious one. It is a time of beginnings, of seeding, of fresh starts. Use the new

Moon period to concentrate your psychic work on future hopes and expectations. Depending in which sign the new Moon falls, take advantage of it to seed your non–conscious with your desires for the future.

The Full Moon

A powerful influence of the transiting Moon occurs when the full Moon occupies the sign of your natal Moon. For example, if your natal Moon is in Scorpio, the full Moon in Scorpio will be a time when your responses to the transiting Moon will be at their peak. Although she will pass through your natal Moon Sign every month, the Moon is not necessarily full in each sign every year. Thus, it might be that you would have to wait for a year to get a full Moon in your natal sign. Should that be the case, you can choose the nearest approximation in a sign before or after your natal sign. As the Moon changes signs every two-and-one-half days, you should not have to wait too long before there is a full Moon in a neighboring sign. Then, a day or two before or after the actual full Moon you will have an "almost" full Moon in your own sign.

How To Do Moon Work

Prior to doing psychic work in relation to the Moon, it is best to perform a cleansing ritual. The Moon is especially harmonious with water. After choosing the Moon time and the subject you wish to concentrate on, prepare to take a warm bath by assembling a candle and scent for the water. Soft warm towels and soothing music will enhance your ritual.

Make sure you can be quiet and undisturbed during the time of your Moon work. Late night hours seem to work best. Fill a tub with warm water (not hot) and scent it with oil or salts. Light a candle. Toss a few flower petals in the water. Now, lie in the warm water and imagine that it is washing away all the negative thoughts and emotions that you have gathered into yourself. You can practice a relaxation technique in the bath and then a releasing technique.

As you relax in the water, close your eyes and let yourself just feel the rise and fall of your breath, allowing the scent to soothe and relax you. When you exhale, consciously let go of all tensions and negativity. Spend at least twenty minutes in the bath, adding more warm water as it cools. Afterward, wrap yourself cozily in warm towels and let yourself dry naturally. Keep a slow pace.

Next, put on a simple soft, loose, and flowing garment of natural fabric—cotton, silk, wool, linen. White is appropriate for a full Moon, blue for a new Moon, rose for relationship work, green for money work. Choose a color that feels right on that particular night.

After your bath, sit facing the direction of the Moon. If you cannot see her, acknowledge her by closing your eyes and imagining the beautiful silver crescent or disk in the sky. If possible, position yourself in front of a window or even outside where the rays of the Moon can shine down on you. Sit quietly for several minutes until you can feel the Moon's energy contacting you. Imagine her white light entering your soul and activating your psychic Self to its utmost potential. Feel the magnetic pull of the Moon on your inner sensitivities; allow yourself to be touched by her softly inspiring light.

When you have reached a state where you feel attuned to the Moon's energy, begin your regular practice with whatever techniques you have a chosen. At this time, focus on the question at hand intently, keeping yourself very clear about what you want to know. Do not let side issues dissipate your concentration.

Center yourself facing the Moon (if you can see it) or simply imagine that you are facing it, and state in one brief sentence a definition of the problem. It should be short and simple, such as, "I want help with my feelings about changing jobs," or "I am starting a new relationship and I want to know its potential," or "What do I need to look at right now in my relationship with _____?" or "What can I do to bring more friends into my life?"

After you have stated your need or question, let yourself remain quiet and concentrate on the energies of the sign the Moon is transiting. On the second night that the Moon is in the same sign, repeat the procedure and expect to receive the answer.

The Hours of Night

Not only is it important for your psychic development for you to be aware of your natal Moon sign and the sign of the transiting

Moon, but it is also necessary to use the hours of night for specific purposes. There are twelve hours of the night (though not all are dark) from sunset to sunrise, and as they progress the psychic vibrations change. You can experience this for yourself by taking an entire night to remain awake and be aware of the differences you feel as the hours of night progress from sunset to midnight, from midnight to four A.M., and from four A.M. to sunrise. Each segment of night has a different psychic energy.

At sunset, night is in its infancy, still attached to day as a newborn is attached to the umbilical cord. As the night deepens toward midnight, it reaches the "pit," or the crosspoint when darkness begins the ascent into light. At midnight our psychic senses are sharp and clear, we are alert to the subtle vibrations of night. As the hours move forward toward four A.M., the psychic door gradually opens wider and wider until the veil lifts of itself and we are able to perceive the innerconnectedness of all things. It is during these hours that psychic experience is most intense, that "magical" beings come forth from within. As night slowly turns into day from four A.M. to sunrise, we are brought to the realization that night and day are but a continuum, as are sleeping and waking consciousness.

When I was director of the "Realms of the Creative Spirit" seminars, I produced a series of all-night seminars specially designed to allow the participants to get in touch with their psychic selves by experiencing the hours of night. As I had at my disposal the resources of a theater, including dancers and actors, we were able to simulate the inner experiences of night in an outer way by theatrically representing figures such as one might encounter in the psychic realm. Starting with a candlelighting ceremony to welcome night, we progressed hour-by-hour through the night-sea journey, with each hour bringing forth that which expressed the essence of that hour. A magical being or a dream figure would appear out of the dark and by word and gesture call us to that inner realm of ourselves. At midnight precisely, we had a supper to feed the "hungry ghosts" and affirm our connection to the living.

As the hours progressed, we encountered strange nocturnal sights—such as a goddess in gold upon a pedestal revealing to us the nature of the Moon. Or a bell-bedecked Indian dancer telling us of the ascent of the beautiful goddess Lotus from her muddy beginnings in the watery abyss. At four, when we were in the sacred psychic precinct, we heard the sounds of a flute cascading around us, not knowing whether it was music heard from within or without. And, as dawn broke over the city, we exited our cave of Night and welcomed Day with a celebratory champagne breakfast.

The participants of those all-night seminars found them to be a special and unforgettable time. Some slept and dreamed part of the night away; others remained alert every minute; even children participated. I wish I could invite you to such a seminar, but you can approximate it for yourself using the method given below.

Your Personal Night-Sea Journey

To experience the hours of the night most fully, choose a time when you can be awake from sunset to sunrise in a quiet and protected environment, preferably one in which you can observe the night sky. For twenty-four hours prior to this exercise, practice sensory deprivation by keeping external stimuli at a minimum—no TV, videos, radio, newspapers, magazines, socializing, telephoning. The purpose is to achieve a state of inner tranquillity prior to your personal night-sea journey.

You can do this alone or with one or more others. Keep occupied during the night hours with light activity such as sewing, cooking, attending to the needs of a pet, simple work like filing or sorting papers, while you remain alert to the nuances of the night hours. *Listen* inwardly to what the different hours are saying to you. If you are a night owl by nature you will have different experiences than if you are a day person. Your experience will tell you a great deal about your nocturnal Self— one you may not yet know very well. Keep a record of your experiences in your personal psychic journal. If you fall asleep and have a dream, be sure to record it. Don't force yourself to remain awake if it is a strain, but do refrain from actually putting on pajamas and going to bed. Arrange a time when you have the next day free to catch up on lost sleep.

At the end of the night, greet the sunrise—the return of the sun god who has been on his night-sea journey. Do something celebratory to mark the end of your conscious passage through Night—take a walk around the block and see how different life seems from a normal day; sing a song; drink a glass of Champagne; treat yourself to an elegant breakfast. Whatever you do, you now will be aware of your psychic Self at a new and heightened level.

The Night Has a Thousand Eyes

Part VI

The Last Frontier

18

Future Mind

Whatever you can do or dream you can do, begin it.
Boldness has genius, power, and magic in it.
—JOHANN WOLFGANG VON GOETHE

Today, with unprecedented advances in all fields of technology, we are in a position to set our dreams of what we can do into high gear. Although the world is advancing technologically at a rapid rate, high-tech methods are not always the best solutions. Experiments with low-tech means have proved successful in fields from medicine to birth control, from entrepreneurship to free enterprise.

Although we have steadfastly looked to and relied upon scientific breakthroughs to solve our burgeoning problems, we are now finding that scientific meddling in the human equation may produce more difficulties than it resolves; or it exchanges one for another. Mechanized farming threatens the rain forests and the traditional ways of life for forest people. Increased fertility and lowered death rates threaten whole nations'—indeed the entire planet's—survival.

Our physical frontiers have been pushed into outer space where, given sufficient light years, we may well one day roam freely, taking our human minds with us. However, while we dazzle and terrify ourselves with the boons and horrors of modern science, we neglect our most precious human resource: the mind. Whereas not every human being is scientifically or otherwise gifted, all come equipped with minds that can be developed.

And, as Charles Lindbergh observed, we may discover that "only *without* spaceships can we reach the galaxies...to venture beyond the fantastic accomplishments of this physically fantastic age, sensory perception must combine with the extrasensory."

A New Scientific Perspective

As we look around at what humans—not God—have wrought—deforestation, nuclear waste, overfished and polluted oceans, oil spills, the proliferation of armaments, overpopulation and the resultant increase in poverty, civil wars with their attendant chaos—we cannot fail to realize we are desperately in need of a new science of consciousness, and of a new consciousness of science. The two must go hand-in-hand if we are to save, and repair, our planet.

Science needs to call upon the new understandings of the psychic/spiritual community to fertilize its researches, and all of us need to call upon the scientists to incorporate new attitudes of mind and consciousness into their conceptions of our being and the world in which we live.

The need is great and the time is short. We cannot go on pursuing separatist lines, like the three blind men attempting to describe an elephant. In this tale, the men encounter the beast and walk around it to determine its identity. The first, feeling the trunk, pronounces the elephant to be a large serpent. The second, encountering a huge leg, disputes the first and insists it is a tree, while the third, at the tail, proclaims it to be a fly swatter. This is not to say that divergent points of view are not to be tolerated, only that we must come together at a deeper level of understanding and tap into our own hidden resources if we want not just to survive, but to thrive.

This radical shift now in progress—and, like an earth fault, it is there whether we choose to recognize it or not—is carrying us with astounding rapidity to the possibility of new states of consciousness, which can produce amazing results, *right now.* Already, peak performances are being achieved in a short period of time by those with no formal training in either meditation or spiritual techniques. Such feats as firewalking, once limited to those who had arduously trained for years, are being achieved by ordinary people from all walks of life.

New technologies are emerging constantly and old tech-niques are being rediscovered. With these, we can now effect self-transformational modes to help us to overcome mental and physical illnesses. It is no longer a question of if such a transfor-mation will take place. It *must*.

We are all in this together, and we all must act separately. Only when, enriching our consciousness with all the informa-tion flowing from spiritual, psychological, and scientific sources, enough of us act to perform our own self-transformations will the New Age truly arrive. What we have now is a tremendous *potential*. Like a newly planted field, we must weed and water, nurture and protect this evolving potential in order to bring it to fruition. As Donald Keys says, in his book *Earth at Omega,*

> This is not to assert that all persons need to become saints...it is quite likely that these times will produce more than the usual quota of graduate humans. What we will need to avoid catastrophe is a critical mass of people....We each have a task to be more aware, more whole...no longer estranged from each other but more aligned with the pulse of life's planetary purpose.

Peter Russell, in *The Global Brain,* echoes this sentiment,

> The transformation of society awaits the transformation of the self—of enough selves, at least—to tip the balance. When the transformed seeker becomes a knower, then he or she becomes a powerful force...[the] being of such a person manifests it, telegraphs it, radiates it throughout the global network of subtle human connectedness.

I can do no better in support of this argument than to quote the final paragraph of Joseph Campbell's *The Hero With A Thousand Faces:*

> The modern hero, the modern individual, who dares to heed the call and seek the mansion of that presence with whom it is our whole destiny to be atoned, cannot, indeed must not, wait for his community to cast off its slough of pride, fear, rationalized avarice, and sanctified misunderstanding....It is not society that is to guide and save the creative hero, but precisely the reverse. And so every one of us shares the supreme ordeal—carries the cross of the redeemer—not in

the bright moments of his tribe's great victories, but in the silences of his personal despair.

We can also turn for inspiration to Ralph Waldo Emerson, the transcendental visionary, who believed that the phenomenal world was a sort of symbolic representation of the inner life and who preached that individual freedom and self-reliance were the keys to that inner life. Emerson's philosophy is newly relevant and as fresh and controversial as it was in 1836, when "Nature" was published. The essay caused a storm of controversy by suggesting that Americans consider the land itself to be an expression of the same living spirit that was embodied in humanity and treat the land accordingly.

One can imagine what this blighted land of ours would be like had Emerson's wisdom been heeded by the rapers of the North American continent, who pursued only materialistic ends. Had it not been for a few other visionaries, like John Muir, it is doubtful that there would still be an acre of wilderness left in America.

In the seventeenth century, Mother Nature was ousted from her role as benevolent provider and terrible mother. Declared to be soul-less, she became a sort of glorified mechanical cow, producing food and animals from predetermined mathematical formulae. As a mechanistic worldview, under the guidance of Darwin and Newton, stepped in and rose to prominence, the Middle Ages concept of Nature as having within herself an unseen but very real productive power, which gave rise to the physical forms we see, was banished, relegated to the level of mere superstition, suitable only for country bumpkins. Triumphantly, Science declared Nature dead.

Even so, the new masters—rational thinkers to a man, with the remarkable exception that they now assigned previously natural processes to the supernatural realm of God—couldn't make everything fit into their new hypothesis. The forces of gravity, for example, were fraught with mystery, and there wasn't much Newton could do to explain away such "invisible forces" that somehow—no one knew how—related everything in the universe to everything else while maintaining a state of equilibrium. Previous scientific thinkers had identified "ether," which incidentally is a concept of Buddhism, but Newton would have none of that.

As time marched on, and the idea of a mechanistic universe gained power, the scientists became like the ogre Procrustes, who had an iron bed upon which he forced the travelers he captured to lie. If they didn't fit, he made adjustments—to them, not to the bed. If too tall, he chopped off some part; if too short, he put them on a rack and stretched them out.

Until along came Albert Einstein, like St. George the dragon killer, to slay the scientific theories of the seventeenth, eighteenth, and nineteenth centuries. Although these theories had allowed humans to understand and control their environment—to exploit Nature mercilessly—they were inadequate to explain what investigators were now observing. It was the beginning of a new scientific framework. A key concept of this new paradigm is that *matter and energy cannot be separated.*

Scientists were, of course, already familiar with gravitational and magnetic fields as organizing principles, but work such as Cambridge biologist Rupert Sheldrake's postulated other, larger, fields, with unique properties. Everything, in fact, had its own field. There was a daisy field and a robin field, and no matter where a daisy or a robin lived or grew, it was always a daisy or a robin and behaved as such, being tuned in to the proper field. What is also becoming evident is that there are feedback loops between the field and whatever is in it—be it atoms or planets. According to this theory, the field and the specific unit in the field are interrelated and interactive. The field influences the individual, and what the individual does modifies the field.

The most interesting extrapolation of the field theory is that *consciousness* fields are being imagined. It was previously held that matter created the field around it. In the new science the field itself structures the matter within it while the matter, by its behavior, modifies the field, in a sort of intertwining of energy and matter, which we now know cannot be separated. In addition to this revelation, scientists are now realizing that fields belong to a different kind of reality than does our ordinary sense/phenomena reality in which cause and effect always take place in that order. The field, it seems, can be the *effect* that produces the *cause.*

Compare the New Age saying, *You create your own reality* (with your thoughts, ideas, emotions, feelings) with this statement by physicist John Wheeler: "We are inescapably involved in bringing about that which appears to be happening."

And this from Nobel Prize–winner Ilya Prigogine: "Nature is part of us, as we are part of it."

None of this is news to those involved in psychic work, and it isn't news to those who work on the land, either. In fact, to some this brand-new revelation from science has always been self-evident.

However, even those who concede that matter and energy cannot be separated balk at the next idea: that matter and *consciousness* also cannot be separated. Not only can they not be separated, but *consciousness and matter are capable of interacting*. While it is true that I cannot think a plant into being, I can have a definite effect on a plant by thinking either positive or negative thoughts about it. I can cause it to wilt by sending it hate vibes, or I can cause it to bloom by sweet-talking to it. It has also been proved that plants can pick up our thoughts and emotions and react to them. We know that positive visualizations can affect an ill or diseased body for the better, that the mental images we make affect our bodies, down to the very cells, and our spirits, in terms of well-being. This is not new information: in the fifth century B.C., Euripides has the nurse in *Medea* warn her mistress that, "Images the mind makes work into life."

However, the idea is still suspect among many, especially those in the medical profession to whom it is anathema to suggest that we can control our own bodies if we so choose. Still, incursions are being made into the mainstream. Witness an article in *Newsweek* of 7 November 1988, titled "Body and Soul," and subtitled, "New discoveries linking the brain to the immune system suggest that state of mind can affect us right down to our cells."

The article went on to say that,

> solid data are still hard to come by. But lately, the doubts have begun to fade. The past ten years have witnessed an explosion of research findings suggesting that the mind and body act on each other in often remarkable ways…a factor called "joy" [remember the "flying monk"?] was the second strongest predictor of survival time. Dr. Steven Locke calls the idea that thinking well helps make you well the "third revolution" in Western medicine—ranking it alongside the advent of surgery and the discovery of penicillin.

Other Worlds, Other Realms

Of the many exciting ideas, theories, and observations coming out of those in the scientific community with the courage to look beyond the tried-and-true, which we have presented in this book, the concept of *parallel universes* is perhaps the most encouraging to workers in the psychic field. Having had personal experience of "visiting" parallel universes, I have no doubt of their existence, and many of my colleagues feel the same way.

Briefly stated, the parallel universes concept, being considered by physicists as an explanation of phenomena observable in the material world, states that, for each of us, an indefinite number of universes exist simultaneously. Each universe may be a slight variation of the next one or may be entirely unrelated. The theory of parallel universes is also a useful way to imagine what can happen in our consciousness field, affecting the flow of events.

In my view, there are many worlds around us, invisible but capable of manifesting into our consciousness. Sometimes these are accompanied by out-of-body experiences, but I also believe that in the dreamworld, which I know to have many more levels than either dream researchers or psychologists have postulated or determined, we can encounter parallel universes. You are the best investigator and witness of your dream experiences.

Scientific support for the parallel universes theory comes from physicist Hugh Everett III, who came to the conclusion that,

> We live in an infinite number of continually interacting universes. Moreover, in this system of an infinite number of parallel universes, "all possible futures really happen."

And Alan Guth, a physicist from M.I.T., says that the concept is actually the simplest interpretation of quantum mechanics.

The Aquarian Transformation

Change is upon us, "more far-reaching than those which emerged from the Copernican, Darwinian, and Freudian revolutions," in the opinion of Dr. Willis Harmon of Stanford Research Institute.

A major change in the way we view ourselves and the world is under way...that will increasingly affect education, business, and life generally....One is our ripening ability to control inner states...probably we will eventually discover that all persons have the full range of psychic phenomena as potentialities, all unconsciously understood.

As we stand on the verge of the twenty-first century, the beginning of the long-awaited Aquarian Age, this stunning possibility comes more clearly into view as the undoubted wave of the future. The "telepathic connection" may ultimately be an ordinary means of communication. The implications are so vast as to be almost unthinkable. Imagine how it would be if you could, instead of picking up the telephone, simply tune into your spouse's wavelength and send the message that you will be late for dinner. We may well learn to use our brains as we today use telecommunication systems. We might even be able to bounce our brainwaves off satellites!

There are those to whom the term ESP smacks of superstition and lack of scientific veracity. To these rational-mind worshipers, ESP is a throwback to times not blessed with technological advances. But psychologist Dr. Carl Rogers thinks that,

> We may be in an evolutionary transition, as major as the one that urged creatures from the sea up onto expanded life on land. "Are we evolving into new spaces, new ways of being? Will we discover new energies and forces?"...by using right-brain abilities, psi abilities, we may come to know directly a different universe, a nonlinear one like the universe our physicists are describing.

Life in the Information Universe of Tomorrow

As the new information superhighway rolls into our living rooms via our computers and TV sets (and who knows what other yet-to-be-invented means), our already oversaturated minds may rebel against this overload of information. However, if we can learn to use our right-brain, nonlinear facilities for processing the myriad of information coming from all around, we will relieve the strain on our linear left brain.

We must learn to let our heavy-duty unconscious mind do the processing, and in order to allow this to happen, we must be able to *trust* in this inner process. My writing of this book is a good case in point. I had masses of material to organize and a short time in which to produce the work. Like most of us, especially those who do mental work for a living, I was used to relying on my logical, orderly left brain to get a book into proper shape. However—due partly to the topic and partly to the need to integrate a great deal of subjective experience into the factual—I soon felt like Psyche, the bride of the invisible god Eros.

This unwitting girl has displeased the great goddess Aphrodite and finds herself out in the cold, saddled with a number of seemingly impossible tasks, one of which is to sort a great heap of tiny seeds—sesame, poppy, lentil—overnight. In despair, she looks at the forbidding mixed-up mound and starts to cry. She exhausts herself and goes to sleep. As she sleeps, ants emerge from around her and busily begin work, neatly and efficiently sorting the seeds into different piles. When she wakes, the job is done and the ants are gone.

The ants, of course, are a symbol for the unconscious process, which sorts and arranges things while we sleep or occupy ourselves with nonrelated activities. This is exactly what happened to me, night after night, day after day, while I was writing this book. I would have no clear idea of the next day's work when I went to sleep. But, each day when I sat down at the computer, I found the next chapter was sitting in my mind, all neatly organized, ready to be typed out. At one point in the work, I dreamed that dozens of couriers were scurrying into a central command post with information from outlying sources.

Future Mind

The future of our minds depends on each individual.

We can no longer look to governments and our social institutions for solutions to our life's problems. We must learn to look to ourselves. And the more of us who do, the greater will be our ability to resolve the important issues that confront us both individually and as societies.

A great deal of confusion surrounds the entire subject of what is loosely called "psychic." To some people, this primarily means ESP, clairvoyance, or seeing into the future. To many the word *psychic* has a magical, mystical ring to it, a not-of-this-world aura. And some turn away from any contemplation, let alone use of psychic ability, because it does not fit into their preconceived notion of what is possible.

As there is no precise definition of *psychic* available to us, we are free to define our experiences as we will. After many years of steady work in this admittedly peculiar realm of endeavor, I have come to think of what happens in what I call "the invisible world," which includes dreams and visionary experiences, as the *unseen real*.

For me, the reality of these experiences is as concrete—sometimes even more so—as the so-called "real world" that we experience through the five senses. In fact, there are times I have difficulty believing that the world of the senses is real at all, so real to me is the psychic realm. Those who claim that in order for experience to be "real" it must be able to be touched, tasted, smelled, seen, or heard cut themselves off from a vast area of human experience common to us all.

Because we all dream (or accept that humans do dream), if we tell a dream no one disbelieves us. But if no one dreamed (or believed they did), who would believe such fantastic adventures? We would be thought mad. No matter how bizarre its content, if we relate a dream we are believed. No one doubts that we have actually had that particular experience, and if it was unpleasant we will receive sympathy for the simple reason that almost everyone has at one time or another had a nightmare. Why should other experiences in the invisible world be different?

Of course, the world of the senses is our *visible* reality, but it is not the only reality. No one has ever *seen* a mood, *touched* a dream, *tasted* an emotion, *smelled* love, or *heard* a gut feeling that either stopped or initiated action. There are other, equally real but infinitely more subtle, areas of human experience available to us through our psychic potential—intuition, dreams, inner experiences of all sorts, altered states of consciousness, and, for some, direct experience with guides who contact us either through our own facilities of perception or through intermediaries such as readers, channelers, and the like. However you might experience the unseen real, know that it is very real indeed. What happens there can change your life.

Unfortunately, some people experience these powers as negative or overwhelming. And, since there is little support in our society for anything not strictly materialistic, those people who have unsettling encounters with the unseen real can become confused and fearful, even in some cases to the point of madness or serious mental illness. This is more than unfortunate, it is tragic. Many who have vivid and life-changing inner experiences keep them secret, for fear of ridicule—or worse. We who know personally about these things from direct experience are often "pooh-poohed" at the kindest level; more often we are looked at askance, as if we possessed (or were possessed by) some dangerous power. To be sure, the power is there, but it need not be dangerous. Like anything else, it can be harnessed for growth and life enhancement. The real danger is in not understanding these powers and how we interact with them.

Currently quite a number of people are being "called" to the psychic experience—some whether they consciously want it or not. To many, these first experiences may seem strange and inexplicable, even frightening. And there are few therapists or counselors available with whom they can safely reveal their sometimes burdensome experience, which is therefore kept hidden as if it were something to be ashamed of.

As we have seen, the mind is an amazing tool of unlimited potential. It is multilayered and multidimensional. There are many exciting facets waiting to be discovered and put to use both for our personal enrichment and the good of humanity. Although centuries of Church-laden restrictions and repressions have convinced us that we are but poor beings, inferior in every way, nothing but unrepentant sinners waiting for a redemption we don't even deserve, these limiting concepts are on the way out. We are now at the point where we can reject them, along with their negative poisons.

Awareness of the vast powers inherent in us has been reappearing—like the little ping of bubbles rising in a yeasting dough starter—across many fields of knowledge, from physics to metaphysics. We now have not only glimpses but positive proof of the mind's untapped resources. We know *what* potentially our minds can do, and best of all we know *how*. Many tools have been discovered and rediscovered—some as ancient as shamanic rituals of music, dance, and meditation; others as new as electronic biofeedback.

All of these techniques have allowed us to make great strides forward in our ability to evolve highly effective ways of accessing our natural abilities through the refocusing of consciousness. We can move inward to develop our latent psychic powers, connecting ourselves in harmony with the universal forces, bringing these outward to make our lives and our world better. We can expand our consciousness and heal our minds and bodies for fuller, more vibrant life expressions. It is time to reclaim our rightful heritage as spiritual beings made incarnate.

Our negative attitude toward psychic experiences has been influenced for centuries by the Catholic Church, whose infamous Inquisition caused the deaths of millions (mostly female) by torture and burning at the stake. The Church to this day staunchly condemns psychic phenomena as the work of the devil. This dogma-encrusted institution, having in 1632 denounced Galileo for asserting that the Earth circled the Sun, forcing him into early retirement, only officially "forgave" him (for being right) in the 1970s—over three hundred years and a moon landing later.

Nevertheless, popular literature—from satanic horror stories to more benign tales of poltergeists and extraterrestrial creatures—continues to reflect the profound need for and interest in the human mind in this subject. Only recently, with the advent of the New Age movement, has the subject of psychic experience been allowed to come out into the open and thrive in the light of understanding and compassion. Even so, many people think it's okay only as scary fiction, sentimental movie-making, or "entertainment," which is what the purveyors of psychic services via TV infomercials are required by law to label their wares. Fraudulent practitioners have damaged credibility, but this law also reflects the lack of seriousness with which the psychic realm is approached by our culture in general.

Nevertheless, it is impossible to continue to deny that psychic experience is part of the human birthright. No matter how suspect it remains in some quarters—despite well-controlled university studies by heavily credentialed academics—it is an ability available to all.

One does not need a postgraduate degree in psychology—or anything else for that matter—to experience profound inner life. Unfortunately, we are habituated to the reliance on authoritative "experts" (those ubiquitous Ph.D.'s) to tell us what it is okay to think and feel and do and experience. The result is that we suspect our own intimate inner world of betraying us and thus distrust our innate intuitive powers. So accustomed have we become to waiting for public approval by a panel of medics and psychologists that we often refuse to take our own experience seriously, denying our empirical evidence, and excluding the use of a considerable part of our inborn mental capacity.

Now is the time to change all that. The relaxation techniques, visualizations, and meditations given in this book are only tools. Use them as you will. Try them out and see what works for you, for you are the only qualified judge. Use your psychic practice time to enhance yourself, make life more enjoyable and exciting, richer, fuller—both materially and spiritually. As you evolve your own inner consciousness, you will love and trust yourself to a greater degree than you previously thought possible. People around you will be affected by this flow of positive energy, which will expand outward in ever more powerful waves, changing not only you but the world in which you live. Embrace your power and learn to use it wisely and well. You will be surprised how every change you make, however small, will spill over into all aspects of your life, and your effort will join with the efforts of all the others similarly engaged, changing the entire world.

I close with the words of Rupert Sheldrake, who, contemplating the "choice of philosophies: the mechanistic theory of nature and of human life, with God as an optional extra; the theory of nature as alive but without God; or the theory of a living God together with living nature," says,

> In the end, we have to choose between them on the basis of intuition. Our choice is influenced by our acknowledgment of mystery and in turn affects our tolerance of it....And those who acknowledge the life of God are consciously open to the mystery of divine consciousness, grace, and love.

The Future Is in Your Mind

Appendix

To Contact the Author

To contact the author regarding personal appearances, group seminars, or private consultations, please write to:

M.J. Abadie c/o Hazelwood Productions
P.O. Box 247
Lenox Hill Station
New York, NY 10021

Please give particulars in your letter about your wishes. Corporate training seminars in intuition development and group seminars for the general public can be arranged with sufficient advance notice.

Computerized Astrological Services

You can order a wide range of astrological services via mail from us. These include a Simple Natal Chart, Personal Profiles (a detailed analysis of your chart), the Relationship Profile (a compatibility analysis between two people), A Child's Profile, and transit lists (including all your exact Moon transits).

In addition, we offer personal astrological services prepared by a professional astrologer specifically for you, on tape. Telephone consultations can also be arranged.

To receive a free descriptive brochure about our astrological services, please send a stamped, self-addressed envelope to:

Hazelwood Productions
P.O. Box 247
Lenox Hill Station
New York, NY 10021

We regret that inquiries that do not include an SASE can not be answered.

Canadian and other non-U.S. correspondents can send an international reply coupon or $1.00 in lieu of SASE.

References

Abadie, M.J., and Claudia Bader. *Love Planets*. New York: Fireside/Simon & Schuster, 1990.

Anderson-Evangelista, Anita. *Hypnosis: A Journey into the Mind*. New York: Arco, 1980.

Bandler, Richard, and John Grinder. *Using Your Brain—For a Change*. Moab, UT: Real People Press, 1985.

Bennett, Hal Zina. *Inner Guides, Visions, Dreams, and Dr. Einstein*. Berkeley, CA: Celestial Arts, 1986.

Benson, Herbert. *The Relaxation Response*. New York: Avon, 1975.

Bohm, David, and F. David Peat. *Science, Order, and Creativity*. New York: Bantam, 1980.

Campbell, Joseph. *The Hero with a Thousand Faces*. New York: Bollingen Foundation, 1961.

_____ Assisted by M.J. Abadie. *The Mythic Image*. Princeton, NJ: Princeton University Press, 1974.

Ferguson, Marilyn. *The Aquarian Conspiracy*. Los Angeles: Jeremy P. Tarcher, 1979.

Garfield, Charles A. *Peak Performance: Mental Training Techniques of the World's Greatest Athletes*. New York: Warner Books, 1984.

Garfield, Patricia. *Creative Dreaming*. New York: Ballantine, 1974.

Harman, Willis, and Howard Rheingold. *Higher Creativity: Liberating the Unconscious for Breakthrough Insights*. Los Angeles: Jeremy P. Tarcher, 1984.

Heisenberg, Werner. *Physics and Philosophy: The Revolution in Modern Science*. New York: Harper, 1971.

Jung, Carl Gustav. "Synchronicity." Foreword to *The I Ching or Book of Changes*, Richard Wilhelm and Cary F. Baynes, trans. Princeton, NJ: Princeton University Press, 1967.

Kerényi, Karl. *Hermes, Guide of Souls*. Dallas, TX: Spring Publications, 1986.

Keyes, Ken, Jr. *The Hundredth Monkey*. Coos Bay, OR: Vision Books, 1982.

Krippner, Stanley, and Joseph Dillard. *Dreamworking: How to Use Your Dreams for Creative Problem Solving*. Buffalo, NY: Bearly Limited, 1988.

Leonard, George. *The Silent Pulse: A Search for the Perfect Rhythm that Exists in Each of Us*. New York: Bantam, 1978.

Lewis, Byron A., and R. Frank Pucelik. *Magic Demystified: A Pragmatic Guide to Communication and Change*. Lake Oswego, OR: Metamorphous Press, 1982.

Orser, Mary, and Richard Zarro. *Changing Your Destiny*. San Francisco: Harper & Row, 1989.

Ostrander, Sheila, and Lynn Schroeder. *Superlearning*. New York: Delacorte Press, 1979.

Peat, F. David. *Synchronicity*. New York: Bantam, 1987.

Ponder, Catharine. *The Dynamic Laws of Prosperity*. Marina del Rey, CA: DeVorss, 1983.

Russell, Peter. *The Global Brain: Speculations on the Evolutionary Leap to Planetary Consciousness*. Los Angeles: J.P. Tarcher, 1982.

Sheldrake, Rupert. *The Presence of the Past: Morphic Resonance and the Habits of Nature*. New York: Times Books, 1988.

————. *The Rebirth of Nature*. Rochester, VT: Park Street Press, 1991.

Talbot, Michael. *Mysticism and the New Physics*. New York: Bantam, 1980.

Toben, Bob, and Fred Alan Wolfe. *Space-Time and Beyond: Toward An Explanation of the Unexplainable*. New York: E. P. Dutton, 1975.

Targ, Russell, and Keith Harary. *The Mind Race: Understanding and Using Psychic Abilities*. New York: Random House, 1984.

Thurston, Mark. *Dream Tonight's Answers for Tomorrows Questions*. San Francisco: Harper & Row, 1988.

Vallentin, Antonina. *The Drama of Albert Einstein.* Garden
  City, NY: Doubleday, 1954.
Watson, Lyall. *Supernature.* New York: Bantam, 1973.
Wilson, Colin. *The Occult.* New York: Viking Books, 1971.